Impacts of Modernities

Other titles in series:

Specters of the West and the Politics of Translation

edited by Naoki Sakai and Yukiko Hanawa
(2000)

"Race" Panic and the Memory of Migration

edited by Meaghan Morris and Brett de Bary
(2001)

TRACES

A MULTILINGUAL SERIES OF CULTURAL THEORY AND TRANSLATION

Impacts of Modernities

Edited by
Thomas Lamarre and Kang Nae-hui

香港大學出版社
Hong Kong University Press

Hong Kong University Press
14/F, Hing Wai Centre
7 Tin Wan Praya Road
Aberdeen
Hong Kong

ISBN 962 209 645 X (Hardback)
ISBN 962 209 646 8 (Paperback)

The name *Traces: A multilingual journal of cultural theory and translation* has been changed to *Traces: A multilingual series of cultural theory and translation.*

British Library Cataloguing-in-Publication Data
A catalogue record for this book is available from the British Library.

Secure On-line Ordering
http://www.hkupress.org

Cover Design: Judy Geib and Aldo Sampieri

Printed and bound by King's Time Printing Press Ltd. in Hong Kong, China

Statement of Purpose

Traces, a multilingual series of cultural theory and translation, calls for comparative cultural theory that is attentive to global traces in the theoretical knowledge produced in specific locations and that explores how theories are themselves constituted in, and transformed by, practical social relations at diverse sites. We eagerly seek theory produced in disparate sites, including that critical work that has often emerged in a hybrid relation to North American or West European 'theory' as a result of the colonialism and quasi-colonialism of the past few centuries. We will publish research, exchanges, and commentaries that address a multilingual audience concerned with all the established disciplines of the social sciences and humanities, in addition to such cross-disciplinary fields as cultural studies, feminist and queer studies, critical race theory, or post-colonial studies. At the same time, *Traces* aims to initiate a different circulation of intellectual conversation and debate in the world, a different geopolitical economy of theory and empirical data, and a different idea of theory itself.

Every essay in *Traces* is available in all the languages of this series. Each contributor is expected to be fully aware that she or he is writing for and addressing a heterogeneous and multilingual audience: in the manner of a local intellectual under a colonial regime, every contributor is expected to speak with a forked tongue. *Traces* is an international series. Yet the international space that it generates and sustains, and to which contributors as well as readers are invited, is fundamentally different from that of an internationalism based on one major language's subjugation of other minor languages. Indeed, it is hoped that the social space in which we argue and converse will challenge the space of the nation and national language. Constituted in processes of translation, among multiple languages and registers, this social space is actualized in our exchanges and debates, and in debates among authors, commentators, translators and readers.

Contents

CONTRIBUTORS

Peter BUTTON is an assistant professor at McGill University, whose research projects include work on the Marxist theorist of aesthetics, Cai Yi. His publications include, with Li Yang, *Wenhua yu wenxue: shiji zhi jiao de ningwang* (Culture and Literature: A Dialogue at the Turn of the Century) (Guoji wenhua chubanshe, 1993). Current research focuses on the problem of the image in socialist realist theory and in post-liberation literature and film.

Kenneth DEAN is Lee Professor of Chinese Studies in the Department of East Asian Studies of McGill University. His books include *First and Last Emperors: The Absolute State and the Body of the Despot* (with Brian Massumi), *Taoist Ritual and Popular Cults of Southeast China* and *Lord of the Three in One: The Spread of a Cult in Southeast China,* as well as several volumes of *Epigraphical Materials* on the History of Religion in Fujian.

Michael GODDARD is a PhD candidate in the department of Art History and Theory, University of Sydney. He is currently researching a thesis on the relations between the writing of Witold Gombrowicz and the aesthetic theories of Gilles Deleuze. He has published on New Zealand and Polish Cinema, poststructuralist philosophy, Polish modernism and film theory.

Harry HAROOTUNIAN is Chair, Department of East Asian Studies and Professor of History at New York University. He recently co-edited with Tomiko Yoda a special issue of *South Atlantic Quarterly* titled 'Millennial Japan.'

HONG Seong-tae teaches Sociology at Sangji University in Wonju, Korea. His research is on issues related to ecology and informatics. He has translated Ulrich Beck's *Risk Society* into Korean in 1997. His own books include *Saibô sahö ûi munhwa wa jôngchi* (Culture and Politics in Cyber Society) published by MunhwaGwahak-sa in 2000, and *Wihôm sahö rûl nômôs* (Beyond Risk Society) published by Saeghil Publishers in 2000.

KANG Nae-hui teaches in the Department of English at Chung-ang University in Seoul, Korea. Publisher of the cultural studies journal *MunhwaGwahak* (Culture/ Science) since 1992 and Director of the Executive Committee of Munhwa Yondae (Cultural Action), he pursues research on aspects of colonial modernity and on issues related to intellectual and cultural movements in Korea. His most recent book is *Shinjayujuûi wa munhwa* (Neoliberalism and Culture) published by MunhwaGwahak-sa in 2000.

Thomas LAMARRE teaches at McGill University. Publications include *Uncovering Heian Japan: An Archaeology of Sensation and Inscription* and *Shadows on the Screen: Tanizaki Jun'ichirô on Cinema and Oriental Aesthetics*. He recently edited a volume of *Japan Forum* titled 'Between Cinema and Anime.'

LAW Wing-sang is an assistant professor teaching at Department of Cultural Studies, Lingnan University in Hong Kong; he has completed his PhD on 'Collaborative Colonialism: A Genealogy of Competing Chineseness in Hong Kong' at University of Technology, Sydney.

Ethan L.J. NASREDDIN-LONGO is a composer and assistant professor of ethnomusicology at the University of California, Riverside, interested in ethnomusicological approaches to Western art music, Urban Ethnomusicology, and Central Javanese Gamelan. Publications include 'Selfhood, Self-Identity, Complexion and Complication: The Contexts of a Song-Cycle by Olly Wilson' (*Journal of Black Music Research*, 1995). Performed compositions include *Σ(and sad)* and *Evocations of Winter Trees and Lost Time* (Contemporary Chamber Players) and *Canzonetta for the Beloved* (X-Tet). Recent compositions include *Symphony for Nine Players - Four Responses to Violence, Liturgy of the Days* and *Meditation for Lili Hahn and Bernard Scholz*, both to premiere in the 2002-2003 season at the California Institute for the Arts. Current composition projects include a *Triple Concerto for Flute, Clarinet, Horn and Strings* and *Lyric of Love and Cancer*, and his current research project is a monograph on autobiography, social praxis and music video, entitled *A Fantasy on Some Themes by Janet Jackson, or The Return of the Red-Haired Boy*.

Jon SOLOMON is an assistant professor in the Department of Futures Studies, Tamkang University, Taiwan. Research projects include the politics of the impossible in Takeuchi Yoshimi, the failure of national institutions of translation in Dazai Osamu, the exilic thought and politics of Chinese dissident Liu Xiaobo, and the non-philosophy of François Laruelle. Among numerous translations of Chinese, Japanese, English, and French texts, the most recent publication is a Chinese translation of Jean-Luc Nancy's landmark essay, *La communauté désoeuvrée* ('The Inoperative Community'). In his lived texts, he has devoted considerable energy—with similar reference to exile, translation, sovereignty without subjectivity, and of course, impossibility—to the invention of a cultural-linguistic alternative to global English and the various others contained within its savage economy of primitive accumulation and unilateral translation.

SUN Ge is a researcher in Comparative Literature in the Institute for Literature at the Chinese Academy of Social Sciences in Beijing. Her books include *The Position of Literature* and *What Does Asia Mean?* (both in Xueshu sixiang pinglun). Her current research centres on the problem of modernity in Japanese intellectual history.

Atsuko UEDA teaches at University of Illinois, Champage-Urbana. Research interests include modern Japanese literature, comparative literature, translation theory, post-structuralism, and post-colonialism. Her recent publications include 'Nakagami Kenji Nihongo ni tsuite ron: bungaku no kurayami' in *Bungaku nenpo*; '"Moji" to iu "kotoba" —Yanji Yuhi o megutte' in *Nihon kindai bungaku* (May 2000); and 'De-Politicization of Literature; Social Darwinism and Interiority' in *The Issue of Canonicity and Canon Formation in Japanese Literary Studies* (PAJLS 1) August 2001.

Introduction: Impacts of Modernities

Thomas Lamarre

Modernity is about certain kinds of change. It suggests the emergence of something new — new modes or modalities, and maybe even new modes of being. Moreover, it commonly implies a positive evaluation of what is new or modern. Accounts of Western modernity frequently revisit the *Querelle des anciens et des modernes*, a debate about the superiority of the modern over the ancient. This debate made clear that modernity is not just about any change whatsoever. It entailed a sense that the new was better than the old, the present better than the past, potentially brighter, cleaner, healthier, freer and richer. Discourses for the new and for the modern dramatically transformed relations to the past, and modernity thus came to dovetail with what are now thought of as myths of progress. The past was no longer what it had been, a high ages, a crystalline source whose waters would continue to nurture and cleanse subsequent generations so long as those generations dedicated themselves to the maintenance of its ancient canals and channels. The past became thick viscous fluid, primordial ooze that demanded constant heroic efforts to step clear of it and to keep it at bay.

Discourses on modernity are, in other words, discourses on change that present a particular set of temporal relations and historical values. There was a time (it is usually thought) when people embraced these discourses for the modern; they affirmed the new; they favoured change as historical progress. Today, however, thinking about change has itself changed dramatically. If it is no longer so easy to affirm the temporal and historical relations associated with modernity, it is because there is something inherently paradoxical about affirming the new. The new never seems to arrive definitively or all at once; it is not exactly now, not quite yet. In which case, something new may appear to be no more than 'just something new,' that is, more of the same. The result is an eternal present in which everything is 'just new' without any particular value. In which case, there is never really anything new. This is the neurosis of modernity diagnosed by Nietzsche: when the new or the modern becomes the dominant value for understanding history, the present no longer succeeds the past but breaks radically with it. Oddly, modernity then becomes a culture of permanent renewal and comes to deny transience or change itself. Everything is constantly renewed; nothing changes. The moderns start to oscillate neurotically between maximizing and minimizing the relation between past and present. If they minimize their relation to the past, they become consumed by the present, by their inevitable and rapid obsolescence. They may then try to maximize their relation to the past, but this is a futile effort to evade obsolescence, one that effectively disavows change. There is, in other words, a temporal anomaly at the heart of the historical relations championed by the moderns. It is this temporal anomaly that ultimately comes to make historical change seem practically unthinkable.

Change is potentially a violent event — especially the kind of change associated with modernity, which is styled as a temporal break or rupture. What Nietzsche identified as historical neurosis appears today as global crisis. One might say that the West (wherever it is) is engaged in desperate efforts to evade its own obsolescence, calling on the maximal glory and sanctity of the tradition of God or Reason or Law or Logos, while the rest of the world is called upon to make good on its break with the past. Thus the rest of the world may be summoned to affirm the unity of the West, which (ironically or neurotically) amounts to a general affirmation of the possibility for unity despite modernity. If modernity is to be sustained, then temporal break, historical rupture, and global crisis must be continually naturalized and disavowed. This is temporal paradox become historical neurosis become the politics of everyday fear: everything breaks, nothing changes, all is crisis.

Now critical discussions of modernity seem to agree on one point — that the problem of modernity is, at some level, one of totalization. This seems to hold true whether commentators cast the problem of modernity as a largely physical problem (a matter of industrialization, imperial expansion, modernization of institutions, and such), or as a more metaphysical problem (modes of rationalization, subject formation, essentialization of identities, and so forth), or both. To confront the problem of modernity — its impacts, as it were — is to confront totalizing forces, processes, structures, formations or logics — a tireless systematization, homogenization, unification, standardization and globalization of resources, exchanges, institutions and peoples. Probably it is an overstatement to say that critiques of modernity 'agree' on this point. For agreement implies some manner of convergence or a common point of departure. Rather the problem of totalization continually arises, maybe not so much as a shared point of departure or debate as an impossible tangle in which discussions inevitably become enmeshed. In any event, the problem of modernity is also that of totalization, that is, modernization.

A number of questions arise, however, about the relation between modernity and modernization. There have been efforts to separate modernity (as cultural modernity) from modernization (as societal modernization). Arguments for the complete autonomy of modernity from modernization remain unconvincing because some degree of complicity is always in evidence. Nevertheless, modernity and modernization are not the same thing. The question is, how does modernity — first and foremost a temporal marker — relate to modernization, that is, to totalizing forces or processes? The answer lies in the notion of a temporal break or historical rupture — one that is somehow total and therefore foundational. The logic of temporal rupture can play into, and even ground, totalizing processes. As Nietzsche noted, an emphasis on the new easily becomes a desire for more of the same, a desire for totality, which totalizes everything in an eternal present — whence, in his view, the need for new non-foundational values.

Second, there is the related question of how a specific kind of temporal relation (modernity) comes to imply a specific configuration of geopolitical relations (the West versus the rest). Clearly, the relation between modernity and its 'antecedents' (antiquity, tradition, the premodern, the classical, the archaic, etc.) has incessantly been mobilized to mark a division between the West and its geopolitical others (constructing such others as the Orient, the East, the Third World, the South, or simply, the Rest of the World). Modernity announces a seemingly indelible division between the West and the rest, and perpetually conflates modernization and Westernization. If modernity as a temporal relation so often becomes associated with geopolitical totalization (that is, Westernization), it is on the basis of a displacement of the operation of modernity as total rupture. Briefly put, temporal rupture is spatialized, which displaces and naturalizes the violence of the rupture. The rupture is no longer within but without — displaced, as it were.

Finally, the question arises of whether there are today ways of dealing with spatial and temporal relations that are not totalizing, that are not modernizing or westernizing. This is a question about whether — or how — one can effectively counter or bypass totalizing modes or logics or formations. It is a question posed insistently in discussions of postmodernity and the postmodern, which have most often been discredited on the basis of their own totalizing gesture — the announcement of a historical rupture with modernity — implicit in the 'post.' There may, however, be other ways of thinking the relation between the modern and postmodern than historical rupture — for instance, as an intensification of a moment within modernity, or maybe in terms of a-modalities.

Nevertheless, the problem of totalization persists in discussions geared toward modernity, and indeed, seems almost fundamental to them. It is not surprising then that discussions of modernity often hinge on diverse possibilities for counter-totalizing tactics, strategic alternative totalizations or non-totalizing differential systems. Crucial to all critical efforts to undermine, overturn or somehow unmake or unravel modern totalization is a demonstration that such efforts are not merely detotalizing. (Or they must at least show some awareness of the problem of detotalization.) For detotalization — a simple quantitative fragmentation or pluralization of the times and spaces of modernity (many smaller modernities) — tends to produce difference as more of the same and to open itself entirely to retotalization — a supermodernity or globalization comprised of comparable nations or consumable locations. The key then is to think breaks that are not so simple, and relations that do not lend themselves to quantification. While speaking in the plural — of modernities and impacts — is not in and of itself a solution to the problem of modern totalization, there is a sense in which such a multiplication of modernities may not be so simple and quantitative after all. If modernity is no longer in or of the West, what will become of it? Maybe this is to start to think change anew.

The general trend in current discussions of modernity seems rather dark and bleak, however. Much criticism lingers, aptly and persuasively, on the crisis and systematic failure inherent in modernity and modernization. It is as if there were no hope for modernity, and that is the best thing about it.

Comparativism and the Production of Space and Place

In the first essay in this volume, Harry Harootunian addresses the problem of modern temporality. The central concern of 'Ghostly Comparisons' is to contest the privileging of space in analyses of modernity. He begins with knowledge about modern time and space produced in the West and gradually enlarges his critique to address the production of knowledge in East Asia. He does not draw a line between the West and the rest. On the contrary, by emphasizing how analyses of modernity have privileged space, Harootunian wishes to call critical attention to how discourses on modernity have generally constructed privileged spaces and essentialized places — nations and national identities above all, but also geopolitical abstractions such as West and East. His aim then is to find a new approach to modernity that does not remain mired in spatial abstractions or totalizations like the nation, or the West.

Of particular importance is his demonstration that the privileging of space entails a systematic unwillingness to deal with temporality. Spatialization, in his account, is not merely a matter of reluctance or inability but of methodology. At the outset, he links this systematic refusal to deal with temporality to a specific discipline — area studies — whose basic methodological framework is comparative and thus spatializing. Drawing on Johannes Fabian's work, he argues that the effect of comparative methodologies, and indeed their founding mission, is to deny the coevalness or contemporaneity of other societies. The observer sees another society as if living in another time, yet that other time remains comprehensible and accessible to the observer because he situates it as a different stage or period of human development or of social evolution — in effect distancing and spatializing it. Needless to say, in Fabian's account, the observer is the Western anthropologist, who establishes the West as the normative standard for the evaluation and classification of temporality of other societies.

Modernization theory, especially the American version that has proved so persistent in universalizing America's strategic interests, could be seen as a variation on the comparative framework. It is a variation that establishes the United States as the pinnacle of modern development, and other societies are mapped in terms of their distance from that normative standard. The historical rupture within the West is naturalized and disavowed as a rupture between the West and the rest. In modernization theory, there is only one path and one aim, and other societies are to pursue that path and to catch up if they can. (They cannot, of course, and the racial and historical disturbances created by the economic success of Japan in the 'bubble years' — such as Japan-bashing in North America and Europe, and Francis Fukuyama's pronouncement of the 'end of history' — show how fragile and precarious modernization theory is, and how violent its responses can be.) Otherwise, if non-Western societies cannot become 'sufficiently' modernized, they should at least be sufficiently amenable to accommodating some degree of Americanization or globalization.

Harootunian contends that accounts of modernity that privilege space or 'spatialize' inevitably side with modernization. Even those accounts that oppose modernization ineluctably reproduce it — so long as they insist on spatializing relations. In effect, Harootunian sees spatialization operating in the same way as modernization: it detotalizes (divides into equal aliquots) only to retotalize (refers back to the West, modernity, or a unitary global time or system). Naturally, because his emphasis is on the production of knowledge (discourses on modernity), he associates this tendency to detotalize and retotalize with disciplinary formations. On the one hand, he finds what might be described as an 'anthropologizing' gesture. The anthropologizing gesture promises to overcome the totalizing forces of modernization by emphasizing local identities. The anthropologizing gesture depends on the establishment of local identities on the basis of places. It makes specific places the sites of unity and identity. Yet, Harootunian suggests, the production of local identities, thus linked to spaces or places, runs the risk of doing nothing more than detotalizing the world in order to enable retotalization — literally deterritorializing in order to reterritorialize. In his account, the emphasis is on the nation as place-identity. Yet he suggests that the same logic informs current trends in cultural theory as well, which strive to dismantle the unity and identity of the nation by fragmenting and multiplying local identities. Indeed, he hints that the recent interest in speaking in terms of global and local may present a simple intensification of the logic of the universal and particular (modernity and the nation, or the West and the rest), precisely because it remains within the same spatializing logic.

In his account, this risk of incessant retotalization or reterritorialization is very great because the anthropologizing gesture relies, however unwittingly, on what might be called (on the other hand) a 'synchronizing' gesture. This gesture becomes most obvious in comparative studies. If identities are to remain identities (that is, self-identical), they must sustain their difference via spatial isolation. Yet, when one compares them, one must assume an underlying or overarching simultaneity or synchronicity, a time frame in which all these different identities exist at once, somehow equally and evenly. In effect, recourse to synchronicity makes different identities the same, equally accessible to modernizing or globalizing processes. Synchronicity produces identical differences. Put another way, the major problems with discourses that privilege space is that they privilege 'difference between societies' over 'difference within societies.' If Harootunian turns to problems of temporality in order to counter spatialization, it is precisely in order to draw attention to unevenness within societies, which becomes especially evident in the everyday experience of 'non-synchronous contemporaneity.' He turns to the temporal disjuncture and dissonance that are experienced and actualized as part of everyday life in 'those places and spaces that have committed their resources to the transformations of capitalist modernization.' He thus proposes that the everyday may afford a new comparative framework for modernity, one attentive to the production and reproduction of difference within and across modernizing societies, one based on rethinking the temporality of modernity.

'Overcoming Modernity,' a symposium held in Japan in 1942 to address Japan's problem with Western modernity, provides for him a prime example of the essentializing of place implicit in thinking modernity spatially. The fundamental problem of 'Overcoming Modernity,' as Harootunian sees it, lay in the equation drawn by Japanese intellectuals between modernity and a spatial unity (the West and especially America as the place of modernity). This forced intellectuals to conceive modernity entirely in terms of imitating or reproducing that model — which naturally proved impossible. Intellectuals then recuperated that impossibility: everything in Japan that did not fit the American model was seen as a remainder and reminder of a lost unity, of authentic traditions and the native homeland. In this privileging of a lost place of timeless authenticity, Harootunian detects complicity between 'modernist' discourses and fascist ideologies.

'Overcoming Modernity' and subsequent responses to it also become the focus of Sun Ge's essay. Sun's central concern is also that of the complicity between intellectuals and what she calls 'official ideologies' or 'national ideologies.' Similarly, she raises questions about the relation between discourses on modernity (modernism) and totalitarianism (fascism). Yet, even as she explores the complicity between intellectuals and official ideologies, she continues to direct attention to the possibilities for difference and resistance within the very problematic of 'Overcoming Modernity.'

On the one hand, Sun emphasizes that subsequent commentators on 'Overcoming Modernity' have largely disparaged it. They see its discourses as not only complicit with totalitarian ideologies but also as continuous with them. In brief, for most commentators, the symposium — indeed the very notion of 'overcoming modernity' — simply entailed intellectual legitimization of the ideologies of total war. Likewise, as if in agreement, Sun herself continually reminds her readers that the historical moment for the symposium, the outbreak of the Pacific War, served to silence all dissent among Japanese intellectuals vis-à-vis Japan's War in Asia. United in their opposition to the West in the wake of the attack on Pearl Harbor, intellectuals came to accept rather than challenge the idea that opposing the West meant liberating the East.

On the other hand, Sun continually asks what it means for subsequent commentators to claim that resistance proved futile, and thus, in effect, to declare that there was no resistance at all. Specifically, she points to commentators who adopt a 'transcendent position' with respect to 'Overcoming Modernity,' reducing it to univocal complicity in order to avoid the difficulties inherent in the idea of Japanese or non-Western modernity. From the outset, she signals a tentative rift between the writers and literary critics who organized the conference, and the scholars and philosophers whom they invited. The writers tended to insist that Japan had already overcome Western modernity through its purification of what they saw as the quintessentially Japanese aesthetic — a sensual, embodied approach to the world exemplified in traditional art and literature — which they linked to the 1930's renaissance of pure literature in opposition to Americanized mass culture. The scholars, by Sun's account, showed greater awareness of the difficulties inherent in claims to have already overcome Western modernity. Sun sees in this rift a play between the relative and the absolute, in which the scholars showed greater awareness that positing Japan as an absolute to which other formations are relative meant repeating not overcoming Western modernity. Yet the scholar's insight came at the expense of a serious account of the everyday and difference in repetition. The scholars, almost by default, endorsed the idea of Japan as a future (Asian) absolute, to which other cultural and geopolitical formations in East Asia would become relative.

Sun thus teases out a sort of 'double consciousness' at the heart of 'Overcoming Modernity,' for she shows how the symposium was at once complicit with, and resistant to, the West. Moreover, she argues that, even if the intellectuals' resistance proved ineffective, subsequent commentators who ignore or disavow the question of their double-consciousness merely foreclose resistance by situating it entirely outside Japan (and thus outside history). Of particular interest is Sun's suggestion that, in and around 'Overcoming Modernity,' the basic problem has been the tendency to think in terms of relative and absolute rather than relationally. She writes, '[s]uch differences are produced in relation, in the process of narrating them, and it is only when awareness of such effects breaks down that differences between Japan and the West tend to collapse (even as they are reified).' When one establishes Western modernity as an absolute, one sets up a situation in which repetition always entails resemblance. Which is to say, to become modern (to modernize) is to become like the West, to resemble the West, to westernize. Japan is never the site of modernity but only that of its negation (as with the writers at 'Overcoming Modernity') or its relativization (the scholars). Their problem was, in essence, one of repetition without difference. The very idea of 'overcoming modernity' set up a play between the relative and the absolute in which repetition could only be resemblance not difference. For the difference of repetition was already captured in resemblance to the West.

Crucial to Sun Ge's rethinking of 'Overcoming Modernity' is the thought of Takeuchi Yoshimi whose importance, in her account, is to have introduced indeterminacy into the question of overcoming modernity. She sees in Takeuchi an insistence on thinking difference within hegemony as well as a willingness to look for resistance to totalitarianism within totalitarianism. This resistance or 'difference within' potentially enables a different understanding of modernity and Japan. Although modernity arrives as shock from without, it must also arrive as a shock from within Japan (and likewise with East Asia), a shock that must be continually renewed. Otherwise, modernity in Japan is little other than modernization as Westernization — gradual process of coming to resemble the West. Yet this experience of shock is not a unitary, once-and-forever 'modern consciousness,' as it were. It is a sort of 'double consciousness' in which repetition is experienced as difference, shockingly, almost traumatically, to the point of losing all hold on resemblance (and thus the self and identity). Sun's Takeuchi speaks as if the result of this loss of self would be the attainment of Japan, that is, a truly modern national subjectivity (one must lose the self to gain the self). Yet this subjectivity, this Japan, is not a 'state' or 'place,' still less a 'home.' Modern subjectivity is, for Sun, a truly critical subjectivity, which entails an on-going process of relating, that is, narrating resistance or 'difference within.'

There are echoes here of something like Derridean deconstruction, much as Law Sing Wang characterizes it in his essay, as 'a double reading encapsulated in the notion of closure,' as a problem of 'discovering how a reading can remain internal to the text and within the limits of textuality without merely repeating the text . . .' It is not surprising, given that modernity is so often set up as a problem of totalization (modernization), that deconstructive tactics should prove so productive in critiques of modernity. For deconstruction does not adopt the stance of overcoming, surpassing or otherwise transcending totalizing tendencies. Nor does it side with, or repeat them, in the manner of a commentary on a text. As Law puts it, 'The signifying structure of a deconstructive reading has to be located at a hinge, which links the double movement between logocentrism or metaphysics and its other. At the same time, it has to enable one to exceed the orbit of conceptual totality. The goal of deconstruction is to locate a point of otherness within logocentric conceptuality and to deconstruct that conceptuality from that position of alterity.'

Part of the appeal of deconstructive readings comes of their attentiveness to the problem of an underlying totality and the risk of recuperation within it or by it. In response to modernity (in its specifically philosophical and juridical register), deconstruction aims to locate points of otherness within it. It avoids the temptation to announce the end of modernity, as some thinkers of the postmodern are often accused of doing. There are, however, many different ways of working with deconstruction in relation to modernity. In this volume, as I will strive to make clear in this introduction, subaltern theory and postcolonial theory frequently provide a point of reference for critique — particularly in relation to the idea of 'alternative modernities.' Yet, despite their continual reference to such thinkers as Chatterjee, Spivak, Bhabha and Chakrabarty, these essays also tend to differentiate themselves from subaltern theory and postcolonial theory, having a very different sense of the politics of deconstruction and alternative modernities. Although such differences can surely be attributed to site specificity and specific disciplinary formations, it is important to raise the question of where specificity arises, and how it works.

One of the operations important to alternative modernities is to question whether one can ever pretend to have supplanted, surpassed or otherwise overcome modernity. One strategy is to submit, as Dilip Parameshwar Gaonkar does, that modernity 'continues to "arrive and emerge."' Indeed Gaonkar suggests that '[t]o think in terms of "alternative modernities" is to admit that modernity is inescapable and to desist from speculations about the end of modernity.'[1]

It would be rash, however, to conclude that this stance entails a simple resignation in the face of an inevitable modernity, a tacit or covert acceptance of its totalizing structures. (There are ways of failing and then there are ways of failing.) Gaonkar, for instance, situates alternative modernities in such a way as to problematize the dialectic of convergence and divergence. Theories of convergence are those that see modernity as societal modernization: regardless of their different points of departure, modernized societies eventually all become the same. Theories of divergence (largely theories of cultural modernity) are those that presume that different points of departure lead to different outcomes, to vastly different modernities. To Gaonkar, the problem with divergence theories is that they entirely ignore homogenizing forces and totalizing logics (modernization). Gaonkar wishes to retain yet complicate the notion of totalizing modernization. 'An alternative modernities perspective,' he writes, 'complicates this neat dichotomy by foregrounding that narrow but critical band of variations consisting of site-specific "creative adaptations" on the axis of convergence (or societal modernization).' Creative adaptation, however, is 'not simply a matter of adjusting the form or recoding the practice to soften the impact of modernity.' Gaonkar sees it as 'an interminable process of questioning the present, which is the attitude of modernity.' He also suggests that it 'is the site where people make themselves modern.'[2] In other words, to speak of alternative modernities is to open points of otherness within totalizing conceptuality ('sites' of 'questioning').

The image of modernity that emerges is not that of simple reproduction or imitation of the unitary Western model. Rather modernity appears as a process of rupture and reinscription; alternative modernities entail an opening of otherness within Western modernity, in the very process of repeating or reinscribing it. It is as if modernity itself is deconstruction. It is not unlike the double consciousness evoked in Sun's discussion of Takeuchi, which comes of a traumatic shock that opens totalizing modernity to the possibility of critical modernity. A question invariably arises, however, about 'site specificity.' What is the relation between these 'points of alterity' or 'sites of questioning' and the place or space of the nation? To Harootunian, the site specificity evoked in theories of alternative modernities reproduces the problem inherent in 'overcoming modernity.' He asks whether the emphasis on site specificity does not simply reproduce and reify national identities. Is the notion of Chinese modernity, Russian modernity, Japanese or Indian modernity so different from Chinese, Russian, Japanese or Indian nationalism? Alternative or alter/native modernities run the risk spatializing 'otherness within' as an alternative place to Western modernity — which amounts to cultural particularism, essentialism or nationalism. Likewise Law cautions at the outset, 'One response to the complexities of modernity takes the form of an increased emphasis on the specificity of site, as in analyses of "alternative modernities." If the formation of those sites is not examined, however, one could easily slip back to a naïve view assuming a natural and coherent spatial entity wherein all sorts of eternal folklores or mythical authenticities could be uncritically asserted . . . . As a consequence, our understanding of modernity has to go back to the question of the relation between modernity and nation formation.'

Gaonkar, however, is cautious on this point. When he speaks concretely of the sites of alternative modernities in his account, he seems to agree with Harootunian. Rather than nations, they are places that have committed their resources to capitalist modernization; in particular they are urban sites and metropolitan modes. Across the 'noise of difference,' Gaonkar sees a 'string of similarities' among modernities — the style of the flaneur, the mystique of fashion, the magic of the city, and so forth. These examples suggest something like urban, cosmopolitan 'non-places' — or, at least, layered and hybrid sites — rather than authentic national traditions and locations. Nevertheless, what does it mean to associate something like 'non-lieu' or 'non-site' with an actual place, be it China or India, or Shanghai or Bombay? What haunts site specificity is the problem of origins. Indeed modernity easily becomes a discourse on origins — a unitary and self-identical origin, an original model, the West.

Gaonkar deals with the problem of origins by proposing that alternative modernities are 'originating' — they entail creative adaptations or variations. Yet the problem of the origin persists: 'Modernity has traveled from the West to the rest of the world not only in terms of cultural forms, social practices, and institutional arrangements but also as a form of discourse that interrogates the present. That questioning of the present, whether in vernacular or in cosmopolitan idioms, which is taking place at every national and cultural site today cannot escape the legacy of Western discourse on modernity.'[3] In Gaonkar's account, the problem of the origin persists in the emphasis on diffusion from the West and on the primacy of convergence. The origin then tends to reappear in the future as a potential point of convergence, albeit in a potentially better, more ethical world. Gaonkar thus asks whether these 'common intensities . . . will one day pave the way for an ethic of the global modern.'[4]

Gaonkar's characterization of modernity as a kind of deconstruction — as an incessant questioning of the present — suggests that modernity is a mode of temporality that always diverges from modernization. Paradoxically, although such divergence characterizes alternative modernities, it has already happened in the West, or rather in the cosmopolitan West. In effect, divergence is always already at the origin. Yet, no sooner does he point to originary divergence than Gaonkar resists it. He insists that only reference to convergence allows an evaluation of the impacts of modernity. (And he tentatively draws lines from cosmopolitan modernisms that converge in the future on global modernity.) I do not wish to underestimate the importance of Gaonkar's evocation of divergence in convergence — surprises, shocks, questions — but rather want to ask whether (or how) alternative modernities would ever allow for their 'originating activities' (creativity) to be done with the logic of unitary origins. This is a question that applies not simply to alternative modernities but to analyses of modernity generally. For it seems that discourses of modernity (or modernities) invariably confront the problem of unitary origins — this becomes especially pronounced when they pose questions about space, place or sites.

It is easy to understand why some thinkers would prefer to be done with the modern and origins. Deleuze, for instance, writes, 'If things aren't going well in contemporary thought, it's because there is a return under the name of "modernism" to abstractions, back to the problem of origins and so on. Any analysis of movement or vectors is blocked. We are now in a very weak phase, a period of reaction. Yet, philosophy thought it was through with the problem of origins. It was no longer a question of starting or finishing. The question was rather, what happens "in between"?'[5]

In discussions of modernity, however, it is commonly and probably necessarily a question of origins, of starting (with the West) and sometimes of finishing (with the globe). Gaonkar's account of alternative modernities potentially complicates the question of origins, by calling attention to divergence — the shocks, surprises, questions and creative transformations that happen in between. At times, he seems far from the notion of a unitary origin and model, and his modernity already seems to be doubled and innovative at its origins. There is always already divergence. Ultimately, however, it seems that the set-up borrowed from Charles Taylor — divergence in opposition to convergence — encourages a continual return of something unitary, as if the impacts of modernity could not be addressed without continual reference to a unitary West — which collapses modernity into modernization.[6] Ultimately, although Gaonkar evokes the difference between modernity and modernization, there is no productive or effective difference between them.

Of particular interest in this respect is the work on Western modernity that appears in a volume edited by Stuart Hall and others, which 'sees modern societies now as a global phenomenon and the modern world as the unexpected and unpredicted outcome of, not one, but a series of major historical transitions.'[7] In other words, to counter the image of modernity presented by modernization theory, in which there was one path and one motor (economic modernization), Hall insists, 'Modernity, then, was the outcome, not of a single process, but of the condensation of a number of different processes and histories.'[8] Hall effectively multiplies, transforms and thus problematizes the origins of modernity. If it becomes impossible to locate modernity in a single space or at a single moment, he suggests that there are nevertheless 'condensations' that merit attention. Yet, somewhat differently from Gaonkar, even though Hall thinks globally, his notion of condensation does not suggest any manner of convergence. Thus it would be a mistake to think of his discussion of modernity as a return to unitary origins, for there is no terminus insight. Rather his is a deconstructive problematization of origins, of starting and of beginnings.

'Deconstruction,' writes Vicki Kirby, 'has a fixation with origins and with their peculiar capacity for innovation, ubiquity and endurance. However the suggestion that a beginning has something of a mutating existence tests our comprehension in a most fundamental way.'[9] If deconstruction tests our comprehension, it is because its insistence that origins are not unitary threatens our ability to orientate ourselves, to locate coordinates that will serve as a point of departure for discriminating, evaluating and making decisions. If origins endure because they are innovative, we have to deal with innovation, change and movement rather than fixed points of departure and arrival. The mutating existence of the origin undermines recourse to a prior fixed system of orientation that would allow us to draw a line between two points, to travel from A to B. We confront deconstruction's paradoxical inversion of the linear temporality of cause and effect: 'a supplement which "produces" what it supplements' or 'an originary repetition' or 'an absolute past that has never been present.' How can we hope to go anywhere if our arrival at B produces our point of departure from A? We are always departing and never arriving.

The mutating existence of origins seems to many commentators to be politically disabling because of its temporal and spatial disorientation. Simply put, it becomes difficult to say definitively when and where Western modernity is. It also becomes difficult to decide, once and for all, who is inside and who is outside. Once one speaks of modernity or of the West, one is paradoxically within it even while one claims to be without. It is impossible to locate and define a position of exteriority. Whence, in a related register, Gayatri Spivak's famous query: Can the subaltern speak? The answer is that, no sooner does the subaltern speak, than the subaltern does not exist. Needless to say, as Law discusses in detail, such a paradox assumes a specifically Western philosophical relation between speaking and being — always already globalized within disciplinary and discursive formations of the modern nation.

In her discussion of subaltern studies, for instance, Spivak looks at how the group 'tracks failures in attempts to displace discursive fields.' In particular, the group shows how Western discursive fields invariably fail in non-Western contexts, and Spivak shows how it is a force of crisis that operates functional displacements in discursive fields — a modern crisis, that of colonialism. She also suggests that 'A deconstructive approach would bring into focus the fact that they are themselves engaged in an attempt at displacing discursive fields, that they themselves "fail" (in the general sense) for reasons as "historical" as those they adduce for the heterogeneous agents they study; and would attempt to forge a practice that would take this into account.' Without a sense of the implications of its own work, the group tends to objectify the subaltern, control him with knowledge, and thus become complicit with what they oppose 'in their desire for totality.'[10] Some readers might object that Spivak's deconstructive approach condemns in advance all resistance, for she generalizes failure not success. She sees complicity in all attempts to speak as the subaltern, to speak for the subaltern, or to have the subaltern speak. Hence 'one must see in their [subaltern studies] practice a repetition as well as a rupture from the colonial predicament.' Analogously, one must also see repetition as well as a rupture at the origin in the metropolitan West. For speech is always failure.

There are, however, different ways of speaking and failing, for historical reasons. There are different failures or different histories, as it were. Context becomes critical, and clearly the context for Spivak is the colonial predicament, or the universalization of Western modernity as metaphysics. It is the universalization of Western metaphysics that informs Spivak's emphasis on the problematic of speech in relation to the subaltern. As Law puts it in his essay in this volume, 'The Western discipline of philosophy, including comparative philosophy, which is supposed to investigate the thought of non-Western worlds, is always instituted as a way to *speak of something*' (emphasis mine). To deconstruction, the history of Western metaphysics is such that speaking is always already conflated with Being, onto-theo-logically. Speaking is inseparable from the assimilatory power of Being. This is logocentricism. To quote Law again: 'Derrida is skeptical of the possibility of overcoming, or finding some leeway for, thinking Being, for he thinks that the assimilatory of Being excludes such a possibility. Derrida is always vigilant about the possibility that the negation of Being will itself be subsumed. It would be moot for him to consider the possibility of *otherwise than Being* without negation to Being.' Yet this problem of speaking 'is not as "speaking in general" or language-in-itself but as the place, the position, the context in which promises or hopes are delivered.' The problem of modernity then is that there are no ways of speaking otherwise than from within Western metaphysics or logocentricism.

Law demonstrates convincingly that the comparative philosophical enterprise is one that makes other traditions of thought speak the language of Western metaphysics. Thus the thought of Chuang Tzu, in one instance, is posited as the site of 'our' (Chinese) logos; and in another instance, Chuang Tzu is seen as deconstruction before deconstruction, as superior deconstruction. Such comparative efforts not only make Chinese thought the equivalent to Western metaphysics but also reduce political critiques of Western metaphysics (such as Derrida's thought) to stylistic play. To counter this kind of failure, which Law aptly characterizes as a whole-hearted capitulation to universalism in the form of national particularism, Law enters into what he tentatively dubs a 'para-comparative' study in which he addresses the difference between the 'unsayable' in Chuang Tzu and Derrida in a philosophically rigorous manner. Law discusses Chuang Tzu as if it were possible for him to speak otherwise than Being. In this respect, his para-comparative study resonates with Spivak's notion of strategic essentialism (or Alberto Moreiras's retooling of this notion as tactical essentialism).[11] For his goal is not to rescue Chuang Tzu from Western metaphysics, nor to use Chuang Tzu to overturn Western metaphysics. Ultimately, Law does not suppose that para-comparative study allows one to speak outside modern comparativism (which would amount to speaking otherwise than Being). Although he attends to the otherness of Chuang Tzu (the historical specificity of what it means to be philosophical), there is a sense in which the historical and philosophical specificity of Chuang Tzu can only be located as a point of otherness within Western metaphysics, within modernity. In other words, Law sees that the para-comparative study also fails. It fails to transcend the place of the nation and the context of modernity. Nonetheless, his is a different way of failing, one that potentially opens new hopes as well as new desires for other histories.

If Law faults other strategies for discussing the impacts of modernity, it is because other strategies continue to evoke sociological explanations of modernity. Chatterjee, for instance, argues that universalism is not equally available to non-Western thinkers, and thus searches for sites outside capitalism and colonialism. Harootunian argues, on the contrary, that the modern nation has long been universalized in such a way as to make 'universalizing' or 'totalizing' gestures available to non-Western intellectuals; there is no outside to capitalist modernity. Law takes issue with Chatterjee for assuming an outside and with Harootunian for ignoring the unevenness in access to universalizing. He detects the residue of sociological explanations of modernity in both stances: the one supposes that modernity's incompleteness allows an outside, while the other supposes modernity's arrival. Thus Law directs our attention to psychoanalytic and philosophical questions about the desire for comparability whose long history continues to frame and colour discourses of modernity, especially those that rely on sociological explanations.

In other words, looking at comparativism, Law sees the mutating existence of the colonial and imperial origins of modernity, which he links to the assimilatory power of Being (Western metaphysics). This means that all speaking is caught up in the production of spaces and places for modernity. Simply put, deconstruction sees speaking as both innovation and assimilation. Speaking continually innovates and produces new sites, but that innovation is also assimilation because innovation merely displaces origins. Speaking otherwise than modernity is bound to fail. This means that Western modernity, as logocentricism, is potentially everywhere there is speaking. This does not mean that modernity succeeds everywhere, however. Rather it fails. Although new places of speaking are always assimilated to an underlying totality, that totality continues to unfurl violently, displacing the origin, producing difference, and generating unevenness. Once again, modernity is an incessant production of difference as the same — which becomes particularly problematized in relation to place and space. Site specificity promises something otherwise than modernity but can never deliver it.

In sum, the first three papers address the impacts of modernity in relation to comparativism, space, and places. Although all three seek points of disorientation or divergence, they do so in order to re-orientate themselves toward those places and spaces very differently. Faced with the production of space, Harootunian turns to temporality. His 'solution' is a tactical essentialism of historical temporality that locates points of otherness in modernity by looking to the temporal anomalies arising around the pasts that modernity unfurls. Sun also calls attention to 'difference within,' in the context of Japanese intellectuals' totalizing bid to overcome Western modernity. Her tactic is to pose the question of a needful yet impossible relation to indigenous traditions — the self must orientate itself in relation to traditions yet cannot do so without losing its self — a self-critical relating and narrating. Law stresses an ethical relation: while it is not possible to speak non-metaphysically, it may be possible to listen. To listen is to find points of otherness within modernity and to acknowledge the violence to the other implicit in that discovery. In many ways, Hong Seong-tae's photo essay on the colonial modernization of Seoul rearticulates these problems.

To avoid unitary modernity, Hong pluralizes modernization. He wishes to contest the idea that the violent rupture wrought by the Japanese invasion and annexation of Korea constitutes just another point of departure for modernity. He challenges that idea that, no matter how modernization starts, it is still the same modernity. Thus he writes of modernizations, with attention to Seoul's colonial history. Although urban spaces around the world may look the same on the surface, he suggests that there are underlying historical differences. The Japanese imperial reconstruction of Seoul — colonial modernization — involved a deliberate erasure of traditional spaces and thus of a historical sense of the city. Contemporary Koreans living in Seoul thus have few clues to remind them of its past, their past. While one solution would to be to reconstruct the city as it was before colonialism, Hong does not take such a simple route. He sees a need to preserve the history of Japanese imperialism. He takes issue not only with the Japanese destruction of traditional space but also with Kim Young Sam's attempt to correct history by removing evidence of Japanese imperialism. Thus two contradictory historicizing impulses co-exist in his essay: to restore the precolonial, traditional past and to preserve the colonial past. This means that the remnants of Japanese imperialism must be at once negated and preserved.

Such an act of remembrance might be thought of as an act of working through, of mourning — in contrast to an amnesiac repetition of the colonial destruction of the past. Yet Korea's current relation to the United States makes this impossible. In light of the American military occupation of Korea, how is it possible to negate and preserve the history of colonialism? Is it possible at this time, under occupation, to negate and preserve historical traces of American imperialism? Hong focuses on one possibility for working through this other layer of colonial modernization: the movement to reclaim and transform the land currently occupied by the American military base. Yet ultimately, Hong calls our attention to the risk of repetition of colonial modernization. For it is not only a matter of getting rid of Japanese or American imperialism but also of working through those histories. In light of the previous essays, one might say that Hong relies on an essentialism of place and identity (the special case of Korea) that pushes toward the production of national identity — within a history of imperial perpetrators and colonial victims without collaborators or bystanders.[12] Nevertheless, given his awareness of urban history as one of both negation and preservation, it is clearly possible to see his emphasis on Korean autonomy as a strategic or tactical essentialism, one that returns with the question, 'What exactly is a strategy or a tactic?' How are we to orientate ourselves politically when the received configurations of speech and place appear to fail in advance?

Speech, Writing and Empire

One of the triumphant narratives of modernization is that of the establishment of mass literacy on the basis of standardized national languages. Sociologically, for instance, the degree of literacy continues to provide an index of a society's civilization and democratization. In recent years, however, this triumphant view of the rise of literacy has been challenged on a number of fronts. Simply put, the transformations in speech and writing necessary to the establishment of a standard national language have been studied in view of their propensity toward homogenization and subjection, toward inventing and mobilizing national subjects, and producing exploitable 'masses.' This stands in stark contrast to the vision of mass literacy, freedom of expression and transparent communication among citizens that had been promoted in stories of linguistic modernization. What is at stake in revisiting and historicizing the production of standardized national languages is not simply to speak of modernization in terms of the rise of unfreedom. Rather at stake is an account of how modern individualizing techniques generate localized disciplinary formations that work in conjunction with totalizing power formations. Which to say, the ability and freedom to speak and write in the national language depends on a prior injunction to speak and write in specific ways, which produces spaces of inclusion and exclusion necessary to modern processes of totalization.

Of particular interest in the three essays in this volume are the links they draw between the establishment of modern forms of writing and the totalizing processes of modern empire. There is little confidence that national language and literature enable local or national autonomies in any positive, effective way. As I will emphasize in my discussion, this stands in contrast to many postcolonial accounts of the novel that emphasize how the non-West's rupture with, and reinscription of, Western literature enables hybrid and indeterminate forms that are not easily or automatically recuperated. One important implication of these essays is that the individualizing techniques of modern writing — and hybridity itself — are productive of national empire or imperial subjects. Moments of difference and divergence are seen as sites of assimilation.

In his essay on linguistic modernity in Korea, Kang Nae-hui historicizes linguistic usages that today appear natural, inevitable and even desirable. In order to counter the tendency to see modern Korean as a natural outcome or as social consensus, Kang outlines different phases in the production of linguistic modernity. He links these phases to the history of Japanese and Western imperialism and the colonization of Korea. For instance, around 1894, when the Japanese army drove the Chinese army out of Korea only to remain as an imperial power, there occurred a major transformation of traditional linguistic and scriptural spaces. A variety of writing practices were subsumed under a binary opposition between 'Chinese letters' (*hanmun*) and 'national letters'(*gukmun*). This opposition also spelled the end of the general prestige of writing practices associated with traditional Chinese learning, and introduced a temporal divide between past and present, tradition and modernity. This divide provided the basis for the totalizing, modernizing processes of separating the present from the past. Of course, such totalization can never be complete: initially, a variety of mixed styles of writing appeared. Yet the overall tendency was toward the purification of 'national letters' through the elimination of all deemed prior or external to them. The impetus for this purification was a desire for national autonomy, but as Kang signals, it was 'a path to autonomous modernization that could only meet with failure.'

Kang also writes of a kind of liminal phase in which older linguistic usages had not yet passed, and new usages had yet to predominate — a period of satire and parody when common people took up the grandiose hierarchical forms of address bequeathed from the past and used them boldly in new public forums. Ultimately, however, such unexpected mixtures of old and new gave way to the establishment of homogeneous and unmarked linguistic modes of address and reception — as if the initial rupture, at once imperialist and modernist, inevitably foreclosed autonomous movements. Crucial was the Japanese annexation of Korea in 1910, after which, Kang notes, a specifically modern formation of subjectivity and objectivity became dominant, especially in novels and newspapers. Characteristic of this modern linguistic mode was an 'unmarking' of the position of speaker or writer. This unmarking produced a new kind of subjectivity, interiority. It also gave precedence to the enunciated, which encouraged naïve realism, and readers came to perceive and believe in the written as factual, objective, and true. Also characteristic of linguistic modernity was a transformation of tenses and temporal relations. The result was a sort of empty, homogeneous linguistic space that emphasized logical and analytical relations (rather than figural, emotional or hierarchical relations), to be mastered by the new modern subject.

One of the interesting points of Kang's account of linguistic modernization is that the linguistic production of an 'unmarked' subject results not only in a politics of inclusion and exclusion but also one of assimilation. On the one hand, insofar as the unmarking of the subject is framed within Korean grammar, the new subject is supposed to be a national subject. Its ideal is sovereignty spread flatly and evenly to the boundaries of the Korean nation, in which all citizens are equally Korean. On the other hand, in linguistic terms, not all inhabitants of Korea are evenly Korean. This means that the linguistic production of national subjectivity must in effect colonize Korea — whence the ambivalent positioning of dialect speakers like Kang himself — at once Korean and not Korean, or potentially of two different Koreas situated differently in the world. National subjectivity is already cosmopolitan and potentially imperial, and one would have to ask whether something like 'modern Korean' is particular or universal, for it acts in both ways. Co-figured with modern Japanese and thus with modern English, modern Korean allows for cosmopolitan and imperial prerogative, even as it produces national sovereignty.

Ethan Nasreddin-Longo's essay on ethnomusicology likewise deals with questions of marking and unmarking in relation to what he styles the 'imperium.' Central to his critique of ethnomusicology is its paradoxical attitude toward its own musical notation. Modern musical notation serves to mark the West from the rest, for only the West is deemed to possess proper notation. Yet, paradoxically, musical notation also unmarks the West, establishing it as an apparently neutral yet authoritative subject. This is analogous to the production of linguistic modernity in Kang's account of modern Korean. For Nasreddin-Longo's account suggests that the production of modernity involved the development of a writing that posed as transparent because it had most thoroughly rationalized the relation of sound to mark. Transparent notation produces an unmarked subject who could mediate all musical cultures, but invisibly, silently. In other words, modern Western musical notation results in a silence that acts — invisible mediation, or more precisely, hegemony — which Nasreddin-Longo calls the 'imperium' to stress its protean relation to diverse modes of imperial appropriation.

Nasreddin-Longo argues that the invisible mediation of Western musical notation serves as the foundation for all ethnomusicological knowledge. Hence Western ethnomusicologists must undermine the claims of other, competing systems of notation. Not surprisingly, however, ethnomusicologists show a distinct preference for musical cultures without systems of notation recognizable as such to the West. Their sense of the immediacy and vitality of these musical cultures that allegedly lack writing recalls for Nasreddin-Longo the persistent Romantic myths about orality and oral cultures — cultures without systematic mediation and thus without alienation, cultures and musics that are 'just there,' eternal and immutable, as if awaiting the Fall into the West. In his critique of ethnomusicology, one of Nasreddin-Longo's central points is that this hegemonic structure of knowledge leans toward racism. This is because it begins with a process of unmarking the West and marking the rest. Yet the West is framed (as self-identical), while the rest are unframed (each equivalent and comparable to the others). Nasreddin-Longo argues that this paradigm leans toward racism precisely because others are marked (usually as coloured) yet unframed (all equally, comparably marked, as non-white). In sum, Western notation remains the naturalized, unexamined basis for ethnomusicology, grounding a disciplinary refusal to look seriously at practices of marking. Maybe it is time, he concludes, that we mark the West itself, as a way to open an inquiry into its marking practices rather than continue to assume their neutrality and authority.

With his parting remarks about marking the West, Nasreddin-Longo seems to call for an end to a certain kind of universalism, one that involves imperial ambivalence (and maybe depth). He shows that, in ethnomusicology, the hegemony of the West lies in its ability to play with marking and unmarking. Western hegemony plays both ends against the middle, as it were. It plays with the marked and unmarked to hide the actual practices that generate those positions. Commonly, it opts for an opposition (writing versus not-writing) to hide the constant play of its marking/unmarking. In this respect, the West is at once marked and unmarked. Thus the call to mark the West ethnically runs the risk of furthering Western interests. Consequently, Nasreddin-Longo's bid to mark the West should probably be seen as a strategy to make visible the operations of imperial ambivalence rather than a definitive solution.

Although Nasreddin-Longo does not consider the production of musical modernity outside the West (national autonomy through the local production of one's own modern notation), his account seems to agree with Kang: this is doomed to failure. Of course, in light of previous essays, I should add that there are different ways of failing, which are potentially other histories. Striking, however, in reading Kang and Nasreddin-Longo is the suggestion that, as different as literature and music are, their recourse to transparent writing produces an unmarked subject whose history is difficult to localize but easy to globalize. Moreover, the problem of modern subject formation is not only or primarily one of signification. It is one of marking and framing, unmarking and unframing. In addition, the hegemonic possibilities of modern subject formation do not lie exclusively in its decisiveness (imposition of meanings, codes and institutions) but also in its ambivalence (sites and times of their suspension).

This is precisely the point of Atsuko Ueda's essay as well. Her essay looks at the profound overlap between discourses on the modern novel and political discourses on civilization, popular rights and 'de-Asianization' in the 1880s in Japan. Ueda calls attention to the discursive production of a new figure, the autonomous intellectual or scholar (*gakusha*). Significantly, she argues that modern Japanese literature would have been impossible without the formation this modern intellectual, which in turn would have been impossible without discourses on the de-Asianization of Japan.

Methodologically, Ueda suggests that literary and political discourses preceded and produced their objects. Which is to say, in the 1880s, geopolitical entities like 'Japan' or 'Asia' or 'the West' had no more objective existence than something like the 'novel' or 'literature.' To produce objects like Japan and the modern Japanese novel, such discourses had to produce and simultaneously repress an 'un-Japanese' and an 'un-novelesque' as well as an 'un-modern.' Of particular importance in the Japanese political discourses of the1880s is the simultaneous production and repression of something called 'Asia.' This was precisely the effect of discourses on de-Asianization — the production of an uncivilized or unmodern to be repressed — Asia. On the side of the production of Asia were all the sociological and political discourses on civilization and rights that posited an uncivilized and unfree Asia. On the side of repression were the military campaigns calculated to subjugate the uncivilized and liberate the unfree. Needless to say, there is something fundamentally tautological and even paradoxical about the discursive production of geopolitical entities such Asia, Japan, and the West — repression and production arise together, as do destruction and liberation.

Ueda suggests that, to contain and naturalize their inherent paradoxes, such discourses demanded specific sites and characters — whence, in discourses on de-Asianization, the insistence on apolitical spaces in which autonomous, neutral intellectuals could transcend interests and exchange ideas disinterestedly. The new, modern intellectual becomes the embodiment of the simultaneous production and repression of Asia. The result, however, was not so much intellectual disinterestedness as double consciousness or ambivalence, which Ueda finds in discourses on the modern novel as well. If such ambivalence ultimately operated hegemonically and imperialistically, it is because the Japanese ambivalence about Asia allowed for a particular kind of relation to the West, which Ueda styles 'mimicry.' Mimicry is not like imitation. Imitation posits a relation between original and copy in which the quality of the copy, its authenticity, is gauged by reference to the original. Imitation thus implies a lag between Japan and the West, which reinforces the logic of modernization: Japan is forever second to the West and behind it. Mimicry, on the contrary, entails a mode of relation in which Japan may act as if it were the West. Its operations are analogous to the simultaneous production and repression of Asia. The operative logic of mimicry allowed Japan to be as the modern West toward Asia — before the fact, so to speak. Mimicry does not involve a studious, step-by-step reproduction of Western institutions and paradigms but rather captures the temporal anomaly at the heart of Western modernity in order to act ahead of time. It is motion capture, as it were.

Ueda suggests that Japan's ability in the 1880s to act before the fact, does not signal a premature, belated, incomplete or otherwise distorted modernity. Mimicry is a fully modern modality. What is striking is how profoundly her account of non-Western intellectuals and mimicry differs from that of Homi Bhabha. To Bhabha, and more generally in accounts of the postcolonial novel, mimicry suggests a process of reinscription that transforms and hence subverts the logic of original and copy. Bhabha evokes mimicry to challenge mimetic models for nationalism and literature. He counters the idea that the non-Western novel is an imitation of the Western novel, an imitation fated to reproduce institutions of national literature. For the logic of imitation establishes the non-Western novel as a site double failure. Not only does non-Western novel fail to reproduce exactly the Western novel, but its failure also relegates it wholly to the formation of ethnic or national identity — it fails to be anything more than an expression of nationness, one that is forever belated or incomplete in relation to the Western norm.

Bhabha's account calls into question that of Benedict Anderson, who sees, with the rise of the novel and newspaper (print capitalism), the production of an empty, homogeneous time that allows for modern nationness. Nationness is a form of subjectivity that corresponds to the ideal of national sovereignty — by which sovereignty is reputed to spread fully, flatly and evenly to the boundaries of the nation. Bhabha evokes mimicry to counter two sociological assumptions about modernity that underlie Anderson's account: first, the nation as a Western model that may be pirated; and second, the novel as the site of production of modernity and modern nationnness. Bhabha is aware that, when one links the novel to the production of modernity via the model of modernization (imitation), the novel becomes trapped in the logic of universal and particular. It is fated to serve the West at the expense of the nation, or to support the nation in opposition to the West. Bhabha turns his attention to ambivalence, to the ways in which the postcolonial novel hovers between the West and the nation. It is both and neither. In this sense, mimicry poses indeterminate hybridity prior to imitation, as the condition of impossibility for imitation and modernization. Ambivalence appears as if prior to operations of universal and particular.

Bhabha stresses the ways in which mimicry thus subverts the logic of universal and particular, of Western modernity and its national formations. Ueda, on the contrary, links it to the production of Japanese empire. Bhabha also sees possibilities for subversion in the ambivalence of cosmopolitan postcolonial intellectuals, while Ueda associates ambivalence with the rise of the universal intellectual. At issue here is not who has the correct view of ambivalence or mimicry. Clearly, the contexts and interests of Bhabha and Ueda differ greatly. Theirs are different histories and different modernities that need not be reduced with a framework of global comparativism. The difference between them is nonetheless instructive because it underscores the importance of context, and indicates that tropes like ambivalence, mimicry and double consciousness are not necessarily or automatically libratory or even subversive. Indeed, in these three essays, the tendency is to associate ambivalence not with zones of autonomy but with the production of unmarked spaces that extend imperial modernity. In all three, something like ambivalence signals the failure of non-Western autonomy. It is as if the production of non-Western civic spaces was merely the point of articulation between quasi-national subjects and an imperial formation. In this respect, the three essays seem to share a critical history and path.

All three challenge the idea that formations of literacy involve liberation or democratization. The very goal of literacy — the production of civic space and universal communication — fails. The production of unmarked spaces, with their claims to transcend ethnicity and local interests, turn out to dovetail with totalizing formations. Not only do these unmarked spaces involve ideologies and fantasies of universal transparency but they also entail the local production of subjects who are subject to national and hence global formations. Crucial are the arguments that literacy does not only subject individuals to local and national formations but also to the global and imperial formations. Universal and particular formations are always already in communication. Local and national formations are not in opposition to global and international formations. An awareness of the complicity of universal and particular imparts a sense of the generalized failure of the particular to resist the universal.

In different ways and to different degrees the essays share this sense of the failure of the particular, because they all detect a productive indeterminacy at work in totalizing formations. Exploring scriptural and discursive formations of literacy, the essays find an underlying totality to modernity — one that subjects. Yet subjection does not work without deterritorializing, without opening unmarked spaces — like those of modern national language, the novel or musical notation. It is as if deterritorialization suspends or subverts the logic of universal and particular, only to bind them more intimately. The resulting image is one of nationalism ever on the verge of empire. Here there are hints that the rise of modern literature and music may not only be written into the history of nations but into formations of global modernity, in which the transparency of communication begins to stage all particulars in the synchronized 'real time' of globalization.

Beyond Sovereignty and Subjection

Another of the key narratives of modernity is that of the rise to prominence of human agency and sovereignty in the construction of the social and political order. With the advent of political modernity, the story often goes, belief in the divine origins of the social order gave way to the notion of humans as lawmakers; people came to see that society was the product of human individuals not deities or monarchs. Crucial to such narratives is some manner of revolution in which humans overthrow the monarch and assume responsibility for, and control over, the natural order (set in motion by a now-distant God whose death approaches). While human sovereignty frequently found its legitimization in the ability of humankind to conquer nature, theories of natural rights and popular sovereignty tended to posit a pre-social state in which humans dwelled together in peaceful contract before various institutions and technologies divided them. In other words, the sovereign individual came to occupy the unenviable position of conquering nature in order to realize its inherently rational and egalitarian order. Political modernity thus is commonly framed as the teleological separation of humans from nature, as the rationalization of nature, or as its dialectical overcoming. In either case, human agency and freedom are established over and against nature.

Of the many challenges to this notion of the sovereign individual, that of Michel Foucault provides a point of departure in the essays by Michael Goddard and Jon Solomon. Simply put, Foucault submitted that we have yet to cut off the head of the sovereign in political and historical analysis so long as we treat the individual as natural and given, as sovereign. In a sense, like Nietzsche, he saw that the death of one sovereign (God) had given rise to another (Man), who in turn needed to be deposed — whence the pronounced anti-humanism of Foucault's early works. One of the ways in which Foucault challenged the notion of individual sovereignty was by radically historicizing the figure of 'Man' and contesting its noble, natural, quasi-divine origins. The figure of Man turned out to be nothing more than a discursive construction, the effect of a historically specific formation of power and knowledge — disciplinary societies, which succeeded the sovereign (that is, monarchical) societies. 'Foucault associated disciplinary societies with the eighteenth and nineteenth centuries; they reach their apogee at the beginning of the twentieth century. They operate by organizing major sites of confinement. Individuals are always going from one closed site to another, each with its own laws. . .'[13] Prison provides the model site of confinement, and carcerality is one of the characteristic discursive formations for disciplinary societies.

Now, as Deleuze notes, Foucault knew how short-lived this model was: 'discipline would in its turn begin to break down as new forces moved slowly into place, then made rapid advances after the Second World War: we were no longer in disciplinary societies, we were leaving them behind.'[14] Nonetheless if Foucault felt that we have yet to cut off the head of the sovereign, it was because the figure of Man continued to organize our thinking of political resistance exclusively in terms of oppositional movements and revolutionary action — that is, on the basis of the individual who replaced yet continued the sovereign. This imagination of resistance continually opposed the particular to the universal, which merely served to advance the universal. Foucault's analysis of the rise of disciplinary societies effectively showed, on the contrary, that the individual emerged through 'subjection.' Disciplinary societies construct self-governing subjects, whose particular interiority subjects them in advance to the laws of each confined space. This is where Michael Goddard's essay begins: with Foucault's attempt to think resistance differently from the model of subjection, beyond the framework of the universal and particular. He shows how Deleuze's concept of 'subjectivation' — which he reads across Deleuze's work on Foucault, on the Baroque and on cinema — continues from Foucault's move away from the model of subjection.

Whereas many read Foucault from the angle of how discourses form, Deleuze emphasizes Foucault's interest in how discursive formations break down. Crucial is the tension between speaking and seeing, between the statement and the visible. Regimes of power and knowledge strive to link, fix and even fuse speaking and seeing, in order to stabilize modes of observation and representation. Yet prior to all relating of speaking and seeing, there is non-relation. There is a force of the outside that disrupts the linking, fixing or fusing of their relation. Goddard writes that there is an inside of the outside — which is not interiority. The subject is not an entity but a process; it remains open to the outside. This means that the subject has an inside 'deeper' than its interiority that comes from without. Neither Foucault nor Deleuze claim that the non-relation constitutes an absolute outside immune to history and regimes of power and knowledge, yet Deleuze especially stresses the ways in which the non-relation intervenes, disrupts and detaches.

Goddard's essay suggests that Deleuze is able to rework the fundamental non-relation between speaking and seeing by taking it to a 'deeper' ontological level. He shifts the non-relation between statements and the visible to the problematic of matter and light (or matter and energy or spirit), to reconsider the (non)relation of body and soul and the process of subjectivation. Leibniz's monad — the fold of a fold — provides the initial model. Deleuze begins with matter as folds, at once continuous and discontinuous. This means that each fold, as a point of continuity in discontinuity, implies a point of view. The subject, as Goddard explains, is what remains in a point of view. It is the fold of a fold — or a co-fold. This differs from a dualistic philosophy in which the subject or consciousness subjectifies matter. Rather, the folds of matter implicate points of view that complicate subjects. Because matter and consciousness co-exist, this makes for an ontology founded on difference (that is, ontogenetic).

In Leibniz, each monad, or each fold with fold, has all of a world, albeit with some regions more or less distinct than others — whence the notion of incompossible worlds based on different monadic points of view. Deleuze differs from Leibniz, however, with regard to the question of whether there exists a point of view that encompasses all others (God or totality). Goddard explains that Deleuze sees the world as infinite potentiality, not as totality. There is no point of view that encompasses the others, God-like. Rather the imcompossibility between worlds is within this world, within each world, potentially. Goddard argues that this allows Deleuze to open the concept of truth to time: '[Leibniz's] concept of incompossibility is an attempt to save the concept of truth by positing different worlds in which a particular event does or does not take place; in one world the battle takes place whereas in another it doesn't so that the contingency of undecidable temporal alternatives is resolved. It is just a question of knowing which incompossible world you are in, depending on whether the event does or does not take place. However, in modern aesthetics these undecidable alternatives or divergent series are located in one and the same world, so that the event both does and doesn't take place in the same world.'

How does Deleuze's reworking of the fold allow a rethinking of modernity? There are (at least) two ways of seeing it. On the one hand, one might think of his reinvention of the Baroque as an alternative modernity, or more precisely, an alternative modernism. The Baroque allows Deleuze to work within a different genealogy, one that bypasses Romanticism and Hegel to arrive at a different theory of change and historical movement. Goddard suggests that, in this respect, Deleuze's Baroque bears comparison with that of another thinker of modernity, Benjamin, who saw in Baroque allegory the liberation of the fragment from totality. However, while Benjamin looked at this disruption from the angle of destruction of historical movement, Deleuze sees in it the creative powers of the false — fabulation. To Deleuze, historical movement is a process of infinite complication that generates divergent series (which bears thinking alongside Derrida's sense of historical movement as abyssal, as infinite regression). All in all, there are infinite incompossible modernities, and even if one insists on thinking in terms of our modernity, the difference between those modernities is nonetheless implicated in ours. Thus Deleuze looks to modernist practices that multiply pasts and futures in the present. Nevertheless, if his approach seems modernist, its lineage diverges from received notions of modernism. Of particular importance is Deleuze's emphasis on 'being for' and 'being with,' which are completely at odds with visions of synchronicity or global simultaneity.

On the other hand, it is possible to ask whether the question of modernity or modernism really matters in this context. Goddard thus ends with the more radical possibility that the important question is no longer 'what era are we in?' but rather 'what practices are we engaged in, and how do they constitute modes of subjectivation?' This is to reinvent the basic question of modernity, by asking how we create new modes or modalities.

Now while Deleuze and Foucault have had a great impact on thinking modernity outside the West, questions often arise about the extent to which their story remains the story of Europe. Timothy Mitchell, for instance, discusses some of the postcolonial criticism of Foucault's work. He concludes that the spatializing tendencies of Foucault's discursive analyses stage a homogeneous time-space that allows for no interruptions from the non-West in the story of modernity.[15] Goddard's account suggests that Foucault began to break with the spatializing tendencies of his earlier work, as he turned toward processes of subjectivation. Yet there is no doubt that Foucault's evocation of Zen and the Orient in his later work continues to posit Japan and China as spaces entirely outside, and even incommensurable with, those of the West. This is, in effect, where Jon Solomon's critique of sovereignty (and Foucault) begins. For he situates his critique at the moment when the outside of the West is no longer discernable as it was in the centuries of Western expansion and imperial conquest.

The extension of political sovereignty to an international league of nations spanning the globe is a recent phenomenon, coming with the processes of decolonization after World War II. Yet, Solomon argues, the result has not been self-determining nations (on the Wilsonian model) or self-governing individuals (on the model of Foucault). Indeed, the model of sovereignty now serves only to mask a new power formation: the sovereign police. Crudely put, the transfer of sovereignty has not been from God to monarch to Man. Sovereignty persists not in citizens but in police forces. The modern problem is not that of self-governing individuals and representational politics that discipline subjects to internalize the laws of separate spaces and spheres of activity (the production of space with the prison as model). Rather it is the dissolution of national boundaries and reduction of individuals to unqualified life or 'bare life.' In essence, Solomon sees a complete dissolution of Foucault's biopolitics of inclusion/exclusion, which afforded sovereignty to those who accepted subjection to it, albeit in the dubious form of protection of their life. The transfer of sovereignty to the police affords no space for welfare. The new biopolitics is that of assuring the complete mobilization of populations.

Solomon's account builds on Agamben to suggest that, if Foucault, like many others, did not see this other biopolitics, it was for geopolitical and historical reasons. Foucault looked at disciplinary societies that reached an apogee in the early twentieth century. At that juncture, Solomon suggests that it was still possible to imagine a spatial divide between the West and the rest, and thus to think modernity spatially in terms of relations, as a problem of representation. While there is some resonance here with postcolonial theory's critique of Foucault, Solomon does not transfer the production of modernity from its alleged centre in the West to centre/periphery or West/rest relations. He does not think in terms of centre and periphery. The real problem, he argues, is our continued inability to think the non-relation in political theory. To this end, he suggests thinking the inclusive exception. Sovereignty is not a matter of relations between friends and enemies (that is, between particulars struggling among themselves to approximate the universal), but a matter of those who are outside (general rather than universal or particular, so to speak). One might see this outside deconstructively, as prior to relations, a supplement that functions as the condition of possibility and impossibility of the system. Solomon, however, does not deconstruct the system based on its points of internal otherness, arguing that these are sites of the system's assimilatory power.

Solomon looks at the contemporary status of Taiwan, posed between America and China as a permanent exception to the global production of national and individual sovereignty. In many respects, Taiwan exemplifies the model for (the failure of) modern sovereignty in East Asia. The rule of extraterritoriality meant that nations tended to conceive sovereignty not on the model of protection of citizens but on the model of policing the native populations to prevent violence against the colonizers. Solomon sees the native populations as the site of non-relation of sovereignty, neither represented politically as citizens nor treated as outsiders — they are neither inside nor outside national sovereignty. In the case of Taiwan, this condition is writ large. Effectively held in a state of permanent exception to national sovereignty, Taiwan is a fictive neo-liberal state whose populations remain under variations on American martial law, in a state of permanent crisis — treaties appropriately refer to 'people on Taiwan' not 'people of Taiwan.' The permanent crisis of Taiwan is not, however, the exception to the rule. Rather, Solomon argues, it is the permanent exception that shows the rules of contemporary geopolitics. Under globalization, we are not all Israelis (as some Americans submitted); nor are we all Americans (as some Europeans suggested). We are all Taiwanese and Korean — in a state of permanent crisis of sovereignty.

In different ways, Goddard and Solomon point to a new condition that demands thinking beyond modernity, that is, beyond subjection and sovereignty. While Solomon describes the contemporary reduction of humans to bare life under martial law and transnational capitalism, Goddard addresses an inability to think subjectivity beyond static spatial models of confinement (or inclusion/exclusion) — models associated with modernity and disciplinary society. When the essays are read together, it seems that Goddard's discussion could be seen as an effort to allow for resistance at the level of bare life (that is, within what Deleuze calls the 'society of control'). Resistance can no longer take the form of liberation from confinement (and maybe never did). Rather we need new forms of resistance, which he begins to conceptualize in terms of 'being for the world' and the co-presence of incompossible worlds. Read together, the essays hint that some prime sites of this non-heroic, non-sovereign resistance will be immigration, the workplace, advanced education, health and nature. Clearly, however, this calls first for a way to think the world beyond sovereignty and subjection, and in some sense, beyond modernity.

Coda

Globalization is sometimes thought of as an intensification of the logic of modernization. It intensifies the modernist production and rationalization of space to the point that everything and every time comes to exist in a single interactive 'real time.' A truly globalized world could only exist in what Nietzsche styled the eternal present, and any temporal experience other than simultaneity or synchronicity would falter and fail. It is in this sense that the temporal rupture of modernity becomes global crisis, and to think modernity inevitably is to think the world. To think the failure of modernity is, on some level, to think the failure of the world, or at least, of one world. Of course, there are ways of failing and then there are ways of failing, for historical reasons. The failure of modernity thus is multiple, and there are as many histories as failures.

One of the important questions raised by this volume is that of whether our diagnoses of these failures are not beginning to converge on a generalized, unconditional failure (manifested as a global disciplinary formation). The point is not that we should return to positive notions of modernity, and think of modernity as merely incomplete yet immanently achievable. Modernity by definition can never arrive, or it is always already here. Rather, it is a question of how critiques of modernity (or modernization or both) must operate with (and within) an underlying totality — in particular, some kind of totalizing prefiguration that implies limits to the subject, epistemologically, ontologically or historically. Crucial sites of the prefiguration in this volume are modern language, culture, discourses, media, institutions — all of which entail impossible yet operative closures — productive failures. If discussions of modernity, regardless of an insistence on specificity of site, tend to converge as if despite themselves, it may be because such discussions have come to share a certain sense of the subject and the world — whence maybe a generalized sense of unconditional failure. Yet, in these essays, this generalized sense of modernity's failure also promises to open critique to the world, with new sense of the world and subjects, attentive to the multiplicity of empire.

In recent years, discussions of modernity have thoroughly challenged the simple diffusion model of a modernity that originates in the West and extends to the world. In cultural, linguistic and historical studies of modernity, close critical attention to processes of rupture with the Western modernity and reinscription of it has challenged prior wisdom about where and how modernity happens. Although modernity, as temporal rupture, inevitably directs attention to the problem of origins, it has become impossible to think modernity without some concept of 'originary difference' or 'divergence at the origin.' Nonetheless, if originary difference challenges the centre/periphery model, it runs the risk of recuperating a world systems model — one in which (to evoke Wallerstein) modernity is a thin net or framework spread over the globe, slowly filling in, becoming denser and more constricting. This is an image of global empire. And as the essays in this volume suggest, to confront such transformations, it may no longer be enough to say that 'modernity is not one *but* multiple' but rather 'modernity is one *and* multiple.' But then this may be to think the world beyond modernity, and the transformative rather than the new.

Notes

1 Dilip Parameshwar Gaonkar , 'On Alternative Modernities,' in *Alter/Native Modernities*, ed. Dilip Parameshwar Gaonkar, Volume 1 in the Millenial Quartet miniseries of *Public Culture* (1999) 11:1, 1.

2 Gaonkar, 'On Alternative Modernities,' 16–17.

3 Gaonkar, 'On Alternative Modernities,' 13.

4 Gaonkar, 'On Alternative Modernities,' 18.

5 Gilles Deleuze, 'Mediators,' trans. Martin Jouhgan, in *Incorporations*, ed. Jonathan Crary and Sanford Kwinter (New York: Urzone Inc, 1992), 281.

6 Charles Taylor, 'Two Theories of Modernity,' in *Alter/Native Modernities*, ed. Dilip Parameshwar Gaonkar, Volume 1 in the Millenial Quartet miniseries of *Public Culture* (1999) 11:1, 153–174.

7 Stuart Hall, 'Introduction: Formations of Modernity,' in *Modernity: An Introduction to Modern Societies*, ed. Stuart Hall et al (Cambridge: Polity Press, 1995), 3.

8 Hall, 'Introduction,' 7.

9 Vicki Kirby, 'Quantum Anthropologies,' in *Derrida Downunder*, ed. L. Simmons and H. Worth (Palmerston North: Dunmore Press, 2001).

10 Gayatri Spivak, 'Subaltern Studies: Deconstructing Historiography,' in *Subaltern Studies IV: Writings on South Asian History and Society*, ed. Ranajit Guha (Oxford: Oxford University Press, 1985), 336–37.

11 Alberto Moreiras, 'Hybridity and Double Consciousness,' *Cultural Studies* 13(3) 1999, 373–407.

12 I evoke the language associated with genocide here, especially Dominic LaCapra's reworking of Freud's notion of mourning, partly because I find Yang Hyunah's rearticulation of the problem of Korean 'comfort woman' in terms of genocide quite convincing. Also, the language seems to fit the tone of Hong's essay. The essay in this volume by Jon Solomon on Taiwan addresses these issues as well, in the context of bare life. See Hyunah Yang, 'Revisiting the Issue of Korean 'Military Comfort Women:' The Question of Truth and Positionality,' in *The Comfort Women: Colonialism, War, and Sex*, special issue of *positions* 5:1 (Spring 1997): 51–72. See too Dominick LaCapra, 'The Return of the Historically Repressed,' from *Representing the Holocault: History, Memory, Trauma* (Ithaca: Cornell University Press, 1994), 169–203; and 'Revisiting the Historians Debate: Mourning and Genocide,' from *History and Memory after Auschwitz* (Ithaca: Cornell University Press, 1998), 43–70.

13 Gilles Deleuze, 'Postscript on Control Societies,' in *Negotiations* (New York: Columbia University Press, 1995), 177.

14 Deleuze, 'Postscript on Control Societies,' 178.

15 Timothy Mitchell, 'The Stage of Modernity,' in *Questions of Modernity*, ed. Timothy Mitchell (Minneapolis: University of Minnesota, 2000), 1–34.

Part 1

Comparativism and the Production of Space and Place

Ghostly Comparisons

Harry Harootunian

Any discussion of modernity and its identification with change will lead to construing the historical process reflexively — temporalizing a moment that immediately and, perhaps, necessarily marks its location from what came before and distinguishes discontinuous time contained within the same chronology.[1] Reinhart Koselleck, quoting from J. G. Herder's *Metakritik of Kant,* reminds us that '(I)n actuality, every changing thing has the measure of its own time within itself. No two worldly things have the same measure of time. There are, therefore, at any one time in the universe innumerably many times.'[2] With this insight, Koselleck proposes that late eightieth century perception already prefigured the practice of investigating historical events and sequences for their own 'internal time.' Yet he could have added (and did elsewhere) that the discovery of internal time — that is, identifying the unique point of time for a specific temporal period — authorized a comparative perspective that would define the vocation of the human and social sciences and thereafter bind its practice to it. In this paper, I want briefly to rehearse the familiar consequences of this comparative framework for practice and especially to look at how it has prompted strategies that have ultimately privileged space.

While area studies were explicitly implemented after World War II to encourage and even foster the development of new comparative perspectives across disciplines and between different culture regions, they were diverted from this vocation by the desire to supply information crucial to the interests of the national security state and then, later, to those of private businesses. Instead of envisaging genuinely interdisciplinary agendas capable of integrating different disciplines, area studies often settled for the regime of a simple multi-disciplinarism as the sign of a comparative method that masqueraded coverage for the work of comparison, with language acquisition for method, and the totality of the nation-state for theory. Too often, area studies became captive of a particular kind of social science that promoted a form of cultural holism, which was made to stand-in for a broader region, even though its true focus was the nation.

This social science, usually some variant of structural functionalism, invariably aimed to 'naturalize time' in such a way as to affirm the primacy of the spatial and the operation of distancing in the classification of societies.[3] What I mean is that the inevitable impulse to compare became fused with a strategy to classify and categorize according to criteria based upon geopolitical privilege. As a result of this principle of classification, societies were invariably ranked according to their spatial distance from an empowering model that was identified with the achievement of industrial and technological supremacy — namely the countries of Euro-America. In this sense, area studies simply replicated the hierarchicizing of political power.

This classification strategy, itself signifying the static synchronicity of the spatial, was mapped onto an evolutionary trajectory that succeeded in apotheosizing the model of natural history and thus defining the task of a comparative agenda which, according to Johannes Fabian, constituted a vast 'omnivorous intellectual machine permitting the "equal" treatment of human culture at all times and in all places.'[4] The appeal to evolutionary time transmuted politics and economics, both intimately concerned with human time, mapping them onto a natural plot line that organized past culture and living societies according to a temporal grid called 'the stream of time' where some managed to move upstream while others were drawn back downstream. Despite the appeal to such concepts as evolution, development, industrialization, modernization, we must observe that these totalizations were more often than not spatially configured rather than temporally marked, more concerned with 'natural' determinations than historically produced forms.

Commonly, the units employed to measure the movement in time result in fixing the quality of states rather than the actual lapse of time. In this way, comparison, implied by the apparatus of 'integrating' several disciplines into a unified approach and a diversity of regional units, is driven by a logic that aimed at naturalizing and spatializing conceptions of time to confer meaning on the distribution of societies in space. Yet the spatial distribution marked by distancing is a transformation of earlier views that had defined temporality as both exclusion and expansion. More importantly, the sense of otherness that must be conceptualized within a theory of knowledge based upon natural history (an Enlightenment project that made possible the comparative method itself) plots all societies in all times on an arc that must designate relative distance from or closeness to the present.

'There would be no raison d'etre for the comparative method,' Fabian writes, 'if it was not the classification of entities or traits which first have to be separate and distinct before their similarities can be used to establish taxonomies and developmental sequences.'[5] Hence the time of the observer's present must be distinguished from the time of the observed, even though the act of observation might be contemporaneous with the object of observation. While the object of knowledge must be expressed as a temporal categorization, the referent is not strictly speaking an object or class of objects but a relationship. This is especially true of ethnographic and historical accounts and indeed of any discipline that is implicated, as are ours, with the task of elucidating a relationship between the West and the Rest.

As a consequence, comparative indices call attention to a classifying system that ranks societies on the principle of gauging distance and separation.[6] The less developed a society, the more distinct it is from the modular paradigm employed to structure the relationship in order to affirm difference. The concept of the late developer, as it was used in modernization studies to describe societies like Japan, China and India, is such an instance. The late developer was produced by this strategy of distancing, and it transmuted what was, in fact, a chronological and quantitative marker into a qualitative one; simple chronology became an attribute. What has been left out in this comparative agenda is history, to be sure, but even more significant is the absence of a sense of temporality that locates practice immanently within the temporality of a modernity, one that embraces the new cultural forms that are developing everywhere and must be considered as coexistent and coeval equivalents, despite the apparent differences among them. Received comparative approaches have consistently disavowed a relationship of coevalness, denying it to precisely those societies targeted for study, misrecognizing a coexistent present we all inhabit — observer and observed — in order to install a perspective that posits a difference of temporal registers between us and the societies and cultures we are seeking to understand, making them 'outside' to our 'inside.' This denial of coevalness implies a refusal to acknowledge that all temporal relations (including contemporaneity) are embedded in socially-, economically- and culturally-organized practices, which are coextensive with capitalism.

If area studies have failed to deliver on their initial promise to produce a viable agenda for comparative studies, the newer cultural studies have offered, in their effort to avoid totalities and essentialisms, ways to rethink the ground of comparability. For they appeal to referents that exceed the units of the nation state that dominated the older approaches. Both poststructuralism and postMarxisms have so overdetermined the text that it probably is no longer necessary to search for a logic capable of integrating the disciplines into a unified approach. In our time, we have to appeal to units larger than the nation state: regions, transnationality, globalization, hyperspace where the diasporic flows of people are said to move across what are misrecognized as 'porous' borders but actually attest to the vast deterritorializing force of capital and labour. Nevertheless, although the newer cultural studies have offered to implement new interpretative modes that promise to avoid the problems manifestly dogging the older developmental model and its binary logic, they have, frequently and unwittingly, recuperated the aporias of the older approach that they wish to succeed. This is especially evident in the spatial turn of cultural studies, its evasion of the role of time. Even among Marxists like Frederic Jameson, time seems to get lost in the fixity of an untranscendable mode of production, despite the status of the mode of production as a primarily temporal category. Fearful of slipping into subjectivistic voluntarism, Marxists inadvertently risk robbing the mode of production of its fundamental timefulness.

Cultural studies, especially its postcolonial inflection, has responded critically to the rapid development of a variety of programs that concentrate on globalization, neo-liberalism, post-Fordism. In fact, they have responded to all those recent signs of the restructuring of global social relations in our time and their consequences for social identity. Spurred by a special urgency provoked by the perception that the nation-state is in process of withering away before the forces of globalization, postcoloniality has turned increasingly toward an attempt to define and even fix identity in an age when older certainties once offered by the nation-state seem to be disappearing. This effort has often been accompanied by a transfer of investment to 'subjects of metahistory and the politics of space and place, and away from their older concerns with (post)colonial subject constitution in psychoanalytic epistemological senses.'[7] Here, Foucault and de Certeau have been hoisted up to replace an earlier privilege accorded to Lacan and Derrida, and genealogy and the specificity of place have been elevated over subjectivity as the principal elements in the construction of identity. Yet we must recognize in this move the primacy of space, especially as it is worked out in the fetishization of place and the lessening importance of forms of temporalization.

While it might be productive to speculate on the reasons for bracketing the temporal (and thus the historical), it is clearly linked at one level to the proliferation of subject positions demanded by consumption on a global scale, which works at the same time to mute the subjectivity of the worker. The really important aspect of this post-colonial preoccupation with space and place lies in its privileging of the conceptual figure of modernity as the sign of a 'hegemonizing socio-historical project' of modernization. In this view, modernity is identified with a specific place, and that place becomes more important than modernity's status as a secular and historical form of temporalization. For the subaltern historian Dipesh Chakrabarty, the categories of 'capital' and 'bourgeois' are simply alternative readings for 'Europe.' The same could be said of 'modernity.'[8] '"The modern" then,' quoting Meaghan Morris, 'will be understood "as a known history, something which has *already happened elsewhere* and which is to be reproduced, mechanically or otherwise, with a local content."'[9]

Like Partha Chatterjee, Chakrabarty worries that this form of modernity will smother native imagination only to recuperate 'the project of positive unoriginality.'[10] Such a program entails a strategy of misrepresenting the modern — the new. It implies an ideological misrecognition of the reproduction of capital accumulation and the deterritorializing force of both capital and labour. But the process is surely as temporalizing — occurring in time — as it is a fixed spatialized identity associated with place. While postcolonial discourse is correct to argue that modernity, as such, is fully compatible with imperialism, it often sacrifices the force of capitalism (sometimes dismissed as another Western metanarrative) as a movement in time that might disturb local certainties but does not necessarily reproduce its original conditions of social existence imperially and mechanically.

By hypostatizing the unity of the 'West' or even 'Europe' as the place of modernity, postcolonial discourse has inadvertently recuperated the worst features of the very binarism that has imperially reduced the rest of the world to the status of a second term to a first that makes everything else look like a pale imitation. Paradoxically, this tactic incorporates the idea of late development as a guarantee of qualitative difference that allows its proponents to envisage something called an 'alternative' modernity. What distinguishes this alternative modernity is its spatial location, a place that is not Euro-America, and thus its claim to an identity that is uniquely different. Once this door is opened, it is possible to imagine all forms of native interiority that have succeeded in remaining immune to the deterritorialization that was forcibly imposed from without — a process which destroys all cultures of reference, as Frantz Fanon presciently observed. Such appeals to cultural resources undisturbed by modernization — a folkloric fiction not worth keeping as Fanon also remarked — are made to offer the surety of an unmovable ground of authenticity on which to construct an identity capable of preserving the autonomy of genuine difference.

The appeal to this illusionary authentic ground, as Japanese misrecognized in the interwar period, seems to offer the promise of 'overcoming the modern,' as they called it, which will configure an alternative to the modernity made in the West. Moreover, the presumption of an alternative modernity reinforces the temporal difference between a putative original and now its 'alternative,' as if the first term will always remain prior, full and primary while its subsequent 'revisions' can only resort to the consolations of difference rooted in a different past and place with claims to native cultural authenticity. In order to offset this spatially inspired asymmetry, some advocates of alternative modernity have looked to forms of identitarian anti-colonial nationalism as evidence of difference resting on the claims of authentic cultural resources that have managed to remain free from contamination. Even here however, we can see the shadow of the time lag and the curious way that the present, a temporal category, conjures up the past.

Recent discussions on the prospects for a proper comparative approach, occasioned by the work of Benedict Anderson, have called into question the status of the modern as a muscular modular metonym dwarfing all before it. The influential *Imagined Communities* put into play the repetition of a mode of modern nationalism based on the agency of print capitalism. Yet Anderson's account was more about print than capitalism, more about communication than the deterritorializing forces of capital and labour. Misrecognizing late nineteenth-century European liberal nationalism based upon middle class literacy as the model for nationalist modernity exported to the Third World, Anderson qualified this fundamentally culturalist interpretation by proposing that it — the model — could be 'pirated.' His accusers, however, have condemned his conception of modularity for having suffocated native imagination and reducing all to 'consumers of modernity.' What seems to have been at stake was the conviction of an 'alternative' modernity that needed to be released from the iron cage of Anderson's Eurocentric model and which could claim for itself the authority and originality of the inner resources supplied by native culture which, perhaps miraculously, had remained undisturbed by modular forms devised elsewhere and imposed by colonial violence. Yet, it is hard not to conclude that the figure of an alternative modernity resembles the reified conception of Tradition once confidently embraced by enthusiasts of modernization theory. Nevertheless, while some of the charges against Anderson border on the tendentious, the critique of an all-empowering model for comparison is on the mark.

In his recent *The Spectre of Comparisons,* Anderson alerts us to one of the excluded possibilities lived by societies outside of Europe but implicated in its imperial expansion, whose modern forms were introduced through the export of capital and colonial deterritorialization. Through a reading of Jose Rizal's late nineteenth century novel *Noli me tangere,* Anderson is able to demonstrate how the author perceived that the gardens of Manila were 'shadowed. . . by images of their sister gardens in Europe. They can no longer be seen in their immediacy but only from a perspective simultaneously close up and faraway.'[11] The novelist names this doubling 'el demonio de las comparaciones' — or the 'spectre of comparison' as Anderson translates it. It may be a bedeviling comparison as well, for the term carries with it the association of a bad or difficult comparison, the dilemma of not knowing which way to look, what I've elsewhere called cultural diplopia.

Anderson, with Rizal's help, designates Southeast Asia as the site of this 'haunting' or devilish vision, housing the spectres, the ghosts of Europe's modernity in replicated forms. He thus sees it as the primary place where this ambiguous optic and the difficulty of comparison have materialized. The haunted house, so to speak, is always the place where the spectres of modernity have taken up residence, which is at the same time the site of comparison. But Anderson could have just as easily seen in the novelistic form itself the sign of the devilish doubling that would prefigure the dilemma of subsequent sister images. For Anderson, concerned with resituating in contemporary analysis the Southeast Asia that has been systematically excluded, the doubling effect (noted also before the war by the Japanese philosopher Watsuji Tetsurô who could not have read Rizal) necessitated thinking simultaneously about Europe and its outside, and mandated the establishment of a comparative perspective in which the act of comparison was always identified with a haunting, the ghostly.

Sustaining this strategy, Anderson further employs the metaphor of the inverted telescope (an up-to-date revision of Marx's camera obscura) that reinforces a comparative method driven by distance and exclusion. By looking through the large lens of the telescope, he sights another image of Southeast Asia that must be smaller, miniaturized, and distant. Since he is in the position of the subject who is gazing through the telescope he has, I believe, magnified his own position at the expense of miniaturizing and diminishing the scene he is viewing. In fact, the distancing implied by the gaze resembles the spatial distance necessary for the formation of the exotic program by an earlier generation of Europeans like Victor Segelan, who always insisted on keeping the object at arm's length. Under this arrangement, there cannot be an equal doubling but only a hierarchicizing of relations between an apparently larger original and a smaller copy, the putative 'sister' image. The determination and distancing of the image means only that it has won its apparent difference from the original by sacrificing the equality of scale and size.

Although Anderson warns us that he is not trading in 'imitations,' 'copies,' and 'derivative discourses,' his appeal to the trope of the inverted telescope more than offsets his logic of 'bound and unbound seriality' and its goal to dispel unwanted 'bogeys.' To be sure, he reminded us in the earlier *Imagined Communities* that idea of the 'nation' could claim no patent since it was continually 'pirated' by different people with often 'unexpected' results. Yet Anderson is closer to his critics than either suspect. On the one hand, there is Anderson who wishes to propose an approach that must take into consideration the role of some form of repetition in the migration of his model to enable the late developer to embark upon the course of capitalist modernization and national liberation. On the other hand, there are his critics who put forth the opposing proposition of an alternative modernity and anti-modern communitarianism free from the corrosion of colonial and thus Western mediations in figuring a modern, national identity. Yet ultimately, both risk recuperating the second term of the very binary they are attempting to avoid. Both, moreover, manage to sustain the primacy of spatial relationships as the vocation of comparative study.

Beyond Anderson's identification of the ghostly as the object of comparative study, there is, I believe, the larger and more important spectrality of societies deeply involved in fashioning a modernity coeval and coextensive with Euro-America, yet whose difference, neither a simple imitation or mechanical reproduction, is dramatized by a different kind of haunting. This is the movement of the revenant, the ghosts of what-has-been-past that coexists with the new in everyday life. Unlike Anderson's spectres, which are more like pale shadows and ambiguous silhouettes, these ghosts of a surviving past — the premodern culture of reference — return from a place out of time or a different temporality to haunt and disturb the historical present, to trouble the stable boundaries between past and present, subject and object, interior and exterior. This haunting requires envisaging a structure of comparability that recognizes the role played by temporally rooted forms in the present. It must also attend to what Ernst Bloch referred to as the contemporaneity of the non-contemporaneousness (*Gleichzeitigkeit der Ungleichzeitigen*), which might also be glossed as 'non-synchronous contemporaneity,' wherein past and present are not necessarily successive but simultaneously produced (as Bergson once proposed), or coexist as uneven temporalities, just as the here and there of modernity are coeval, even though the latter is forgotten in the former.[12]

What comparative practice has excluded in its desire to narrativize a cultural aspiration associated with Euro-America is the relationship between its modernity and the modernities of the world outside of it that must share the same ground of temporality and agencies of transformation. To deal seriously with this ground of temporality, we must address the question of how our present shows itself to us, and we must find in it a minimal unity provided by everyday life that has organized the experience of modernity. In this way, we confront the larger and immanent framework of capitalist modernity and its incessant transformations. Such an approach has the advantage of redirecting our attention to the role of capitalism, in its many manifestations throughout the world, rather than merely displacing it onto modernity or repressing it. It serves to alert us to the relationship between lived experiences of everydayness and the regime of the commodity form, surely one of the principal agencies in the production of contemporary historical formations.

Making this move also allows us to bypass the dangerous misrecognition that identifies capitalism with universalism, a misrecognition that arises when a culturally-specific context fixed in a geopolitical space is made to stand in for all subsequent manifestations, or when it is replaced with a spatializing process that involves placement in time to mark the historical difference of various formations. The point, as Pierre Vilar observes, is that capitalism was 'born of colonization' and the 'world market,' and has subsequently 'universalized' history only insofar as it has established systematic relations of social interdependence on a global scale, which have eventually encompassed non-capitalist societies. In this regard, capitalism has managed to fix a standard of measurement — world time — produced by a 'single, global space of coexistence' within which action and events are subject to a single, quantifiable chronology. But, because different social and cultural practices remain outside this abstract measure, capitalism has not 'unified' history.[13]

In sum, everydayness constitutes a cultural form that shares with modernity the experience of capitalism and thus is coeval with it. Both everydayness and modernity are also temporal categories that derive their broader importance from their historical forms. If we can represent modernity as the ever new, everydayness then must be seen as the durational present, the site of vast temporal economic and cultural unevenness, incomplete but 'situated at the intersection of two modes of repetition: the cyclical, which dominates in nature and the linear, which dominates in the processes known as rational.'[14]

For the prewar Japanese thinker Tosaka Jun, in a manner analogous to Lefebvre, everydayness manifested a mode of temporalizing that was different from the modern mode and combined the presentness of the Heideggarian Now with repetition. At one level, everydayness thus served as the intersection of all repetitions — received and recent, past and present — and constituted the site of 'recurrences,' that is, 'gestures of labour and leisure, mechanical movements both human and properly mechanic, hours, days, weeks, months years, linear and cyclical repetitions.'[15] It was also 'material culture,' clothing, and (especially for Tosaka) life, furniture, houses, neighbourhoods, and environment — the solidity of filled space, Heidegger's 'there' (*Da*), the world of the present. This is what Lefebvre, Tosaka and the Portuguese poet Pessoa thought of as the 'veiled,' as a kind of hidden, shadow existence.[16] It stands in contrast to Anderson's ghosts, what he designated as the haunt — the place of comparison. It allows us to envisage an everyday that is genuinely the spectral, where the shadows of another life constantly act upon and are acted upon by the ever new, the modern.

The modern reveals this everydayness in its immediacy, while this everydayness is constantly mediating the new. Moreover, as the everyday, the 'practically untellable,' meets the modern, the modern now appears as the endlessly novel, worldly, transitory and spectacular. In this momentous encounter, the new, now strategically misrepresented as modernity, begins to function as 'repetitive gestures' that mask the regular cycles of everyday. Thus the monotony of everydayness contains the shock of the new. Yet, as Tosaka Jun saw, this remained an explosive encounter, filled with 'possibility.' And Lefebvre discerned in such repetitions the place where 'everything changes.'[17]

If the figure of unevenness stands at the heart of everyday life, it is because, as Marx observed in *Grundrisse*, the insertion of capitalism into societies at differential moments and different rates of intensity results in the coexistence of different forms of economic and cultural practices.[18] We can agree with Henri Lefebvre and David Harvey that capitalism in the twentieth century has survived principally by necessarily expanding into space, by 'producing space.' But it should also be added that its success has been based upon its capacity to generate vast unevenness along its route, not just between societies but also within them. In other words, this spatial movement demands a reconfiguration of the relationship between time and space. As a consequence, any effort to construct a comparative framework must be capable of grasping the manifestation of modernities. In fact, the expansion of capitalism, whether carried on within a national society or overseas, is inextricably linked to the production of unevenness. This was not only articulated by Lefebvre but also by Bloch in the concept of a contemporaneous non-contemporaneousness.

It seems to me that one of the ways of thinking about this new reconfiguration is to concentrate on how unevenness, the experience expressed paradigmatically in the Blochian idea of contemporaneous non-contemporaneousness, is actualized in those places and spaces that have committed their resources to the transformations of capitalist modernization. What I am suggesting is that the contemporaneity of the non-contemporaneous allows us to return to the question of temporality and the forms through which it is expressed in those societies whose appearance has been spatialized by the capitalist nation-state. Initially resulting from overseas expansion, this sense of a dissonant temporal asymmetry, as it is then experienced in the everyday, supplies a possible framework for constructing a comparative framework on a global scale, one that might account for local differences without exceptionalizing the location of space as an 'alternative' to a prior, original model.[19]

The geographic opening of the globe and its subsequent colonization brought about the recognition of co-existing cultures which, through a kind of synchronous classification, were then ordered diachronically — in an effort to make a 'civilized' Europe appear ahead of an 'uncivilized' Asia and Africa. Yet, if such comparisons promoted the emergence of an experience of a possible world history in terms of 'development' and 'progress,' they also set the stage for reconsidering and reconfiguring the contemporaneity of the non-contemporaneous in such a way as to highlight the production of difference — that difference that any society would experience as it confronted the unevenness caused by the interactions of its past in its present. It was, I believe, precisely this observation that led Bloch to account for the arrival and success of fascism in Germany, even though his analysis never exceeded that cultural and historical horizon or even acknowledged the larger geographical origins of such an insight.

With Bloch, the argument stalled in a comparison of Germany, France and England, which came to function more as alibi than explanation. German capitalism, he was convinced, became hostage to late development and therefore failed to integrate the social, political, and economic realms. The lack of integration gave way to the continuation and surfacing of older practices and mentalities — the non-contemporaneous — which was something that fascism successfully appropriated, while Marxism misunderstood it. By confining this form of temporalizing to Germany, however, he unintentionally and inadvertently exceptionalized the German experience of modernization, thus reinforcing an argument already made by the fascists whom he held in derision.

On the other side of the world, Tosaka Jun was observing a similar phenomenon in Japan, which he called 'archaicism.' Tosaka, however, clearly recognized that 'archaism' was merely a local manifestation of a wider experience to be found throughout the industrializing world of the 1930s. It is, in any case, interesting to note that Frederic Jameson has recently resuscitated the concept of contemporaneous non-contemporaneousness, attributing it to modernism. In his analysis, modernism functions ideologically to conceal unevenness, which a later postmodernism will supposedly eliminate with the establishment of a putatively full and even modernity. Yet this argument seems to have more to do with vesting the West with an exceptional endowment than with the logic of capital or the history of the world outside Euro-America. (Jameson thus furthers the never-ending myth of Western unity, envisaged of course from the perspective of 'Western Marxism' but not from the perspective of those who were enlisted to give meaning to this concept.) If the instance of unevenness has invariably attended the historical spread of capitalism everywhere, it still must continue to occupy a commanding 'space of experience' in our analyses because unevenness continues to constitute one of capitalism's principal conditions of reproduction.

In the 1920s, the Japanese native ethnologist Yanagita Kunio already named this combined development (that he was already recording in Japan) 'mixed or hybrid civilization' — which, he acknowledged, could be found throughout East Asia.[20] At the same time the Indonesian nationalist Soetomo was acknowledging the constant unevenness of life produced by the interaction of the past with his present. Both could have just as easily been describing that process everywhere by which modernity and everyday life were responding and corresponding to each other. While such a focus on the development of uneven temporalities within modernities may easily slip into the space occupied by a fixed place (that still fails to conceal its status as the second term), it may also serve to shift our attention away from the singularity of the nation and its counterclaims to uniqueness that, it now seems, has always been trying to bridge the difference between modernity and everyday life. For, if categories of historical analysis like capital and modernity are to have a particular effect, they will have to be examined in the cultural and social forms in which history is lived everywhere as a continuing and never completed but ever explosive conjuration of the past in the present.

Notes

1. Reinhart Koselleck, *Futures Past: On the Semantics of Historical Time,* trans. Keith Tribe (Cambridge: MIT Press, 1985), 94.
2. Ibid., 247.
3. Johannes Fabian, *Time and the Other: How Anthropology Makes Its Object* (New York, Columbia University Press, 1983), 16.
4. Ibid., 16–17.
5. Ibid., 27.

6 Ibid., 26.

7 Lazarus, 'Hating Tradition Properly,' in *Nationalism and Cultural Practice in the Postcolonial World* (Cambridge: Cambridge University press, 1999), 28.

8 Dipesh Chakrabarty, 'Postcoloniality and the Artiface of History,' in *A Subaltern Studies Reader, 1986–1995*, ed. Ranajit Guhaa (Minneapolis: University of Minnesota Press, 1997), 267. See, too, Dipesh Chakrabarty, *Provincializing Europe* (Princeton: Princeton University Press, 2000).

9 Meaghan Morris, 'Metamorphoses at Sydney Tower,' *New Formations* 11 (Summer 1990), 10; and Meaghan Morris, *Too Soon, Too Late : History in Popular Culture* (Bloomington and Indianapolis:, Indiana University Press: 1998), 16. Also cited in Dipesh Chakrabarty, 'Postcoloniality and the Artiface of History,' 283.

10 Ibid. I am thinking here of Partha Chatterjee's *The Nation and Its Fragments* (Princeton: Princeton University Press, 1993).

11 Benedict Anderson, *The Spectre of Comparisons: Nationalism, Southeast Asia and the World* (London and New York: Verso, 1998), 2.

12 Ernst Bloch, 'Non-contemporaneity and Obligation to the Dialectic,' in *The Heritage of Our Times* (1932), trans. Neville and Stephen Plaice, (Cambridge: Polity Press, 1991).

13 Pierre Vilar, 'Marxist History, A History in the Making: Towards a Dialogue with Althusser,' *New Left Review* 80 (July/August 1973), 105. See, too, Peter Osborne, *The Politics of Time: Modernity and the Avant-Garde.* (London and New York: Verso, 1995), 34.

14 Tosaka Jun, 'Fûzoku no kôsai' (1948), in *Tosaka Jun zenshû* (Tokyo: Ito shôten, 1971). Henri Lefebvre, 'The Everyday and Everydayness,' *Yale French Studies* 73 (1987), 10.

15 Henri Lefebvre, *Everyday Life in the Modern World* (New Brunswick, NJ: Transactions Publishers, 1994), 21–22.

16 See Fernando Pessoa, *The Book of Disquiet*, ed. Maria Jose du Lancastre, trans. Margaret Jull Costa (London: Serpent's Tail, 1991).

17 See Osborne, *The Politics of Time*, 196.

18 Karl Marx, *Grundrisse* (1859), trans. Martin Nicolas (London and New York: Penguin Books, 1973), 105–6).

19 Koselleck, *Futures Past*, 256.

20 Yanagita Kunio, *Teihon Yanagita Kunio zenshû vol. 25* (Tokyo: Chikuma shobô, 1965), 279.

In Search of the Modern: Tracing Japanese Thought on 'Overcoming Modernity'

Sun Ge

— *Translated from Chinese by Peter Button*

In 1942, following the outbreak of the Pacific War, a prominent group of intellectuals in Japan held a symposium entitled 'Overcoming Modernity.' The symposium itself did not directly discuss the war, with the exception of a small number of papers by individual participants. Its topics included the fundamental problems brought on by European and American modernity, the effects of Western modernity in Japan, and the question of rediscovering the Japanese spirit. In his concluding remarks on the symposium, the chair, Kawakami Tetsutarô, emphasized that the central issue of the meeting lay in spreading knowledge about the spiritual power that had been concealed under the propaganda slogans for the Greater East Asia War. He stressed that, in an age of great ideological pressure, the idea of 'being unable to speak one's mind' amounted to little more than an emotional soliloquy. 'Overcoming Modernity,' he went on to claim, constituted neither an ideological slogan nor an emotional soliloquy; it sought to address the question, 'How are we to become modern Japanese?'

Although the symposium faithfully adhered to this agenda, it nonetheless ignored a certain brutal reality. It was not merely that the two-day discussion took place far from the battlefield in the relative luxury of a hot springs resort. Rather, the symposium, despite its physical distance from war, was not afforded any discursive distance from it. Between the official ideologies and opposition to them, it found no substantially different third way. Moreover, because oppositional ideologies did not truly exist at that time, it became all too easy to muddle independent intellectual engagement and the official ideology. And on the surface at least, intellectual work had to take the form of tacit acceptance of, and cooperation with, the official ideology. At the symposium, intellectual work and wartime ideology were, in fact, conflated. As a consequence, subsequent generations of Japanese intellectuals, despite their individual differences, have almost unanimously characterized the symposium in terms of a relationship of complicity, however complex, with the fascist and militarist ideology of the era.

Paradoxically, in light of their subsequent, nearly universal opprobrium of it, later Japanese intellectuals have consistently praised the symposium in comparison to other important symposia of the era, and have repeatedly cited and analyzed it. This subsequent series of renewed analytical efforts hint that much remains for subsequent generations to think through. The later analyses suggest that 'Overcoming Modernity' entailed something more than mere ideological fuss, something that continues to speak beyond its time and place. Maybe because it continues paradoxically to pose new challenges, some commentators have tried to transcend the symposium itself, to reduce it to an ideological expression of its time.

In any event, the symposium has continued to provide a point of departure for extracting a fundamental problem in Japanese thought in the World War II era, and even thereafter. As a result, even as 'Overcoming Modernity' fulfills a certain symbolic function (deemed representative of its era and limited to it), it has been forced to bear the weight of a historical and ideological content that far exceeds its actual limits. One can thus pursue 'Overcoming Modernity' as a coherent line of thought, from the symposium into the series of subsequent commentaries by postwar intellectuals. 'Overcoming Modernity' now refers to a relatively complete and independent set of issues that arise around the symposium and around the subsequent debates on it, which today help us to trace the thought of modern Japanese intellectuals on the problem of modernity.

Overview of the 'Overcoming Modernity' Symposium

A group of men associated with the journal *Literary Society* (*Bungakkai*) convened 'Overcoming Modernity' — as an interdisciplinary symposium.[1] While primarily devoted to literary topics, *Literary Society* had gained a reputation for the broad range of its discussions, and so it is not surprising that this journal should have attempted an interdisciplinary event like 'Overcoming Modernity'. From among those associated with the journal, however, the writers were responsible for conceiving and sponsoring the symposium. As a consequence, while interdisciplinary in appearance, the symposium in fact retained what might be described as an essentially literary framework. This was most evident in its emphasis on the Renaissance and on everyday life, as we will see.

The symposium presented quite a broad range of topics, such as the modern significance of the Renaissance; modernity in science; the relationship between science and theology; our modernity; modern Japanese music; historical development and stasis; the problems of civilization and specialization; the essence of Meiji civilization; the West within us; Americanism and modernism; and, the possibilities of the modern Japanese people. Even a brief perusal of this list of topics should suggest that the aim of the symposium — an overcoming of modernity — was based on a discussion of the inherent limits of Western modernity. Equally salient is its emphasis on the superiority of that culture deemed to be indigenous to Japan. Otherwise, the list tells us very little about the actual contents of the symposium. This is not only because different participants pursued these topics in very different manners, but also because many discussions were foreclosed in advance, preventing any development in depth. We must thus go beyond the kinds of discussion implied in the program and explore the *manner* in which topics were actually discussed.

A comparison with another prominent symposium 'World Historical Position and Japan' provides an excellent point of departure for exploring the manner in which 'Overcoming Modernity' pursued its program. 'World Historical Position and Japan,' a symposium organized by the Kyoto School in the same year, similarly aimed to challenge Western modernity, and also in a manner that was easily confounded with the ideology of the Greater East Asia Co-Prosperity Sphere. Moreover, the two symposiums also presented some significant overlap in their participants. In addition to those associated with *Literary Society* and the scholars representing various disciplines such as theology, natural sciences, and music, two Kyoto School scholars were particularly important participants in 'Overcoming Modernity' — the philosopher Nishitani Keiji and the historian Suzuki Shigetaka — both of whom also participated in 'World Historical Position and Japan.' What is more, the symposiums were drawn together in subsequent publications and discussions. For instance, while 'World Historical Position and Japan' initially appeared in three consecutive issues of the journal *Chûô Kôron*, it was later, in the postwar years, compiled in a collection with 'Overcoming Modernity' under the general title *Overcoming Modernity.* [2]

Nevertheless, despite such overlaps, the efforts at rigorous argumentation and polished discussion that characterized 'World Historical Position and Japan' also serve to highlight the fundamental confusion that surrounded 'Overcoming Modernity.' The confusion was such that it is impossible to think of 'Overcoming Modernity' as a successful example of interdisciplinary discussion. Basically, many of the aims and assumptions that came with the literary framework of 'Overcoming Modernity' tended to disrupt extended theoretical discussion on important issues.

For instance, one of the first questions posed by the chair for 'Overcoming Modernity' (Kawakami Tetsutarô) concerned one of the important themes of the program: 'The Modern Significance of the Renaissance.'[3] The above-mentioned Kyoto School historian, Suzuki Shigetaka, was appointed as a commentator on this topic. Significantly, even though Suzuki tried to address the topic in question, he nonetheless had made clear in his paper proposal that he had grave doubts about this topic as a point of departure. As an historian, Suzuki attempted to redirect the topic toward specific academic complexities that arise within the discipline of history. Then he stressed that '[t]his is highly specialized knowledge. I doubt that the average person has any need to delve into such questions.'[4]

While the Kyoto School scholars did not hesitate to expound the official ideology, they also tried to render it more theoretically rigorous. It was precisely such theoretical rigor that made their questions ones into which the average person had no need to delve. This became the very premise for 'World Historical Position and Japan.' At 'Overcoming Modernity,' on the other hand, Suzuki's academic style immediately met with interruptions and objections, which forced him to draw overly rigid and simplified conclusions. While Suzuki continually strove to lead the discussion back to something more theoretically rigorous, the writers made clear their lack of interest in that kind of rigor. Generally speaking, the historians saw the French Revolution and the Enlightenment as the proper point of departure for the question of modernity (*kindai*) and the nature of the contemporary (*gendaisei*). Kawakami Tetsutarô, for instance, assigned the Renaissance a central position, independent from later developments, establishing it as a point of departure for discussion of the nature of the contemporary. Yet his approach ran so dramatically counter to Suzuki's that Suzuki continually tried to direct discussion toward the Enlightenment and French Revolution. He gently refuted Kawakami's stance, pointing out that it was inappropriate to define the Renaissance as the origin of modernity. Although beset with interruptions and objections from the literary contingent, both Suzuki and Nishitani Keiji struggled to direct the discussion on the Renaissance toward that of the relation between the medieval and the modern, thus striving to introduce greater continuity into the discussion of historical periods.

For the writers, however, the Renaissance remained the point of departure for an account of modernity. Their preference for the Renaissance can be better understood by seeing the way in which it echoes one of the major literary movements of the period. During the 1930s, especially in the four-year period from 1933–37, as the Marxist and proletarian culture movement waned, journals devoted to 'pure literature' began to make their appearance. Because many writers produced their finest works at this time, the period later became known as one of 'literary renaissance.' In other words, for the literary figures behind 'Overcoming Modernity,' the Renaissance seemed to promise a Japanese modernity based on the flourishing of vernacular arts (particularly literature). It was, however a vernacular revival that was to stand in opposition to the contaminating influences of popular or mass culture (which were associated with Westernization), hence the notion of 'pure literature.'

At 'World Historical Position and Japan,' Suzuki Shigetaka, together with three other speakers, again delved into the problem of the Renaissance, but in a manner that differed significantly from that allowed for in the context of 'Overcoming Modernity.' In this discussion, the Renaissance was not only deemed unworthy of independent discussion but modernity itself also required considerable qualification. Briefly put, the Renaissance was seen as but one link in the knowledge of European and world history, and not as the point of departure for modernity. Its position could only be determined in relation to others, not in isolation. It was simply a constitutive element of modern Europe with no absolute value independent of other historical periods.

This comparison with 'World Historical Position and Japan' reveals another important aspect of 'Overcoming Modernity.' The writers associated with *Literary Society* wanted simple answers from the scholars — just some brief explanation with useful conclusions. Once the scholars introduced greater complexity into the dialogue and departed from easily comprehensible conclusions, the role of the writers seemed to lie in interrupting that kind of discussion. All of the confusion around 'Overcoming Modernity' results from this basic format. 'World Historical Position and Japan' presented a format in which scholars pursued a coherent line of inquiry without interruption, thus elucidating a highly authoritative theory of world history. In sum, the completely different structuring of the two symposiums led to profound differences in what they could achieve.

Equally important were the ways in which participants in the two symposiums situated themselves in relation to modernity. Both symposiums attempted to negotiate the position of Japan in the world during the fiercest period of the Asia-Pacific War, insisting on, and even boasting about, Japan's superiority and its right to a position of leadership in Greater East Asia. Yet participants situated themselves very differently with respect to the position of Japan in the world. Participants in 'Overcoming Modernity' tended to take a personalized approach, hence highlighting the questions about subjectivity. Speakers at 'World Historical Position and Japan' tended to raise questions about their objects of theoretical investigation as such. The previously-mentioned division of intellectual labor that tended to develop at 'Overcoming Modernity' reinforced such trends: scholars were expected to explain the fundamental problems of Western modernity on the first day, then on the second day, the literary figures associated with *Literary Society* were to discuss Japanese modernity. They gradually began to stress their own experiences. It was implied that Japanese modernity could be framed in terms of personal experience (while Western modernity remained a prickly problem). Moreover, it was implied that experience was properly the domain of literary types rather than scholars. This tension became most evident in the conversations that Kobayashi Hideo (a renowned literary critic and cultural commentator from *Literary Society*) had with Suzuki and Nishitani. All three were in agreement on the issue of overcoming historicism, yet to Suzuki's query 'Where could one observe the stasis amidst historical change that you discuss?' Kobayashi felt it sufficient to answer, 'It is part of everyday experience.'[5]

Everyday experience had no place in 'World Historical Position and Japan.' Due of their rigorous training, Kyoto School scholars invariably appealed to the authority of the text even to express their own point of view. While such a gesture did not guarantee the objectivity of their position, it did nonetheless assure that everyday experience (at least in the guise of personal experiences) was barred as an intellectual ground for debate. For debate, as Suzuki emphasized in his discussion of the Renaissance, 'I doubt that the average person has any need to delve into such questions.' For the literary figures involved in 'Overcoming Modernity,' however, everyday experience was of central importance. While this did not mean that they could claim to represent so-called average persons and their experiences, they truly brought a perspective on modernity in which everyday experience became available for observation and thought.

Much of the confusion surrounding 'Overcoming Modernity' lies in this emphasis on everyday experience. Yet this is also why the symposium has garnered the praise of subsequent commentators, especially in comparison to other symposiums. While the Kyoto School scholars understood the symposium topics in terms of their theoretical significance, the associates from *Literary Society* had, in a rather journalist fashion, organized the symposium around a series of seemingly crucial questions drawn from daily life as they imagined it. As a consequence, the symposium tended in two directions, on the basis of the same questions. On the one hand, the literary figures tended to associate the 'anti-modern' with an affirmation of a native 'pure tradition.'[6] On the other hand, the scholars saw the discussion of the superiority of Japan as a constitutive element in the narrative of world history. The discussions on the subject of 'the West that exists within us' that occurred on the second day are characteristic. In these exchanges Kobayashi Hideo criticized Nishitani Keiji and some of the other participants for their lack of a sense of the physical and corporeal, a sensibility deemed to be characteristically Japanese. Nishitani retorted that he 'really didn't have the luxury' to indulge such a sensibility. This was because 'in comparison with the question of whether or not the people of Japan could understand what scholars were writing,' he felt that the 'desire to break through the dead end of the Westerners was far more urgent.'[7]

Behind the differences expressed by Kobayashi and Nishitani are traces of fundamental differences among Japanese intellectuals' responses to Western modernity. From the Meiji period, with its drive for modernization and a desire to construct a nation to rank with the Western powers, Japanese intellectuals tended, however indirectly, to take the West as an object of emulation. Nishitani's sense of the urgency of confronting the West runs through all the activities of the Kyoto School. For Kyoto School scholars, the native traditions that were of such importance to the writers constituted nothing more than the ingredients necessary to the project of breaking through the dead end of the West. In the grand, world historical narrative of the Kyoto School, while 'Japan' had been placed in the important position of replacing the modern West, 'Japan' was never regarded as the end point of discussion or of history. In other words, the titles for the two symposiums manifest the subtle differences in orientation with respect to resistance to the West. For the literary contingent, resistance became fully embodied in a Japanese sense of the physical, sensuous world. For the scholars, on the contrary, resistance to the West, situated in a world-historical framework, meant there was no time to indulge such a sensibility.

In the historical context of 1942, however, the underlying connections between these apparently opposed positions became clearer. First, the outbreak of the Pacific War itself forced a certain degree of agreement with respect to Japan's military aggression. Here the posture of challenging the West served to conceal a sense of guilt and anxiety that had been openly expressed by progressive intellectuals in Japan at the time of earlier invasions of neighboring countries in East Asia. In the wake of the surprise attack on Pearl Harbor, however, Japanese intellectuals spoke unanimously in favor of the war and the Greater East Asia Co-Prosperity Sphere. Second, there arose a certain form of consensus around the question of how to deal with the West. Around the drive for modernization in Meiji Japan developed an opposition (and complex admixtures) between a position that centered on Japan and one that centered on the West. The outbreak of the Pacific War tipped the scales toward a unified position that centered on Japan. In sum, at this pivotal moment in the Asia-Pacific War, it became possible to set aside differences regarding the shock produced by Western modernity in Japan, at least temporarily.

Although the hard-won cooperation between writers and scholars could only occur in the context of the difficult 'cultural identity' forced on them by the advent of the Pacific War, the real interest of 'Overcoming Modernity' derives from its stark manifestation of the differences that had apparently been set aside. It was most manifest in the inability of its scholars and writers to work together and to think alike, despite all the exhortations for cooperation. (In fact, in the postwar period, the journal *Literary Society* was never again able to call on Kyoto School scholars to participate in their discussions.) The symposium thus revealed the illusory nature of the persistently promoted identity of Japan that was to replace the West and become the superpower of East Asia. Even though war never became central to its discussion (but served only as background), the symposium nonetheless showed the violence of war more clearly than any other discussion, exposing more powerfully the effect of this violence on the intellectual as it forced spurious cooperation and unification.

This unification in the last instance serves as a reminder that the binary opposition — Japan versus the West — must not be accepted at face value as a self-evident opposition. In fact, there are no inherent differences between Japan and the West, or between tradition and modernity. Such differences are produced in relation, in the process of narrating them, and it is only when awareness of such effects of relation and narration breaks down that differences between Japan and the West tend to collapse (even as they are reified). For this reason, while there did not exist any real difference of position among Japanese intellectuals of the 1940s, a single problematic held sway: that of *how to narrate* 'Japan' and the 'West' within the putatively larger narrative of modernity. It was precisely such fundamental differences about 'how to narrate' that subtly influenced the later debates about 'Overcoming Modernity.'

Takeuchi Yoshimi and Ara Masahito's 'Overcoming Modernity Debates'

In the postwar years, fraught as they were with a nationwide stance of repentance or disavowal, the debates on 'Overcoming Modernity' became a source of 'secret anguish' for scholars associated with the Kyoto School, who ignored or suppressed them in their subsequent work. Yet their 'Forum on Japanese Culture' continued the concern for a narrative of world history, albeit one with official sanction and thus rather conservative tendencies. While almost all of the same Kyoto School scholars participated in this forum, the writers from the *Literary Society* had severed all ties with this group. What had once been an obstacle between differing orientations based on the narratives of 'World History' versus those of 'Overcoming Modernity' coalesced into a veritable barrier. Because the Kyoto School scholars had disavowed and displaced their former concerns, recollection of the symposiums fell entirely to the writers. Thus in the April 1952 edition of *Literary Society*, transcripts of the symposium were published, and Kawakami, Kobayashi, Hayashi Fusao and others once again raised questions about 'Overcoming Modernity,' but with the caveat that it was a personal, private pursuit.[8] Postwar criticism of, and reflection on, wartime Japan treated the symposium as a negative example of how Japanese intellectuals had cooperated with, and promoted, fascist ideologies, and so the very idea of 'Overcoming Modernity' was thoroughly censured. Gradually, however, this censure provoked an interest in returning to the rationale behind the symposium.

It was under such circumstances that Takeuchi Yoshimi, in November 1959, published his essay on 'Overcoming Modernity.'[9] At the outset, Takeuchi signaled that intellectuals had produced the phrase 'overcoming modernity' for intellectuals; it thus differed dramatically from the popular conception of it as a simple ideological campaign. Nonetheless, he wished to point out that, from the standpoint of historical memory as it confronted the intricate mesh of war and fascism, the phrase 'overcoming modernity' had indeed functioned much as popularly imagined. Takeuchi noted that, although those responsible for the symposium surely lacked the wherewithal to conduct an ideological campaign, the symposium nevertheless came to be seen an ideological effort, despite its actual heterogeneity. As a result, for any Japanese intellectual over the age of thirty, the phrase provoked extremely complex responses. One might say that Takeuchi's essay grew out of the complexity of responses to 'Overcoming Modernity' among intellectuals.

Subsequent commentators thus felt obligated to deal with the ideological charge of 'Overcoming Modernity,' and evaluations tended toward oppositional stances, either striving to recover their truths or to negate them. Yet, in so far as both positions were fundamentally critiques of ideology, they had much in common. Takeuchi took Odagiri's critique of 'Overcoming Modernity' as representative of the position of left-wing intellectuals. While it 'could not persuasively deny the demand for recovering the truths behind "Overcoming Modernity," neither did it possess the critical force to negate those truths.'[10]

Thus Takeuchi stressed the importance of getting the intellectual facts straight. 'To get the facts of so-called ideology straight means to investigate how that ideology strives to determine its topics, how it reaches for resolution in concrete instances, or how it remains unresolved.'[11] Of course, what Takeuchi meant by 'ideology' did not simply encompass those ideologies deemed correct but also those deemed incorrect or pernicious. Which is to say, he introduced a certain degree of relativity and autonomy into the question of ideology, showing that any ideology had a relative power of influence, to some degree autonomous of the political order. The influence of ideology on society arose outside the political order. 'Overcoming Modernity' and 'World Historical Position and Japan' entailed precisely such 'ideologies.' What, then, is the ideology that we should approach factually in 'Overcoming Modernity'?

In Takeuchi's account, the two symposiums had, in essence, served to transmit the spiritual condition of the Japanese intellectual community at that moment when the Pacific War broke out. It not only served to highlight the impotence of the 'liberal' anti-war thought that held sway throughout the previous ten years of Japan's war of aggression in Asia. It also showed how difficult it was under those historical conditions to distinguish between war of aggression and war of resistance. The Japan of the Asia-Pacific War — unlike that of the Sino-Japanese war (1894–95) or Russo-Japanese war (1904–5) — mobilized the entire population within the form of 'total war,' which effectively blocked any space of opposition to the war of aggression that did not adopt its terms. 'While, on the one hand, people subjectively resisted and loathed the myths, the very same people were drawn into the myths due to those myths' layers of complexity — this evaluation probably applies most to intellectuals.'[12]

Just prior to this passage, Takeuchi quotes from Takasugi Ichirô, who was the editor of *Literature* when the Pacific War broke out. On the very evening when the news of the surprise attack on Pearl Harbor came, Takasugi found at home an English-language special issue of *International Literature*, published in Moscow, which was devoted to the Soviet counter-attack against the invading German army. He decided then to edit a similar issue of *Literature* devoted to reflections on the will of the Japanese people to fight. The next day he issued a call to various contributors. Not one declined his call for manuscripts. On the one hand, Takeuchi pointed out, Takasugi sided psychologically with the Soviet Union, and loathed Nazi Germany. On the other hand, intellectually, he despised Japan's invasion of China. Yet this intellectual disagreement could exist only in repressed form for Takasugi. Due to the 'sense of liberation' that attended Japan's posture of actually declaring war with the outbreak of the Pacific War, Takasugi, without the slightest sense of contradiction, viewed the Soviet Union's defensive attack on Germany as identical to Japan's defensive attack on the United States. For Takeuchi, the complexity of Takasugi's response speaks volumes about the possibilities for resistance. Takeuchi reasoned that, with very few exceptions, there were no real possibilities for taking a stand against the war, other than standing on the sidelines or deserting.

For precisely this reason, Takeuchi seized on Kawakami Tetsutarô's words from the conclusion of 'Overcoming Modernity': 'our Japanese blood, the force that truly motivates our intellectual activities, has until now been in a state of mutual repulsion with respect to the intellectual framework of Western Europe that has been forced upon it, a situation from which it has been impossible for our intellectuals as individuals to extricate themselves.'[13] With the declaration of war, Takeuchi showed, this sense of mutual repulsion encouraged the transfer of enthusiasm for the Soviet Union into wholehearted support for the Pacific War. It united Japanese intellectuals in their sense of being historically non-Western, that is, Asian. It all but erased the question of whether the war was justifiable. As a consequence of these peculiar conditions, distinguishing between resistance and submission became impossible, at least on the surface.

With the complete reform of the global order in the postwar period, a new opposition — socialism versus capitalism — replaced that between Europe and Asia as well as the wartime opposition between the Axis and Allied forces, which served to efface the historical memory of those prior oppositions. This meant that the 'blood of the Japanese' needed to find new veins in which to flow. Takeuchi knew very well that the leftist critique in postwar Japan had not in fact succeeded in surmounting this basic problem. The leftist critique thus lacked the power to deal with the persistence of the notion of a unitary 'Japanese blood' in the postwar period, which resulted in layers of complexity that allowed different oppositions to become strategically aligned (as with the association of the Soviet Union versus Nazi Germany with Japan's Asia versus the West).

'Japanese blood,' however, is definitely not homogeneous. It was the assumption of its purity and unity that was a major source of the confusion inherent in 'Overcoming Modernity.' It was the major achievement of Takeuchi to undertake a critical evaluation of the symposium even as he delved into the concrete circumstances of its historical situatedness. He showed that people participated in the war not because they were following the orders of militarists but rather because they were willing to give their all for the national community. Herein Takeuchi also located the hypocrisy of the so-called 'anti-war forces' constructed after the war. He aptly observed that a truly anti-war position could only be constructed within the dominant ideology, for, outside that ideology, there existed no other ideological force capable of exerting an influence over the basic reality of the people's total participation in the war.

Having established that 'Overcoming Modernity' utilized the dominant discourse and thus in effect tended to bolster the wartime ideology, Takeuchi then proceeded to look for the anti-war moment in 'Overcoming Modernity.' Within this discursive space, he submitted, there still existed possibilities for transforming it from within even while deploying it. Of particular interest are the challenges that he posed to our conception of totalitarianism — these are of greater importance than the specifics of his analyses (although the Japanese White Terror during WWII offers useful documentation). Takeuchi suggested that, in the so-called totalitarian nations, the possibility of true democracy does not lie outside the system, formed as a mode of opposition to it. Rather it lies within the system; it is born only with great difficulty as a mode of 'reform' from within. For this reason, from the standpoint of the dominant ideology, what truly threatens it is not the formation of 'anti-establishment' forces but rather the heterogeneity within the system itself.

Nonetheless, it was not in 'Overcoming Modernity' that Takeuchi located the possibilities for such developments. He saw a simple effort to forge an intellectual tradition under extremely restrictive conditions, an effort that ultimately failed, because crushed by those severe restrictions. While the symposium presented, in a concentrated form, all the major dilemmas of modern Japanese history, it failed to confront them, and in effect, erased them, making 'Overcoming Modernity' appear as nothing more than a commentary on the official view of the war. In Takeuchi's opinion, this problem remained unresolved in the postwar era. Not only had 'Overcoming Modernity' failed to confront these dilemmas, but postwar intellectuals similarly had failed to confront and resolve them. This resulted in what he called the 'prostrate condition' of postwar Japanese thought. Indeed, in the late 1950s, theories of Japanese superiority resurfaced. In the context of the 'Japanese Culture Forum,' various speakers began to describe Japan as a leading country in East Asia. In short, postwar Japanologists fell into the same bind as 'Overcoming Modernity,' and progressive intellectuals had clearly not found a way to use the resources of Western theory to deal effectively with this situation. This crisis spurred Takeuchi to re-open the issue of 'Overcoming Modernity,' in an attempt to locate new possibilities within this thoroughly discredited moment in Japanese intellectual history.

His essays immediately provoked a number of responses, among them those of Tsurumi Shunsuke and Ara Masato. At a symposium on this topic convened by

Takeuchi, Tsurumi placed emphasis on the way in which children had been raised in Japan from at least the Meiji period, by which they were inculcated with a reluctance to act aggressively. Therefore, in his opinion, possibilities for opposing war lay within the people themselves, and it was erroneous to claim that the notion of total war existed in the some fundamental way within the ideology of the Japanese people. Thus he opposed the search for healthy nationalism, suggesting that, at the risk of oversimplification, emphasis should instead fall to peaceful opposition to war. He called his position 'the theory of calculated peace.'[14] Normally polite, Takeuchi rather rudely pointed out that Tsurumi had lived in the United States until the outbreak of the Pacific War and thus had no real understanding of the experiences of the wartime generation; nor did he understand the subtler effects of December 8, 1942, or its emotional impact. This exchange gives evidence of the differences that arose even between intellectuals who both espoused progressive positions. Takeuchi wished to address the experience of people during the war, and what he wished especially to point out was that people's experiences could not be calculated, explained or summoned in a logical and rational manner. Tsurumi, on the contrary, wanted to take up the possibility of deducing and applying a correct theory.

Ara Masato, for his part, wrote a series of six articles on 'Overcoming Modernity' for the journal *Modern Literature,* in which he pointed out that Takeuchi had a rather idealized image of the symposium and thus tended to adopt a transcendent perspective on it. He noted that Takeuchi had constructed an eccentric grouping around 'Overcoming Modernity,' including some who did not participate and ignoring others who had. Ara suggested that this method did not lend itself to a discussion of the actual symposium.[15] His criticism, though correct, only served to reinforce that the basic concern of Takeuchi resided in the ambience of that period rather than the actual contents of the symposium per se.

Ara's critique of Takeuchi became fiercer when he turned to the Pacific War, challenging the notion of 'being unable to rely on the imperialists to overthrow the imperialists.' From this standpoint, Ara argued, one would not be able to locate the anti-fascist struggle of the Soviet Union. Herein lay an important distinction. For Takeuchi, something like the anti-fascist struggle of the Soviet Union did not come to the fore with any specificity. His account of war and modernity focused on how East Asia had responded to the shock of Western modernity. He saw Russia largely in terms of a breakup within Western Europe, a position that suited his argument. Russia, indeed, was always a blind spot in Takeuchi's thought.[16] At the same time, Takeuchi saw the Tokyo war trials as a critical moment, insisting that these showed that the relation between Japan and the United States was not one of civilization versus barbarism, or of righteousness versus aggression, but rather one of imperialism versus imperialism.[17] Ara, by contrast, had always taken Russia as the perspective from which to assess the Second World War, deriving from it this proposition: the United States, as an ally of Russia and China, had in fact supported wars of national unification and had struck back at Japanese fascism. He felt that one could understand WWII from a number of angles but with fascism and anti-fascism as the guiding thread.[18] With this point of departure, Ara undertook a critique of capitalism, pointing out that, in so far as 'Overcoming Modernity' had failed to offer a critique of capitalism, it had definitely not overcome modernity.

Ara made some excellent points. It was, however, Takeuchi's essay that became the seminal one. For some reason, whether for its political stance or its close reading of the debates on overcoming modernity, Takeuchi's essay lived beyond its immediate circumstances, becoming one of the most cited essays in Japanese intellectual history. Takeuchi's insight was to break with the binary classification that prevailed at that time, by which to be progressive meant to be internationalist, and to be reactionary meant to be nationalist. Takeuchi appealed to wartime experience and emotional memory in search of a more fluid understanding, precisely because abstract explanations of the war tended to conceal the subtler points of difference. If it were possible to erase such differences through the subsequent application of an alleged correct theory, then Takeuchi felt it necessary to pose these questions: What resources were available then to the Japanese to establish an intellectual tradition, and how could they affect daily life and indigenous experience?

As Takeuchi's line of inquiry was gradually transformed into a movement to seek out and purify those intellectual resources deemed native to Japan, he encountered more resistance from left-wing intellectuals than from right-wing intellectuals. As far as Takeuchi was concerned, theory was not the beginning and end for knowledge of a given situation — theory could only be sustained within the situation. Unlike Ara with his drive for fixed principles, Takeuchi sought fluid, transforming principles. Perhaps such differences are themselves matters of principle, and it is the inability to resolve such differences in principle that lay behind the rift between Takeuchi and Ara, and which continues to generate differences today. When, in the 1970s, Takeuchi announced his retirement from the forum, he left behind this difficult, unresolved problem that could not but arouse the attention of later generations.

Hiromatsu Wataru's 'On 'Overcoming Modernity''

Beginning in 1974–1975, the leftist philosopher Hiromatsu Wataru published a series of essays entitled 'On 'Overcoming Modernity'' in the journal *Currents* (*Ryûdô*). By the time his essays appeared in book form, Takeuchi had passed away.

In the seventh chapter of the book, Hiromatsu Wataru launches into a critique of Takeuchi, to clarify that Takeuchi's problematic did not serve as a point of departure for his own. His critique has two main points. First, Hiromatsu takes issue with the way in which Takeuchi focused on the 'Overcoming Modernity' debates to the exclusion of the war and fascist ideology. Hiromatsu argued that, even if the Kyoto School stance was nothing but a dogmatic one that demonstrated the rationale for the declaration of war, this in itself sufficed to make the Kyoto School an instrument of war and fascism. While they did not have the power to have an ideological impact on reality, ideology does necessarily have to have such an impact to function ideologically. Second, Hiromatsu felt that it was still impossible to produce an adequate analysis of the duality that underlay the events that led from the Great East Asian War to the Pacific War. He thus implied that the intellectual community in Japan had yet to deal with its dilemma in its own terms. This involved a misreading that was only in part unintentional: Hiromatsu attacked Takeuchi's reading of the 'dilemma' and 'duality' behind 'Overcoming Modernity' as if Takeuchi had addressed only the form of the symposium — but it was precisely its formal duality and dilemma that corresponded to the needs of wartime ideology.[19]

Hiromatsu's critique shared some points (and problems) with Ara's critique of Takeuchi. As one who had experienced the war directly and had failed at that time to search for other kinds of legitimacy and development within the concept of the Greater East Asia Co-Prosperity Sphere, Takeuchi desired to recuperate some manner of 'critical state' within the 'Overcoming Modernity' symposium. He also wanted to transform, under very specific circumstances, the conditions necessary for this critical state. Hiromatsu, who had been a child during the war and thus only experienced it indirectly, sought to render a verdict on the past — which was precisely what Takeuchi wished to complicate. The problem of deconstructing the newest version of 'Japan-centrism' was of the utmost importance to Hiromatsu because he had faced the problem of student rebellions against the status quo in the late 1960s and saw himself confronted with the demands of a new version of Japan's 'overcoming modernity.' He did not feel, however, that there had existed in Japan the intellectual resources to deal with the problematic of modernity. Thus, in his effort to construct an adequate narrative of 'Overcoming Modernity,' one as ambitious as that of the Kyoto School in its own way, Hiromatsu overlooked the most fundamental insight in Takeuchi's discussion, namely, the need to situate oneself within the historical object, to locate its historical tensions.

His premise was a firm belief in the ideological function of 'Overcoming Modernity,' which entailed a refusal to look for instances of intellectual experimentation or conceptual breakdown. As a consequence, Hiromatsu attempted an ideological cleansing of the symposium from Japanese history. Lumping together 'Overcoming Modernity' and 'World Historical Position and Japan,' he uncritically reduced the subtle differences between the two into an instrument in the service of the dominant ideology. Moreover, he ignored their internal logic, completely transforming the discussion of 'Overcoming Modernity' into a critique of the Kyoto School alone in relation to the political and social history of Shôwa Japan (1926–1989). Such a displacement of concern onto the Kyoto School entailed a covert theoretical shift, one that extended 'Overcoming Modernity' to the entire intellectual history of the Shôwa period. This was consonant with Hiromatsu's main concerns, namely, the ideology behind state monopoly capitalism that took the emperor system as the pinnacle of its social structure.

Hiromatsu took issue with Takeuchi's 'critical procedure' for being too narrow, for treating problems exclusively within the domain of theories of culture and civilization. Hiromatsu, however, placed too much emphasis on the role of the Kyoto School, maintaining (despite evidence to the contrary) that only the Kyoto School scholars had been in line with the basic tone of the symposium. Thus he made the symposium take on far greater socio-historical significance than it actually had, focusing his analysis entirely on an ideological critique of

'Overcoming Modernity.' Yet even his most brilliant analyses of Shôwa social history fail to achieve the ideological purification that he pursues. Rather than overcome 'Overcoming Modernity,' he concentrates on refuting the narrowness of Takeuchi's arguments. Unfortunately, as a result, he misses Takeuchi's subtle sense of restraint, and ends up ignoring the important issues to which Takeuchi called attention, including Takeuchi's focus on the discussion of the specific spiritual condition that permeated the intellectual community at that time. Instead Hiromatsu reduces this spiritual condition to a 'cynicism mediated by a hopelessness about the present,' and 'a self-aware aestheticization of national essence that worked hand in glove with a knowledge seeped in the civilization of Western Europe.'[20] All in all, Hiromatsu merely expanded (and reduced) the symposium to its operation as a sign of the times.

Hiromatsu thus hastily writes off the central, difficult questions that Takeuchi explored, such as why intellectuals saw Japan's Pacific War as similar to the Soviet Union's fight against fascism. Most importantly, the problem of 'everyday experience' raised by Kobayashi and Nishitani drops out all together. The problem is not that of whether Hiromatsu recognizes the danger of the 'tumultuous present.' Rather it lies in the spurious manner in which he responds to this problematic. In many ways, Hiromatsu's account falls into the same trap as that Takeuchi found in Japanese Marxists, namely, that they used 'external' and 'theoretical' modes to simplify and displace the complex reality of Japan. This is why Hiromatsu's critical fervor and sense of responsibility toward reality are never put at risk by the historical object.

On March 16, 1994, in the 'Culture' column of the evening edition of *Asahi Shinbun*, Hiromatsu Wataru published a review article with the title 'East Asia is to become the main actor in history.' The article claims,

> The right wing once monopolized the Greater East Asia Co-Prosperity Sphere. Now the course taken by Japanese imperialism has been put aside, and only Japan's opposition to Europe and the United States receives any attention. Yet today, the stage of history has already taken a dramatic turn. Establish a New System in East Asia along a Japan-China axis! Let it provide the basis for a New World Order! The time has come in which, provided it is conjoined with a radical reexamination of Japanese capitalism itself, this could well furnish the slogan for the anti-establishment left wing.[21]

This short piece in the Asahi Shinbun is not so far from his account of 'Overcoming Modernity' in its logic. For Hiromatsu submits that, if one does not thrust oneself into the situation in question, one cannot find effective intellectual weapons to transform that situation. Yet, when circumstances do suddenly change, even the critic may succumb to the logic of object under scrutiny. Indeed, in December 1996, not two years after Hiromatsu's call to the Japanese left wing to renew the concept of Greater East Asia Co-Prosperity Sphere, another organization emerged that called for a positive reassessment of it. The organization was called 'The Council for Writing New History Textbooks.' Their call to rewrite wartime history stemmed from the desire to put an end to what they felt was a 'self-persecuting historical view.' (In fact they simply adopted yet another 'pre-theoretical state of mind' that raised again the proposition for Japan's 'Overcoming Modernity.') The gist of their argument was that the criminal acts during WWII were no worse than those of other countries in the world. Moreover, through economic indemnities, the old accounts had been settled. The Japanese people should now put an end to their oscillation between self-abnegation and self-pity, and establish a new, third way — a liberal historical view. As theoretically unsophisticated as it appears, this intellectual trend provoked an enthusiastic response, particularly capturing the imagination of a new generation of Japanese youth. As for the progressive intellectuals who struggled to critique this intellectual trend, they found their greatest difficulty lay in finding a good critical arsenal. Clearly, the questions left unresolved by Takeuchi had been left hanging too long.

Coda: Nishio Kanji's History of the Japanese People

In October of 1999, Nishio Kanji, chairman of the 'Council for Writing New History Textbooks,' published *The History of the Japanese People*. Lengthy yet accessible in style, the book runs some eight hundred pages, and ten million copies have already been printed. Nishio paints a picture of Japan that possessed self-respect, behaved reasonably, and deserved trust; within the complicated web of international relations in modern times, Japan had largely experienced vexation and grievance. Nishio lays stress on the fact that the Western powers controlled the global arrangement of international relations, and so, even though Japan had conscientiously abided by the international treaties that they drafted, Japan met repeatedly with criticism and abuse. Instances of Japan's aggression — the annexation of Korea and the invasion of China — were simply efforts to rescue neighboring countries from the predicament of becoming colonies of the white race. International power politics produced such results. Japan had actually done nothing wrong. *The History of the Japanese People* accuses the United States of constantly setting up Japan as an enemy, and emphasizes that the true hegemon in modern international politics and economic relations is the United States itself.

Nishio then appeals to the silence of the Japanese upon their defeat, conjuring up an image of 'silent dissent.' In his opinion, such silent dissent had till then been the attitude of the majority of Japanese as they confronted the hostility of the outside world and the criticism of intellectuals within Japan. Basically, *The History of the Japanese People* strives to construct an autonomous subjectivity for Japan, one that was independent of China in ancient times, one now independent of the West. Furthermore, because the Japanese people are implicitly the real victims of modern history, the book calls for an end to moralizing judgments about history. Rather, one must again approach history 'objectively' in realm of international power politics.

As a concerted reaction against the efforts of the Japanese intellectual community to grapple with the shock of modernity, this kind of book throws into sharp relief the difficulties today faced by the progressive intellectual elite (who probably did not deign to read it). The book presents, in its purest form, the Japanese imaginary that has consistently met with criticism and deconstruction. Its very basis is the traumatic experience of the Japanese people during WWII, and it renews the hero worship that underlies much writing about the Japanese nation. By appealing to such suppressed memories of the war, this book tries to reshape the everyday experience of contemporary Japanese citizens. Moreover, it asserts a challenge to progressive intellectuals who resort to Western theoretical resources.

This is precisely the kind of situation that Takeuchi addressed in his desire to 'snatch the chestnuts from the fire' — that is, to sustain a sense of the complexity of the wartime experience by excavating traditions. Unfortunately, a book like *The History of the Japanese People* serves to make clear the counterproductive effect of abstract arguments against Japanese nationalism, for it is precisely such abstractions that eliminated Takeuchi's search for a Japanese subjectivity.

For Takeuchi, the 'modern' was not a substantial object but a moment of self-negation and self-renewal. If one did not enter into the history of the Japanese war and thus experience the spiritual and psychological complexity of the Japanese at that time, then, in his opinion, a truly critical subjectivity could not emerge, and its real possibilities would not appear. Yet he did not approach this problem in such abstract terms as East versus West or tradition versus modernity. He always located himself in the situation. Of course, the risk of 'snatching chestnuts from the fire' is that of appearing politically incorrect, of seeming to side with the object of critical inquiry. This risk itself is an instance of the shock of 'modernity' at its greatest intensity, to Japan and even to the rest of East Asia. For with the advent of modernity in East Asia, the theoretical resources of the West have constantly been transformed into specific elements of revolutionary thought. While the transformation is complex, it is usually accompanied by a certain simplification of meaning and by political correctness. Schemas such as 'tradition versus the West,' for instance, are the simplified results of these kinds of theoretical transformations. The excavation of traditions likewise involves various simplifications. In response to the impact of Western modernity, native culture becomes substantialized as a concept in opposition to the West. Unearthing native resources is therefore always part of a conservative, even reactionary tendency. If one wishes to excavate indigenous resources, one must take care to clearly distinguish oneself from conservative trends. The great difficulty, then, resides in the continual necessity for differing with the intuited and substantialized native imaginary. And one also runs the risk of falling behind the current of the times. Indeed, in order to combine Western and native intellectual resources, one must incessantly adopt the posture of being half a step behind the times.

Even if the specific problems faced by Chinese intellectuals vis-à-vis the formation of an intellectual tradition differ from those of Japanese intellectuals, 'snatching chestnuts from the fire' is nonetheless an equally necessary procedure. And in this respect, Takeuchi remains important. Takeuchi became especially aware of such difficulties through his detailed study of the specificity of Lu Xun, whom he saw as an 'historical intermediary.' He saw clearly how the nations of East Asia had to assume the risk of losing themselves in order to become themselves. In his discussion of the tradition of modern Chinese literature, Takeuchi wrote, 'Lu Xun alone lived and died with the modern literary tradition, starting before the 'literary revolution' and pursuing it to the end. How did he come by such enduring vitality? Lu Xun was not a visionary.'[22]

Nor, for that matter, was Takeuchi. Yet, as the passage of time has weeded out one visionary after another, these 'historical intermediaries' reveal their true power. For instance, Takeuchi elucidated a principle alien to Japan in particular and to East Asia in general: although the shock of modernization, as a kind of political, economic, and military invasion, had arrived from outside East Asia, nonetheless the shock of modernity itself had to occur in East Asia. Thus, Takeuchi declared, where there is no resistance, there is no modernity. Modernity in East Asia, mediated by resistance that he sought, will unfold within a renewed effort to understand and to take account of historical events similar to those of 'Overcoming Modernity.' Today, when right wing intellectuals produce a Japanese imaginary that threatens to eliminate the moment of resistance, and when men and women on the intellectual left adopt postures that tend to sweep away the possibility of resistance, Takeuchi serves as a reminder that, should we abandon the effort to 'snatch chestnuts from the fire,' we may ultimately lose our modernity itself.

Notes

1. The transcript of the discussion was published in the October 1942 issue of the journal, *Literary Society* under the title, 'Overcoming Modernity.' In July of 1943, Sôgensha published the transcript as a single volume under the same name, with an initial printing of six thousand copies.
2. The symposium actually met on three separate occasions. And in addition to Nishitani and Suzuki, the philosophers Kôsaka Masaaki and Koyama Iwao also participated. The journal *Chûô Kôron* published the manuscripts in the issues dated January and April 1942 and January 1943, under three titles: 'World Historical Position and Japan,' 'The Ethics and Historicity of the Greater East Asia Co-Prosperity Sphere,' and 'The Philosophy of Total War.' In March 1943, Chûô Kôron Publishing House published the transcripts from the three discussions in a single volume, with a first edition of 15,000 copies. From the standpoint of scholarly achievement, 'World Historical Position and Japan' seems to dwarf 'Overcoming Modernity' with a published edition some one and half times as voluminous. Yet later generations of scholars tended to ignore this symposium, unless discussing it in relation to 'Overcoming Modernity,' whence its subsequent inclusion in a general volume devoted to 'Overcoming Modernity.'
3. This was, in fact, the first sub-topic of the conference. See Kawakami Tetsutarô and Takeuchi Yoshimi, *Overcoming Modernity*, 6th Edition (Tokyo: Fûzambo Hyakka Bunko, 1994), 175.
4. *Ibid.*, 177–78.
5. *Ibid.*, 231.
6. *Ibid.*, 244. The words are Kawakami Tetsutarô's.
7. *Ibid.*, 248–249.

[8] 'Twenty Years of the *Literary Society,*' in *Literary Society* (April, 1952), 108–111.
[9] This article and the conference are also included in *Overcoming Modernity*, 274–342.
[10] *Ibid.*, 282.
[11] *Ibid.*, 283–84.
[12] *Ibid.*, 301.
[13] *Ibid.*, 166.
[14] See *New Japanese Literature* 5:154 (1960), 134–149. For Tsurumi's discussion, see especially pages 135 and 139; for his rebuttal, see 137. Sasaki Sôichi (co-organizer) and Itô Sei also attended the conference.
[15] Ara Masahito, 'Overcoming Modernity: Part 1' in *Modern Literature* (March 1960), 8.
[16] Among early scholars of Asia, there were some who tried to participate in Russia's social transformation. Yet, when Takeuchi dealt with the problem of Asianism, this element basically escaped his attention. Needless to say, when Takeuchi pondered the problem of Asia, he unconsciously preserved the historical memory of the Russo-Japanese war, which, at that time was construed by East Asian countries as a war in which 'people of color defeated white people.' Russia was seen wholly as a part of the West.
[17] In the discussion cited in note 14 above, Takeuchi very clearly raised this point. He emphasized that, although in terms of its relationship to China, Japan's crimes could not be discussed together with those of the United States, in terms of the problem of colonial conquest, the United States and Japan were equally guilty (*New Japanese Literature* 5:154 (1960), p. 139). When the symposium progressed to the question of whether nationalism might hasten Chinese great nation chauvinism and radical nationalism in smaller countries, Takeuchi said that the key to the problem lay in an assessment of Western European modernity. He especially emphasized that the Japanese people had great difficulty adopting an attitude of skepticism and distrust for Western Europe, yet that such an attitude had to be established. He even went so far as to claim that a lack of faith in Western Europe was the basis for the legitimacy of the Pacific War (147). This reminds us of the essay Takeuchi wrote at the outbreak of the Pacific War, entitled 'The Greater East Asian War and our Determination,' an essay whose theoretical foundation was this lack of faith in Western Europe.
[18] 'Overcoming Modernity: Part Two,' in *Modern Literature* (April 1960), 3.
[19] Hiromatsu Wataru, *Kindai no chôkoku ron* (Tokyo: Kôdansha,1989), 171–172.
[20] *Ibid.*, 182.
[21] Hiromatsu Wataru, 'Tôhoku Ajia ga rekishi no shuyaki ni; ôbei chûshin no sekaikan wa hôkai e' (*Asahi shinbun* Evening Edition, March 16, 1994).
[22] Takeuchi Yoshimi, 'Lu Xun,' in *The Collected Works of Takeuchi Yoshimi*, Vol. 1, 9.

'Our Logos?' — A Reading for Unsayable Ethics between Chuang Tzu, Derrida and Levinas[1]

Law Wing-sang

Introduction

Our understanding of modernity has taken a great leap forward in recent years. Diverse critiques under the name of, or influenced by, intellectual currents such as post-structuralism and post-colonialism have shifted our understanding of modernity away from the monolithic conception of a linear progression, that is, modernization. The recognition that modernity has been, and continues to be, realized as a complex historical reality, has encouraged a shift in scholarly attention to the investigation of modernity's complex origins, to its formation and re-formation across different sites. One response to the complexities of modernity takes the form of an increased emphasis on the specificity of site, as in analyses of 'alternative modernities.' If the formation of those sites is not examined, however, one could easily slip back to a naïve view assuming a natural and coherent spatial entity wherein all sorts of eternal folklores or mythical authenticities could be uncritically asserted. Under the aegis of different, yet ultimately nation-bound modernities, a monolithic view of modernity might effectively be reinstated — only this time as variations on the same theme. As a consequence, our understanding of modernity has to go back to the question of the relation between modernity and nation formation. In recent years, two notions — the 'invention of tradition' and 'nation as imagined community' — have posed a challenge to the primordialist view of the nation. Benedict Anderson has forcefully put forth the later notion in *Imagined Communities,* which analysis he has recently revised in *Spectre of Comparisons,* a book that has prompted a new round of debates and discussions about the reinvigoration of comparative study and even a new comparative methodology.[2]

Comparison, of course, is not a new thing. There are various kinds of comparative studies, spanning the gamut of comparative religion, comparative culture, comparative literature, comparative philosophy, and so forth, and some of them came into being with the emergence of Western modernity. Although some of those disciplines have undergone substantial changes, and although some of the foundational beliefs on which these comparative studies are based have been severely criticized, enthusiasm for comparative studies has never ceased to grow, especially in some non-Western societies. In China, for instance, journals, conferences and associations in the name of comparative studies dramatically increased in number during the last years of the century just past, recalling the intellectual rage of the mid-eighties called 'Culture Fever.' This passion for comparative studies provides additional confirmation of an idea cited by Anderson in his new book. The idea, drawn from Pramoedya's novel, is that there exists a 'dissatisfied restlessness in *the world of comparison,*' and those people who do not have comparison are to be lamented for 'their narrow destiny.' Summarizing Anderson's emphasis on communication and technology in creating possibilities for endless comparison, Pheng Cheah writes 'these material developments have created quotidian universals that make everything comparable for every one, and cause everyone to compare everything.'[3] Is it truly the case, however, that everything is comparable to everything else? Lydia Liu explains that Ku Hung Ming was able to liken the Empress Dowager to Queen Victoria because of the impending and imposing positivist interpretation of international law.[4] But what conditions made it possible for CNN to caricature Wei Jinseng as a Chinese Nelson Mandela after 1989?

If the innovative notion of nation as an imagined community sets up a scenario in which the national imagination becomes possible everywhere (predicated on the global spread of modern communications, such as print technology), it also implies that a totally wild imagination is impossible. A nation can only imagine itself in a certain way. Similarly, the idea of comparison, as introduced in Anderson's new theoretical and methodological frame, cannot be construed as giving license to wild comparison either. The question then becomes: Which is comparable and which is incomparable? Thus the question of comparability moves beyond Chatterjee's query ('What is left to be imagined?'), because imagination has become realizable within enumerable and identifiable grids.[5] This prompts us to ask: What are the 'comparative schemas'? Where do they come from? What are the standards, objectives, scope and references, etc. of comparison? How are these comparative schemas produced and circulated?

Among the various comparative enterprises, comparative philosophy has a history of generating remarkably neat demarcations between what is comparable and what is not. It thus produces comparative schemas for other academic disciplines as well as popular understanding. It generates essentialised cross-cultural conceptions, which in turn enter into the respective imaginations of nations. For example, all students of Chinese philosophy know how enduring is the distinction between 'intuition' and 'postulation', as a marker of the putative difference between the Eastern and Western ways of thinking. This distinction, propagated by Charles Moore, has recently found an echo among the Neo-Confucianist thinkers such as Tang Chuan I, Mou Chun Shan and the whole contemporary Neo-Confucianist movement originating in Taiwan and Hong Kong. Although such naïvely totalizing and polarizing an approach now has largely lost all importance in the Western academies, readers of Chinese are surely aware of how pervasive this approach has become in popular designations of the so-called 'Chinese personality.' Those readers of Chinese who read popular psychology or philosophy, bent on improving their own self-understanding, have proved avid consumers of such ideas. The polarizing, totalizing approach has also become a daily presence in newspapers, lending a somewhat theoretical outlook to various kinds of cultural and political analysis. We may trace this product of the 'universalist' phase of comparative philosophy to a very precise location: the comparativist framework of the First East-West Philosophers' Conference held in the East-West Center at the University of Hawaii in 1939.

While Indian and Chinese thought had long been presented to European readers via various Orientalist studies, their 'philosophical' appearance in the early half of the twentieth century became possible with the grand project of building a unified global philosophy. This global philosophical project entailed synthesizing the ideas and ideals of 'the East and the West' in the search of 'the unity of the human mind'. This ambitious task gradually lost support, paving the way for the next phase, what J.J. Clarke called the 'comparative phase.'[6] The emphasis fell less on finding a 'synthesizable' unity and more on discussing the specific concepts and ideas of an individual thinker. Yet, obviously, the site on which this new phase of comparative philosophy was normally conducted tells us a lot about the extent to which 'comparison for the West' remained (and remains) the guiding logic. Wilson Organ rather bluntly declares that, while the original motivation for comparative philosophy was intellectual curiosity, '*our* motivation now is *survival*,' and '*we* need to look beyond the West for *therapy*' (my emphasis).[7] Hopes continue to run high for a series of 'new' objectives and re-orientations that will allow comparative philosophy to get away from unwelcome universalistic assumptions ('orchestrated unity,' 'grand narratives' and such) and to move towards 'improved mutual understanding,' dialogue and appreciation of differences and otherness. As Gerald Larson puts it, '[it is time] to get away from talking *to* one another... in favour of talking *with* one another' (original emphasis).[8]

But what is a dialogue? Can difference be communicated? How can otherness be grasped and then respected? What is talking *with*? Can a comparison be made between two thinkers if at least one of them believes in total incommensurability between different thoughts? Should we not first clarify what is comparability before we set off to compare? Obviously, such vicious hermeneutical problems have to be 'bracketed' first to make comparison possible — but at what price? Before we can answer these philosophical questions *philosophically*, however, we remark that, with the recent interest in precisely such questions, Derrida and Chuang Tzu have already been made to meet with each other in various comparative exercises.

Partly as an attempt to answer some of the questions raised above, and partly to foreground some of the problems related to the recent revived interest in comparative study, this essay is a para-comparative reading between Derrida and Chuang Tzu (with forays in Levinas as well) — in order to mount a critique of some comparative exercises that have already been done on them. Derrida and Chuang Tzu lived over a thousand years apart, but the telescopic comparison that is emblematic of the kind of modernity in which we are living insists on somehow drawing them together. Although this essay does not aim to provide a systematic analysis of their thought, it will venture to highlight some of their paradoxical features and their respective modes of treating the *unsayable*, for these aspects (paradox and the unsayable) are what motivate many of the current East-West comparisons centred on them.

Richard Rorty sarcastically characterizes this motivation as coming from the 'bit of the ascetic priest' in all philosophers, a desire for 'a language entirely disengaged from the business of the tribe,' which sets the ascetic priests apart from the people because of their 'inability to be in touch with something Wholly Other.'[9] However, the reading given here has more in store than giving Rortian cynicism a run. It first aims to foreground discussion of the different ethical and political implications of these writers, implications that are, in some current modes of comparison, in danger of being suppressed — first, philosophically and second, comparatively. The essay will subsequently put the philosophical readings in their historical context, touching upon some issues related to why and how the comparisons between them have been made possible in certain ways but not in others. It will also explore the implications of (in)comparability in relation to some of more general questions about comparison, nation and colonialism raised in debates around Benedict Anderson's book.

Derrida and Negative Theology

Derrida's philosophy is an attempt to deconstruct the Western metaphysics of identity, of the presence of the self to itself in consciousness. He notices that there has always been a fear of difference of the other underlying all philosophical systems whose aim is to reduce the experience of multiplicity to the unity beyond or behind. He insists that deconstruction is not a method that serves only to perpetuate the totalizing practice of philosophy. *Différance* is instead a move to open up language and thought to a 'play' that will undermine the stability of identity. It is neither a concept, nor an origin, still less a metaphysical determinant of the forms that Being takes. It is a thought that is characterized by the moves of negation against any onto-theology.

Philosophy, however, has been so obsessed with its other that one can hardly find any negations of philosophy that can stand outside it. While other poststructuralists like Deleuze and Guattari appear to offer a counter-ontology in which heterogeneity, not homogeneity, is primary, Derrida remains very sensitive to the possibility of creating a simple mirror image of totalizing philosophy by way of negation. He takes the philosophy of Levinas as illustrative of this danger.

Levinas is acutely aware of the violent structure of metaphysical language. In order to shake off the language of metaphysics and to open up a space for ethics,

Levinas resorts to the irreversible power of a face. He differentiates his approach from positive religion and the tradition of ontological thought, calling his thought a metaphysics of the trace. In order to reverse the priority of categories over heteronomous experience, he resorts to the most formalized description to inscribe the structure of alterity. He contests the now-entrenched notion of Being, redefining it as Exteriority. An early book, *Totality and Infinity,* is premised upon a theoretical rationality that produces the incoherency of the absolutely other.

In an early essay 'Violence and Metaphysics,' Derrida criticizes Levinas for betraying the ethical intention at stake in his proposing a non-theological and non-ontological idea of infinity, which Levinas supposes to reside not in categories but in the humanly face-to-face. Derrida sees that, insofar as Levinas maintains the ethical relation to the Other as one based upon discourse, Levinas inevitably presupposes the very ontological language that he claims to have overcome. This is because, as soon as the Other enters discourse, the Other is reduced to the same.[10] To Derrida the 'unlimited power of envelopment' possessed by the Greek *logos* has indeed come back, even in the works of Levinas who made some of the most dramatic attempts to leave behind the Western philosophical tradition. Derrida writes, 'That it is necessary to state infinity's *excess* over totality *in* the language of totality; that it is necessary to state the other in the language of the Same; that it is necessary to think true exteriority as *non-exteriority,* that is, still by means of the Inside-Outside structure and by spatial metaphor...there is no philosophical logos which must not *first* let itself be expatriated into the structure Inside-Outside.'[11]

In this connection, Derrida points to the apophatic structure of Levinas' thought. Derrida describes it as a residual negative theology, which for Derrida designates a certain typical *attitude towards* language. It consists in 'considering that every predicative language is inadequate to the essence, in truth to the hyperessentiality (the being beyond Being) of God; consequently, only a negative ("apophatic") attribution can claim to approach God and to prepare for a silent intuition of God.'[12]

Unlike the classical counterparts who try to redefine categorical terms as being rooted primarily in attitudes arising from experiential encounters with the Other, Levinas insists on the centrality of language as the medium of the experience of alterity. Yet according to Derrida, the disavowal of language by means of language cannot transcend the circularity and auto-reflection of onto-theological thought. Levinas' unsayable infinity is suggesting in every way an apophatic movement toward an idea of God.

Derrida does recognize that negative theology is not confined to the order of religion. He admits that one would find some traits of, or family resemblance to, negative theology in every discourse that seems to return in a regular and insistent manner to the rhetoric of negative determination. Derrida has also been once accused of being a negative theologian because his notion of *différance* is subjected to the same rhetoric in which the defenses and apophatic warnings of 'neither this nor that' endlessly play. Yet Derrida does not allow the association of his thought with any negative theology. He writes, 'The detours, locutions, and syntax in which I will often have to take recourse will resemble those of negative theology, occasionally even to the point of being indistinguishable from negative theology, and yet those aspects of *différance*... are not theological, not even in the order of the most negative of negative theologies...'[13]

The reason is that *différance* is not concerned with disengaging a superessentiality beyond the finite categories of essence and existence to recall and acknowledge a superior, ineffable mode of being. He explains, '*Différance* is not only irreducible to any ontological or theological — ontotheological — reappropriation, but as the very *opening of the space* in which ontotheology-philosophy produces its system and its history, it includes ontotheology, inscribing it and exceeding it *without return*.'[14]

For Derrida, negative theology is indeed not negative enough. The name of God or Being would always come back to neutralize the interruptive move as the hyperbolic effect of that negativity of all negativity. As a result, the metaphysics of presence will win its revenge after long detours. Derrida is always clear enough about the likelihood of this threat of revenge. He says, 'What *différance,* the *trace,* and so on "mean" — which hence *does not mean anything* — is "before" the concept, the name, the word, "something" that would be nothing, that no longer arises from Being, from presence or from the presence of the present, nor even from absence, and even less from some hyperessentiality. Yet the ontotheological reappropriation always remains possible and doubtless *inevitable* insofar as one speaks, precisely, in the element of logic and of onto-theological grammar.'[15]

One way in which the onto-theological reappropriation or revenge can be realized is perhaps comparative philosophy.

Comparative Philosophy (I): Différance as Tao

If what Derrida says is right, we actually have no other language except our metaphysical language. Therefore, speaking itself is always a move to render present what is present. Therefore, although *différance* has no name in our language, it nonetheless has to be named by the speaker who speaks of it. So too is any truth of or about the unsayable. No matter how painstaking Derrida is in pointing out that *différance* is neither a word nor a concept, terms such as 'traces', 'hymen', and 'archiécriture' that he soon provisionally brings forth only to cross them out, will be resurrected one way or the other in philosophy. Every time philosophers call upon such terms to make sense of them philosophically, they are inevitably recuperated. Thus the wheel of onto-theological reappropriation has to be (re)started time and again. Since there is a whole order of meaning always already being set up under a given system of discursive practice, the unsayable or ineffable has to be turned into unsayab*ility* or ineffab*ility*. In this light, the unsayable is not that unsayable after all. If this is true in the academic discipline of Western philosophy, it is more so in comparative philosophy. A telling example of such a transformation of the unsayable into unsayability can be found in comparisons of Chuang Tzu and Derrida that seize on their 'parallel' emphases upon the 'themes' of paradoxicality, skepticism and even mysticism.

In 'The Deconstructive Way: A Comparative Study of Derrida and Chuang Tzu,' Michelle Yeh likens Derrida to Chuang Tzu on the basis of their anti-traditionalism, spirit of freedom, provocative style, concern with language, and impact upon literary criticism.[16] Yeh's major thesis is that, despite some differences (which include Derrida lagging behind Chuang Tzu for he fails to see oneness as already being implied in deconstruction), Derrida's *différance* is but another name for Chuang Tzu's Tao.[17] Her title 'The Deconstructive Way' neatly encapsulates this thesis.

According to Yeh, despite the fact that both Chuang Tzu and Derrida do not set out to create a general theory or systematic thought, what makes them comparable is the paradoxicality at the center of their thinking. Both present challenges to any 'conventional thought, the common denominator of which can be termed dualistic conceptualization.'[18] Yeh then proceeds to elucidate similarities between the two thinkers with respect to their undoing of binary opposites. She interprets Derrida's *différance* as a strategy to 'uncover' the 'double moment' or 'double marking.' Similarly, Chuang Tzu asserts 'the law of difference, in which dualistic terms are reversible and interchangeable.' To substantiate these characterizations, Yeh writes that '[t]he *theme* of the deconstructive polemics can be summarized in this way: "If one is always bound by one's perspective, one can at least deliberately reverse perspectives as often as possible, in the process undoing opposed perspectives, showing that the two terms of an opposition are merely accomplices of each other." '[19]

In this statement she cites extensively from Spivak's 'Translator's Preface' to Derrida's *Of Grammatology*, in which Spivak describes a Nietzschean practice that constitutes only 'a version of Derrida's practice,' yet Yeh presents it as 'the theme' that allows for comparison.[20] To further substantiate her claims about the comparability of Derrida and Chuang Tzu, Yeh also stresses an association once made by Derrida between *différance* and *frayage*, which latter 'carries a strong sense of "opening up or clearing out of a pathway."' The image of the Chinese word Tao as Way comes forth as the mysterious ground for staging the encounter between Chinese Taoism and Derridian deconstruction. This close encounter only happens, however, after Derrida's *différance* is construed as 'the originating principle.'[21] Although Yeh insists that *différance* bears no onto-theological implications, and thus should be 'understood beyond the metaphysical language,' she does not hesitate to construct a parallel with the Taoist 'possibilizing principle.' She abstracts this from the famous dictum in Lao Tzu's *Tao Te Ching*, which says, 'Tao gives birth to one, one to two, two to three, three to the ten thousand things.' Such random cross-referencing between Lao Tzu and Chuang Tzu is problematic, to say the least, even if both writers are classified as Taoists. There are differences between them: while Lao Tzu's *Tao Te Ching* is obviously more concerned with the question of metaphysics, one can hardly find in *Chuang Tzu* a similar emphasis on the importance of taking Tao as leverage to make a statement about metaphysics.[22] Conflating these two Taoist thinkers effectively grafts the metaphysical interest of Lao Tzu onto Chuang Tzu. It is much like Yeh's conflation of Nietzsche's jugglery with reversing perspectives and Derrida's deconstruction. Given that such conflations are not uncommon in philosophy, particularly in contemporary interpretations of classical Chinese philosophy, what bears examination is the effective subordination of both Derrida and Chuang Tzu to the problematic of ontology — which is what Yeh's comparative exercise in establishing Tao as 'Deconstructive Way' ironically effectuates.

Lao Tzu's Taoism is well known for its mysticism, for its mystic ontological statements. Lao Tzu describes Tao as not-form (*wu-hsing*), not-having (*wu-yo*), not-striving (*wu-wei*), not-knowing (*wu-chih*), and not-name (*wu-ming*). In short, it is unnameable. Lao Tzu insists that the act of naming would only destroy Tao. Yet, even before we may begin to ask in what ways this unnameable Tao functions in Taoist thought, including Chuang Tzu's and Lao Tzu's writings, the comparative philosopher has foreclosed difference between this unnameable Tao and the kind of negative theology that concerns Derrida. In other words, even before we inquire into the workings of different mysticisms, the court of metaphysics has summoned both Derrida and Chuang. Just as different mysticisms are rendered 'the same' and subsumed under the *theme* of 'paradoxicality', so Derrida and Chuang Tzu are also singled out for their style of writing and their common concern with the problematic of language. Such conceptual reductions are necessary to render deconstruction and Taoism as presence, to construe them as chiefly rhetorical exercises dealing with dualistic conceptualizations. Yeh effectively displaces Derrida's concern with the 'metaphysics of presence' (which he insists is characteristic of the Western philosophical tradition), making it a more general philosophical problem, not specific to place. Yeh thus characterizes *différance* and Tao as indicators of 'a disruption, a transgression, or a stratification of *any metaphysical-dualistic* concept.'[23]

To be sure, we are not here witnessing a simple dilemma for philosophical writing (we cannot escape from metaphysical language) but an example of how modern academic disciplinary mechanisms function: namely, if comparative philosophy is possible, the first rule is to thematize the undecidable or the ambiguous in order to prepare the ground on which comparison may take place. Yeh's thematization of 'paradoxicality,' for instance, is a foregrounding condition for her characterization of a common project, that of undoing dualistic conceptualizations. Thematization is a condition of possibility for comparative philosophy, without which Yeh could not conclude that 'With the exception of the difference in emphasis, Chuang Tzu and Derrida make *essentially* the same statement...'[24] Her exercise illustrates vividly how onto-theological reappropriation is intrinsic to comparative philosophical practice, which must exorcise the ambiguous and the mystic and accord to each of them a comparative schema tagged with an implicit hierarchy between the ontology of paradox and its rhetoric.

Comparative Philosophy (II): Logos as Tao

In a similar manner, in his comparative study, Zhang Longxi makes possible an encounter between Chuang Tzu and Derrida, albeit through the much grander project of East-West intercultural hermeneutics. Yet, interestingly enough, although Derrida's thought is commonly received as the most devastating critique of logocentrism (which critique allows Yeh to equate deconstruction and Tao), Zhang links Tao to what it is supposed to counter, namely, Logos. In *The Tao and the Logos,* Zhang claims that what the Chinese call Tao is but the Western Logos.[25] What motivates Zhang to pursue this hypothesis to its logical conclusion is not Derrida's critique of logocentrism as onto-theology but Derrida's unscrupulous attitude vis-à-vis the Chinese language. In *Of Grammatology,* Derrida, by 'sleight of hand' (as Zhang describes it) credits Fenollosa and Pound for their 'break' with the Western tradition of phonocentrism. Zhang finds Fenollosa and Pound guilty of misunderstanding Chinese language, mistakenly seeing it as composed solely of ideograms. According to Zhang, Derrida is perpetuating, or 'not safely guarding itself against,' a long-standing Western bias, 'a sort of European hallucination,' by which Chinese becomes a 'mute language,' an incommensurable other. Yet a patient reading of the passage in question will find that Derrida is actually taking to task the old Sinological prejudice against Chinese language, represented by Gernet, which conceives it as merely 'primitive scripts,' that are 'eclipsed' by writing, having never 'reached' a phonetic analysis of language as 'normal outcome,' as an historical telos. Derrida clearly does not share Pound's fascination with the Chinese ideogram, but he calls for an account of 'its historical significance.'[26] Evidently, Zhang's attention is not on how this Sinological myth serves as an example of the power of logocentric thought to subsume differences into a teleological schema. Rather what displeases Zhang is the discovery that China has been kept out of the phonocentrism and logocentrism, which are defined by Derrida as the sole property of the West. In a complete reversal of the historically-embedded Chinese prejudice, Zhang announces that logocentrism should not be seen as that which defines the West as the West. Rather it is a universal problem. Zhang asks, 'Is it possible that logocentrism or metaphysical hierarchy with regard to thinking, speaking, and writing also exists in the Eastern tradition? Do the nonphonetic Chinese scripts really mark the outer boundaries of all logocentrism? And finally, Is there a Chinese word that denotes, as the word *logos* does, something equivalent or similar to the Western metaphysical hierarchy?'[27] And apparently with delight, he answers his last question with: 'By a most *curious coincidence*, there is indeed a word in Chinese that exactly captures the duality of thinking and speaking.'[28]

The word is Tao. In a breath-taking hermeneutic exercise, cross-referencing writers of different generations, countries and styles of thought, Zhang finds in Schopenhauer a citation from Cicero saying that the Greek word *logos* means both *ratio* and *oratio*. Zhang finds further support in Stephen Ullmann's condensation of two major elements from the ambiguous word's diverse meanings, namely, thinking and speaking. Subsequently, Zhang finds that Derrida, despite his insistence on the importance of difference, (re-)joins Gadamer in dispelling Plato's fear of writing. What qualifies Chinese thinkers to join in this play of (not exclusively) Greek tragi-comedy is Lao Tzu's enigmatic statement 'The Tao that can be tao-ed is not the constant Tao.' Zhang interprets this remark as displaying the same tension as that which arises between the Platonic constant idea (read as 'thinking') and ever changing and unreliable names (read as 'speaking').

The stage is thus set for Chuang Tzu, whose poetic notion of 'non-word' has been waiting in the wings, to join the heroic combat against the fear of writing, against the same metaphysical hierarchy, and against the same 'concern over loss of "inner reality" by "outer expression."' The only difference is that Chuang Tzu offers a more profound 'use of silence' in overcoming Homer's anxiety over invoking the muse to tell the will of gods. He offers a more earthly answer to the puzzle of poetic articulation, one that baffled the modern poets like T. S. Eliot, Mallarmé and Rilke. If Derrida, in his terse anti-logocentric reading of Mallarmé, risks 'confusing literary indeterminacy with mystic obscurantism,' then Chuang Tzu, in this putatively universal crisis of representation, is instrumental in rescuing meaning in honour of facilitating a 'Chinese hermeneutic theory.' Zhang puts it thus: 'Theory opens a new vista for comparative studies, but a theoretically informed study must put different cultural traditions *on an equal footing*.'[29] There is no doubt that making a global theorist of Chuang Tzu qualifies as an attempt to conduct 'East-West dialogue' 'on an equal footing.'[30]

Differences among Ways of Thinking Difference

In this global scramble to offer a solution to 'the universal problem of language' (reduced to the problem of representation), it probably makes no difference whether Tao is likened to Logos or to *différance*. These exercises in elevating Chuang Tzu or any other Taoist to the status of a 'global theorist' for modern or post-modern humanities are only possible when we disengage Chuang Tzu's and other Taoist thinkers' complex ways of relating their epistemology, ethics and ontology. We must also be prepared to reduce Derrida's deconstruction to literary or philosophical theory.

Before rushing to equate Tao to *Logos* or *différance*, we should first clarify the discursive context of Taoist literature in which Tao has been described as a way of articulating the ultimate reality. Before we can impose on Chuang Tzu or Taoism the problematic about the tension between Being and beings (the theoretical horizon within which Derrida set off his deconstruction of *Western* logocentrism), what do we make of the complex and intriguing question of Taoist ontology? Let us begin by looking at Chuang Tzu's thought from the angle of ontology.

Although Chuang Tzu, unlike Lao Tzu, does not take metaphysics as his central concern, there is no doubt that ontological implications can be discerned in his writings. In his careful reading of *Chuang Tzu*, Wu Kuang Ming avoids the very common and hasty take on Taoist nonbeing as a ready answer to the question of being. Instead, he carefully distinguishes between 'nonbeing' (without hyphen) and 'non-being' (with hyphen). The former is a simple nonbeing opposed to being; it is simply nothing. The latter is a '[there] *is not-yet*' kind of nonbeing, which is not opposed to beings; rather 'there *is* a *not* yet beginning to not yet being [even] to be nonbeing.'[31] While the first type is simply nothing, intelligible as something opposed to being, the second type is truly mysterious and epistemologically perplexing, insofar as intelligibility is possible only in the realm of being and its opposite. It is only non-being of the second type that is the origination and alignment of being. Wu compares this non-being to the Magnet and the Matrix by mean of which alignment of things *is* and is seen to be intelligible.[32]

Insofar as non-being is invisible and unintelligible, however, it can only be named by an allusive bynaming. That is why Chuang Tzu called this the 'Beginning of beginnings,' 'Void of void,' 'that non-being which is beyond the absence of nothing,' or 'the Great Void.' It is not expressed either in words or in silence.

Operating within a quite different horizon, that of the critique of metaphysics and onto-theology, Derrida's thinking offers quite different characteristics. Derrida's thinking about an unsayable truth can hardly be equated to that of Chuang Tzu.

In the Judaeo-Christian onto-theological tradition, paradox always refers to what reason cannot handle. As Kierkegaard says, it is the torment of the Unknown as a limit inflicted upon the passion of Reason. The Unknown is an undifferentiated realm, the boundaries of which are set by Reason. However, as Reason itself has no set boundaries, Unknown can only be the absolute difference or unlikeness. It is a negation of Reason, or the move in which Reason negates itself. Kierkegaard points out the dilemma for Reason. He writes, 'The Reason cannot negate itself absolutely, but uses itself for the purpose, and thus conceives only such an unlikeness within itself as it can conceive by means of itself, it cannot absolutely transcend itself, and hence conceives only such a superiority over itself as it can conceive by means of itself.'[33]

Kierkegaard sees that this lack of specific determination to difference paves the way for paganism to proliferate. The idea of difference will be thrown into a state of confusion. In the Christian tradition from which Kierkegaard speaks, the discovery of this self-irony of Reason gives rise to his notion of the leap of faith. Yet, what puzzles Derrida is not the clarification of belief but the enveloping power of Reason, the language of Being. The Derridean notion of *différance* thus addresses a set of problems that Chuang Tzu did not face, and it is perfectly conceivable that Chuang Tzu's idea about a realm of *non-being* as an alternative to the order of being has never emerged from Derrida's thinking. This is because, for Derrida, *différance* is not other than Being, it is 'older' than Being.[34] This 'older than' gives evidence of a temporality with which Derrida is forced to deal, but Chuang Tzu may dismiss with a somewhat parodic statement of this sort: 'There is being, there is nonbeing. 'There is a not yet beginning to be nonbeing. There is not yet beginning to be a not yet beginning to be nonbeing. Suddenly there is nonbeing. But I do not know, when it comes to nonbeing, whether it is really being or nonbeing.'[35]

Furthermore, *différance* for Derrida is not different from Being, it is, as he puts it, the difference between Being and beings. It is the simulacrum of a presence that dislocates itself and displaces itself. In describing what he terms the play of the trace, he says that the play of a trace no longer belongs to the horizon of Being. Yet he adds that '...[the] play transports and encloses the meaning of Being.'[36] Clearly, regardless of the metaphors he deploys, he is not speaking of an order other than Being. To a large extent, Derrida is skeptical of the possibility of overcoming, or finding some leeway for, thinking Being, for he thinks that the assimilatory power of Being excludes such a possibility. Derrida is always vigilant about the possibility that the negation of being will itself subsumed. It would be moot for him to consider the possibility of *otherwise than being* without negation to being.

Ineffability, Origin and Difference

For Chuang Tzu, who wrote outside of the Judaeo-Christian tradition, Tao as non-being is ineffable not because it is absolutely transcendent or absolutely different from being. Unlike the negative theology which makes ineffability equivalent to the inability to speak about Being — which is how Kierkegaardian angst arises — non-being in Chuang Tzu actually allows 'being' and 'nothing' as 'words' to *disclose* the silent meaning of non-being. No matter how much Derrida and Chuang Tzu may seem to resemble one another in various aspects, surely Chuang Tzu's enabling view of silence is at odds with Derrida. To be sure, within Western philosophical and theological traditions, there are modes of thought in which silence does signify. In various kinds of mysticism, silence represents the attainment of a mute vision that makes mystic union with God possible. Derrida, who sees speaking as always obligatory, pronounces that even silence remains a modality of speech.[37]

However, before we make generalizations about the different ways in which silence mean, and before we intuitively define silence as the absence of speech, we should remark that, in Chuang Tzu's thought, the silence in which non-being discloses is not a mute vision; nor is it the absolute limit haunting Reason. Rather, it occurs when the speaker speaks as if he has forgotten words.[38] Our ignorance about non-being does not call for an irrational leap of faith, as in Kierkegaard, nor a joyful fall into the abyss, still less a moment of aesthetic or poetic sublimation. Rather, ignorance, understood as forgetfulness as well as quiet acknowledgement, is evocative of non-being, which is not to set against being; it pervades and enables being as well as nothing.

Wu Kuang-ming describes Chuang Tzu's metaphysics as a parent-metaphysic: 'Non-being differs *from* being, *to* which it is related, as the mother differs from and is related to her child.'[39] It is not merely a preparatory stage for being to arise and subordinate itself to being. In the significative silence of non-being, inexpressiveness 'signifies' the flexibility of life that is not set against being or nothing. While this is surely a double negative, it is not a movement of double negation that leads to dialectical sublation (*aufhebung*) or a negative theology.

In contrast, Derrida claims that *différance* is 'older' than metaphysical difference or the truth of Being. Yet even so, the meaning of the word 'older' cannot be associated with any generative logic — with the Platonic conception of receptacle or with Chuang Tzu's mother logic, let alone with an 'originating principle' (as Yeh does).[40] Despite such basic differences, the fascination with arriving at a cross-cultural law or principle has nevertheless animated comparativism. Such fascination underlies both Zhang's effort to establish a universal logocentrism and Yeh's attempt to equate *différance* and Tao. Both attempts turn the 'white mythology' into a *universal* myth in order to particularize Derrida and Chuang Tzu, in an effort to solve the puzzle of the 'unavoidable' logocentric language. But in what sense can we assert that speaking metaphysically is 'unavoidable'?

The Secret, Speaking and Place

In 'How to Avoid Speaking: Denials,' Derrida poses a series of questions: How is it possible to avoid speaking? How, if one speaks of something, to avoid speaking of it? How to avoid speaking of it without rhyme or reason? These questions come in response to allegations that deconstruction is related to negative theology. Derrida's answer to these questions is that he cannot just avoid speaking. Even before speaking, he knew that he was committed to doing it. Before speech or any discursive event as such, there is necessarily a commitment or a promise. The promise is there *as if in spite of myself.*[41] Speech is therefore unavoidable, an obligation. The only question then is whether one can only speak from a prescribed mode. He finds it extremely difficult not to speak of negative theology in a negative theological mode.

To speak of negative theology is obviously to become involved in a paradox because negative theology is that about which one cannot speak. Derrida addresses the problem of negative theology as a general problem regarding the necessity and difficulty of speaking about the negative itself. It is the necessity to speak about what essentially is not and yet must be articulated in another syntax or a different language. For Derrida, this is the double bind: to speak of *différance* and to render it present. He likens it to the revelation of a secret. The paradox is that, as the secret is revealed, it is no longer secret. However, Derrida is obliged to speak of the secret. There is no way to avoid speaking (of it), in as much as no one can avoid speaking indefinitely. The secret cannot be kept indefinitely for no one is sure when and whether the dissimulation has taken place. This is not because everything manifests itself but simply because, as he says, 'the nonmanifestation is never assured.'[42] This is because there is always the trace.

The problem of the secret leads to the question of the *place* proper to the experience of the secret. In other word, what speaking, as a divulging of hopes, promises ('the secret') is performatively related to a particular context always preconfigured by power and continuously contested by politics. An initiatory politopology or topolitology governs the relation between the *beyond* of that which is beyond Being and the place of speaking of that secret, for the question of the place is also the question of order. The divine promise is also an injunction, an injunction about the place where God dwells. Therefore, as Derrida says, the figures and rhetoric of the sacred symbols are also political strategems. The question 'how to avoid speaking?' is always already too late because what makes it possible *has taken place.* This always-presupposed event is also immanent in every interpretation that calls for origin or *oeuvre.* In other words, the choice between speaking and silence is always already haunted spectrally by those sacred words. Speaking or not (or meaning or non-sense) is always already institutionalised in a particular place of speaking.

The Western discipline of philosophy, including comparative philosophy, which is supposed to investigate the thought of non-Western worlds, is always instituted as a way to speak of something. It is a response to the desire for meaning, for cause and for origin. It happens and is always happening in a particular politopological setting that 'always has a past that was never present and yet remains unforgettable.' However, is it philosophy's inevitable fate to speak the language of ontology? Derrida discusses several paradigms in the Western tradition that resonate with his own non-Greek and non-Christian thought.

First, in the Platonic principle concerning the idea of the Good beyond Being and essence, he sees in Greece the tradition of analogical continuity maintained between Being and what is beyond Being. Mediation between the two realms thus calls for a schema of the *third* that has in the past led to the thought of dialectics and logos, in which non-being can be received as *other* and nothingness is transcended. Another bridge between the negativity and the articulation of the unsayable is located in the Platonic *khora* ('place'). This unintelligible and non-sensible place in which the God dwells can receive all and allow itself to be marked by what is inscribed, yet it remains formless and without proper determination. It is already there and beyond time. It is neither this nor that, neither intelligible nor sensible, yet participates in all of these. It is where the demiurge organizes the cosmos by cutting and impressing images. Yet it receives not in the manner of a medium or a container, not even in that of a receptacle. It is genuinely unsayable because even metaphor is inadequate for designating it, because metaphor always already inherits the distinction between the sensible and the intelligible. As it is ineffable, it is a place always associated with what Derrida calls the secret of denial and a denial of secrets.

The experience of such a secret place of singularity, which appears as the irreducible other, poses a problem related to the Christian tradition of praying. A Christian prayer is always a mode of address to the absolute Other. In contrast to the experience of *khora,* however, the mystic tradition (even though it sees God as beyond predication) inevitably links the secret manifestation or 'secret gift' to the promise of an event, the injunction of an order and the opening up of a history, which necessitates a passage, a transfer or translation, such as a Christian prayer. Derrida clearly links the difficulty of avoiding speaking in the language of ontology explicitly to the modern condition structured by legality inextricably bound up with (Western) theological traditions — and not to what Zhang conceives as 'universal' metaphoricity. To reduce the problem of representation to a 'metaphoricity of language' found in all cultures is a common way of reducing Derrida's thinking to a literary problematic. Posed in this way, Derrida is easy to grasp. Yet the crucial *political* problem is thus ignored, since whenever Derrida attempts to deal with the problem of speaking, it is not as 'speaking in general' or as language-in-itself but as the place, the position, the context in which promises or hopes are delivered. He has to posit a non-site known as *khora* in which speaking is not rendered susceptible to onto-theological reappropriation. The extent to which Derrida is successful in avoiding this reappropriation remains an open and *political* question.

Speech, Silence and Tao

While Derrida likens what is unsayable to the secret that has to be denied, Chuang

Tzu does not have anything to hide. Speaking, for him, is not exclusively about keeping a promise; nor is it the only access to the highest truth. The problem for Chuang Tzu is not how to speak to, or speak under, the sign of the absolute Other. The truth of life and nature is not disclosed primarily through speech or philosophical reflection. Rather, speaking is by nature a spontaneous business with no ultimate destination. Sometimes Chuang Tzu appears proud of the great wisdom he has attained, looking down upon the people who, like frogs in a well, can't match his understanding. At other times he confesses that there is no end to the weighing of things. Chuang Tzu's speech is not about the search for the truth, the highest one of all the highests, neither in a positive or negative manner. He seems perfectly aware of the uses and the abuses of speaking. Yet he does not rely on words to tell him or anybody the genuinely significant differences in the world. He says, 'The speaker has something to say, but what he says is not final. Has something been said? Or has something not been said? It may be different from the chirping of chickens. But is there really any difference? Or is there no difference? How can Tao be so obscured that there should be a distinction of true and false? How can speech be so obscured that there should be a distinction of right and wrong? Where can you go and find Tao not to exist? Where can you go and find speech impossible? Tao is obscured by petty biases and speech is obscured by flowery expressions.'[43]

Obviously, Chuang Tzu dismisses the importance of engaging in the game of 'speaking *the* truth.' Insofar as neither speech nor silence in itself bears any predetermined positive or negative relation to Tao, Chuang Tzu does not think we can discriminate right from wrong and thus settle disputes about truth with words. He writes, 'I have just said something [about being and non-being], but I don't know if what I have said really says something or says nothing. Since all things are one, what room is there for speech? But since I have already said that all things are one, how can speech not exist? Speech and the one then make two. These two and one make three...'[44]

If there is a secret of the Tao, it is not something that human speech alone can divulge, let alone futile efforts to deny that there is one. Although Chuang Tzu deems knowledge of many kinds necessary, for him the effect of speech is to make things more complicated. This does not mean that Chuang Tzu would underestimate the extent to which language frames our mind and gives order to our life through the categorization and differentiation of things. For he says, 'In reality Tao has no limitation, and speech has no finality. [But] because of speech, there are clear demarcations. There are the left and the right; there are discussions and theories; there are analyses and arguments; there are competitions and quarrels . . . The sage keeps it in his mind while men in general argue in order to brag before each other. Therefore it is said that argument arises from failure to see [the greatness of Tao].'[45]

In this light, Chuang Tzu is not a skeptic who doubts the existence of any truthful statement. Statements are never final, always intersubstitutable, and sometimes they are simply irrelevant. Furthermore, proving the validity of a statement belongs too narrowly to the realm of making statements. Therefore, it would be wrong to classify Chuang Tzu as a relativist or to treat him as a thinker who indulges himself only in mute and mystical thought. For the debates with Hui Shih on his knowledge about the happiness of fish indicate clearly that it was Hui Shih who, indulging in arguments with words, winds up as a relativist. Chuang Tzu rebuts Hui Shih, reminding him that his question 'How do you know?' already presupposed that he knew the answer; and, further, he adds that he knew [the happiness of fish] by standing there beside the Hao River. Speaking, language and epistemology cannot stand alone, dissociated from real life encounters; the validity of speech has to be evaluated in context, but context cannot be reduced to pure textuality. Chuang Tzu enjoys speaking and debating and fosters an unambiguous sense of truth, although he never forgets to be self-critical and self-erasing.

Play, Forgetfulness and the Self

Frequently, philosophies of decadent eras are not only accused of having a mystical ontology but also of indulging in an irresponsible hedonism, said to be evident in their 'playful style.' Thus, while Derrida's play of the trace is often taken as wordplay, Chuang Tzu's double negatives are simply taken as an 'attitude of equivocation' by which opposite terms become 'easily' intersubstitutable.[46] When unfamiliar thinking practices are reduced to a matter of style or a 'manner of expression,' they can easily be cast aside as irrelevant to serious moral pursuits. Derrida thinks he is obliged to speak of negative theology, because his allusions to the negativity of the secret and the secret of negativity leave him open to accusations of speaking only for the sake of speaking. Such talk is prone to be denounced as a bastardized resurgence of some form of esoteric sociality. Either it is conceived as hiding a 'real' secret or as pretending to have one in order to organize itself around a bid for social power, which is seen as founded on the magic of speech.[47] Not surprisingly, playfulness is usually taken as an ingredient of such 'magic.'

Yeh, for instance, finds in Chuang Tzu and Derrida a common impenetrability of the deconstructive style that stems from a shared penchant for 'mixing of seriousness and non-seriousness' and for avoiding assertations. Similarly, Zhang worries that Derrida's deconstructive reading involves 'mystic obscurantism.' He prefers the sublime aesthetical silence of poetry that (he claims) transcends the predicament of finding no-word to speak. For these two commentators, as for other (comparative) philosophers, obscurantism and impenetrability is undoubtedly a form of hiding. What is hidden must be a secret — either a secret feat or a secret law. If not, Derrida and Chuang Tzu must be pretending in play or playing in pretension, thereby giving a false or irresponsible promise to their readers who are all thrown into disarray.

To be sure, Chuang Tzu has no intention to make a promise, either in the content of his words or his style. He would not be particularly drawn to the Derridean play of the trace; such grammatological hair-splitting would surely seem to him futile and tedious, when compared with rhetorical happy meandering. Nonetheless his playfulness cannot be taken as just a matter of style. His 'play with words' is an extremely solemn business. The figure in his parable, Cook Ting, who looks so tranquil, cut up an ox with an immense craftiness, in which even his perception and understanding have come to a stop momentarily. He would never get his work done if he lacked the seriousness to care for life. Life, as play of music harmonizing with heaven and earth, has nothing to do with an impenetrable (style of) the secret. Writing style concerns more than style as such. The commitment to non-commitment, the engagement with non-engagement in life, is neither a preference for play over seriousness, nor an escape from, or an excuse to avoid, serious matters, including serious speaking. It is for this reason that Chuang Tzu, while condemning the value of debate, still enjoyed his debates with Hui Shih. Therefore, in Chuang Tzu's thinking, playfulness cannot be set in opposition to seriousness, any more than non-being can be set in opposition being.

If, in Derrida, play (of the trace) is a political, aesthetic and epistemological subversion and negation (of logocentric language and the world of modernity), then, in Chuang Tzu, play is an affirmative act (of life) against the entanglement of the self in futile pursuits of evanescent social values. For, in Chuang Tzu, the play of words with words in an attitude of self-forgetfulness is predisposed to a cognitive openness in which the silent voice of life can resonate. It calls for a life in which people can 'forget the passage of time (life and death), putting aside the business of the distinction between ultimate right and ultimate wrong, [in order to] relax in the realm of the infinite and make it home.'[48] In other word, self-forgetfulness is a gate to temporalities other than the one that binds life to the spurious assemblage of justice as violence and violence as justice.

One point on which most philosophers would agree is that one cannot play seriously if one does not lose oneself in play. Heidegger and Gadamer, for instance, make a great deal out of the concept of play. Gadamer speaks of play as 'the clue to ontological explanation.'[49] Gadamer's rich phenomenological description of play and games presupposes, however, a Platonic conception of truth as a horizon. Posed as a critique of the enlightenment conception of subjectivity and self, Gadamer's play seems to have its own essence independent of the player's consciousness. He writes, for example, 'The structure of play absorbs the player into itself, and thus takes from him the burden of the initiative, which constitutes the actual strain of existence.'[50] He also submits, 'Play fulfils its purpose only if the player loses himself in his play... The players are not the subjects of play: instead play merely reaches presentation through the players.'[51]

Chuang Tzu, too, talks a lot about self-forgetting and the forgetting of the self. Instead of the self being absorbed in giving presence to the play itself, the process of self-forgetfulness is simultaneously one of self-attainment. For the self before the forgetful play with non-being is a selfish, not true, self. It is only through the play of mutual piping and meandering in and out of cognitive ambiguity and openness that one becomes visible to oneself again. The attainment of an enlightened self by playing in and out of a chaotic world of moral and textual ambiguities is intrinsic to Chuang Tzu's politics of subjectivity. Chuang Tzu distinguishes carefully between two modes through which reflection of subjectivity is made possible. The first is looking at oneself *through looking at others* (*chien pi*); the second is not looking *at* oneself but looking *of* oneself *(tzu chien)*.[52] For Chuang Tzu, looking at oneself demands that the self first be harmfully split into two. Because, strictly speaking, one cannot really look at oneself except through reflection in the light of the other, others and others' perspectives might become intrusions. For this reason, morality without the care of the true self is only enslavement by the others. Chuang Tzu maintains that only the non-intrusive self-ishness in playful forgetfulness can do neither violence to oneself nor to others.

However, the path followed by Heidegger, Gadamer and even Derrida makes very different presuppositions about the nature of subjectivity. To the extent that the player loses his or her self, play is taken as the presencing of a pre-structure or pre-understanding. The critique of the solipsistic subject is based upon a model of an enlarged self that takes tradition, history and language into consideration. Chuang Tzu's playful forgetfulness is very different, because to him the play of words by man can never be reduced to a scene in which the word (itself) plays. What Derrida asserts as the 'always-already happening' of language is too solemn for Chuang Tzu's somewhat 'instrumental' and 'playful' view of language. Chuang Tzu says, 'Traps are for the rabbits; once they are got, traps are forgotten. Words are for the intended meaning; once the meaning is got, the words are forgotten. How can I get a man who has forgotten words to have a word with him?'[53]

Using and forgetting language is definitely not just slippery play. Every forgetting of language is simultaneously a remembering of the intersubstitutability of the self and language. In contrast with some of the conventional Confucian ethics based on 'rectification of names,' Chuang Tzu's view entails an anti-literalism that goes beyond conventional morality. In a dialogue between Yen Hui and Confucius, Chuang Tzu makes a remarkable point about 'sitting in forgetfulness.' Only until humanity and righteousness, ceremonies and music, are all forgotten while sitting can one have no partiality and be part of the process of transformation.[54]

Different Paradoxes

Chuang Tzu's paradoxical assertion of ethics is homologous with his paradoxical ontology and epistemology. He writes, 'Great Tao has no appellation. Great speech does not say anything. Great humanity is not humane. Great modesty is not yielding. Great courage does not injure.'[55]

This may seem parallel with what Augustine called the simultaneously negative and hyperaffirmative meaning of the word *without.* As the harbinger of the tradition of negative theology, Augustine said, 'God is wise without wisdom, good without goodness, powerful without power.'[56] In these characterizations of God, the singular attribution is not merely dissociated from the essential generality, namely, wisdom as *being-wise* in general, or goodness as *being-good* in general, or power as being-powerful in general. Instead, the word *without* transmutes its purely phenomenal negativity into affirmation.

However, in a manner counter to negative theology, Chuang Tzu's non-being is not arrived at as the destination of this apophatic movement, for there is never a promise of the place. What even Derrida has to put into the metaphor of a past happening, or an 'immemorial past,' is not what has obliged Chuang Tzu to speak. In addition, what Chuang Tzu is after is certainly not 'the highest of the highest' but what is *otherwise than* the highest. Although undoubtedly Derrida too is struggling to get away from this apophatic movement, he is acutely aware that he is not, and cannot be, operating totally in a different language cleansed of metaphysics. This is not a matter of Derrida's inability but of strategy. Derrida makes clear that even an 'immemorial past' is still modeled after, and dissimulated as, a past. The longing for the hope above all hopes would still be rendered as one of the always-failing hopes. Erasures are still and always will be leaving marks of trace as promise. In this respect, Derrida is aware of the fact that he is not really playing a free play. Speaking is indeed the playing-out *of something.* He may not be able to speak *around* that something, and anyhow, he is *obliged* to speak *of* that something. In such a situation, space can only be created by denials; projects of hopes have to be biodegradable, so to speak.

In dissociating his thinking of *différance* (as a principle of interruption and limit) from Wittgenstein's dictum about the unsayable, Derrida signals an old onto-theological trace. While Wittgenstein in *Tractatus* says, 'concerning that about which one cannot speak, one must remain silent,' Derrida draws our attention to the 'one must,' for it indeed inscribes an injunction to silence into the order or the promise of 'one cannot speak.'[57] Insofar as this old order of promise is also a promise of order, Derrida also knows which alternative positions are (already) available for his or all those enigmatic symbols. In discussing the topolitology of negative theology, he thus writes, 'Without the divine promise which is also an injunction, the power of these *synthemata* would be merely conventional rhetoric, poetry, fine arts, perhaps literature.'[58]

In the modern world devoid of a divinely ethical promise but with prescribed positions always ready within the academic disciplinary mechanisms as part of 'the order,' it is no surprise that both Derrida and Chuang Tzu's unsayable hopes have been received mainly, if not exclusively, in terms of their playful style *as* literature or rhetoric; or sublated into divulgations of 'the secret of style.' For example, Zhang in his chapter "The Use of Silence," praises Tao Qian, a fourth-century Chinese poet, for making good use of Chuang Tzu, claiming that Tao Quian 'turns the linguistic skepticism of a mystic-philosopher into a positive solution to the problem of language.' Moreover, in explaining the 'use' of silence to which Chuang Tzu contributed, Zhang writes, 'that is why in great works of literature, as in great music, we often find that the *climactic* moment is one of pause or silence.'[59] It is in this way that echoes of Chuang Tzu in Tao Qian's poetry can be posited as completing no more than the Hegelian dialectic of Aesthetics, something that Mallarmé in the late twentieth century had just begun to achieve. It rings more like the grand finale of a Wagnerian symphony than a moment of unsayable silence. Yet it is truly a tragedy: even the unsayable cannot help from being sublated onto-theologically at the expense of the moment of ethics and politics.

Ethics and the Unsayable(s)

Fighting hard against the onto-theological reduction of ethics into moral codes and moral philosophy, Levinas consistently asserts the dissociation of ethics *from* philosophy. Speech about morality to him risks collapsing the infinite responsibility of the concrete individual into themes of conceptual truth. Like Chuang Tzu and Derrida, he seeks to abandon speaking and writing without giving in to mystical experience like the negative theologians; he opens a space for his ethics in the distinction between Saying and the Said. While the truth of the latter belongs to the order of ontology, the truth of the former is unthematizable thought, which always precedes the latter, and as a response to the asymmetrical 'command' issued from the face of the other in proximity, exceeds it.

To Levinas, genuine and universal ethical language is possible only in terms of such extreme unsayable particularity. Levinas thinks that it is by asserting this prophetic moment that the egoism underlying the whole Western philosophical tradition will be overcome. He feels it is necessary to re-establish absolute *subjectiveness* by abolishing the language of subjectivity, including phenomenology, such that ethical values more fundamental than freedom and autonomy can stand up again. To Levinas, a truly ethical self, a being-for-the-other, is the self without concept. The relationship between the self and the other is not one of mutual constitution; it is not even governed by reciprocity. Subjectivity can only be given a new existence by the other's judgment, and the singularity of an individual can only be attained by being awakened to the responsibility to the other's face.

Levinas's is an *unsayable ethics,* for the ethical supremacy of Saying comes from the *beyond,* which is intelligible only as the trace. It is also a deconstructive attempt to displace ethics and think it anew by locating its condition of possibility in the relation to the singular other. However, as the possibility of this unsayable ethics has to rely paradoxically on a 'conceptual' distinction initiated largely within the realm of language and philosophy, Derrida interrupts to indicate the trace of residual metaphysical categories and thus negative theology in his thinking. While Derrida thus criticizes this attempt, he does not disagree with the intentions of such an ethical theory. To him, the problem remains: if ethics is defined in terms of respect for alterity, how is alterity respected in a discourse established upon that alterity? In other words, a discourse about reconciling with otherness will create its own otherness. How then is an ethics toward the other possible?

Derrida's *sayable heterology* is about a double reading encapsulated in the notion of closure. Closure is the double refusal, a refusal to remain within the limits of tradition and a refusal of the possibility of transgressing that limit. The 'methodological' problem becomes that of discovering how a reading can remain internal to the text and within the limits of textuality without merely repeating the text in the manner of a 'commentary.' Textual space has to be opened up to create a certain distance between deconstructive reading and logocentric conceptuality. The signifying structure of a deconstructive reading has to be located at a hinge, which articulates the double movement between logocentrism or metaphysics and its other. At the same time, deconstructive reading has to enable one to exceed the orbit of conceptual totality. The goal of deconstruction is to locate a point of otherness within logocentric conceptuality and to deconstruct that conceptuality from that position of alterity.

It is in this light that Derrida finds himself situated in a relation to the double tradition of negative theology similar to that articulated by Dionysius. On the one hand, there is the unspeakable, secret, inaccessible and mystical, and on the other hand, the philosophic, demonstrative, capable of being shown.[60] He characterizes his speaking as located at the intersection (*symploke)* of these two modes — which intersection is the hinge. This amounts to saying that he must both preserve and name the secret, yet it is impossible except by incessant denials of the secret. Furthermore, for this Derridean play of doubleness to be ethical, he has to rely on an unconditional claim or a claim of unconditionality, which he acknowledges in *Limited Inc.* There he writes,

> In the different texts I have written on (against) apartheid, I have on several occasions spoken of 'unconditional' affirmation or of 'unconditional' 'appeal'. Now the very least that can be said of *unconditionality (a word that I use not by accident to recall the character of the categorical imperative in its Kantian form)* is that it is independent of every determinate context... It announces itself as such only in the *opening* of context. Not that it is simply present (existent) elsewhere, outside of all context; rather it intervenes in the determination of a context from its very opening, and from an injunction, a law, a responsibility that transcend this or that determination of a given context. Following this, what remains is to *articulate this unconditionality with the determinate* (Kant would say, hypothetical) conditions of this or that context; and this is the moment of strategies, of rhetorics, of ethics, and of politics.[61]

For Derrida, this moment of ethics is contingent upon situations and yet remains unconditional. It is literally con-textual. It is neither thematizable nor unthematizable. Because it is based upon a belief that there is nothing outside of a context, yet there is always a non-closure, an opening of the context. He continues, 'The structure thus described supposes both that there are only contexts, that nothing *exists* outside context, as I have often said, but also that the limit of the frame or the border of the context always entails a clause of *non-closure.* The outside penetrates and thus determines the inside.'[62]

To Chuang Tzu, ethics is chiefly the pursuit of a harmonious rapport with every kind of life encounter (as nature) by earnest effort to achieve an emptied but responsive self. There is nothing more unnecessary to him than the claim that there is nothing outside a *con-text,* let alone the inclusion of responsibility or ethics exclusively there. This is because Chuang Tzu thinks that there is abundance of possibilities outside text or textuality in and out of which speech and silence can continuously play. Putting all things unconditionally in *con-text* would seem to belittle the violence of text, insofar as textuality is not so much the source of hope as roots of problems. To Chuang Tzu, what is truly paradoxical and contradictory of Derrida is that he (like Levinas) claims that language is imbued with violence, so how could he still hold that ethics is dependent upon the clause of non-closure in context, the opening up of which is another speech? Derrida himself finds in Levinas residual violence, from which the only refuge is apophatic movement. Yet one may still ask how far Derrida himself has moved away from this.[63] Or, to put it politically, rather than simply philosophically, one may ask whether Derrida *chooses* to move away from the play.

For Chuang Tzu who does not conceive speaking as constrained in the double bind between divulging or preserving any secret, ethics does not lie in finding a speaking place like the Platonic *khora* in order to conceive the intersection of double movement. Hence, doubleness is not primarily of a grammatological nature but is implied in his view of language and in his ontology of mutual transformation. As Edward T. Ch'ien puts it, 'Language use as a self-erasing practice is anchored in his ontological vision...in its discursive specificity as both statements and counterstatements and in its very being as both speech and silence... Just as things transform from and into one another and just as statements and counterstatements implicate and produce one another, speech and silence are mutually involved and substitutable. There is speech in silence and silence in speech. Because there is speech in silence, silence is capable of erasing itself to become speech. Conversely, because there is silence in speech, speech is also capable of erasing itself to become silence.'[64]

Therefore, an ethical life is not one in which there is an obligation for everyone to speak, nor to remain in silence, but to 'follow two courses at the same time,' to enable responsive transformations between silence and speech as well as between the self and the other. The ethics of language and life is then an unsublated dialectic between speech and silence, self and other, engagement and non-engagement. This *responsive* rather than *responsible* ethics is made possible only by a 'hinge'. Yet unlike the Derridean hinge that serves only as an intersection of two different realms of textuality, hinge (*tao shu*) for Chuang Tzu is rather the hollowness of the self that enables unlimited responses. Setting himself apart from the pursuit of intellectual intelligibility weaved by textualities, Chuang Tzu is definitely not the heir of the Platonic tradition of analogicism, which is bounded by the pursuit of intelligible 'truth'; he never developed an angst over mimesis. (As a consequence, to call on Chuang Tzu for assistance in solving the tension between 'inner reality' and 'outer expression' entails a simplistic imposition of a Romanticist image of the self.) Language in Chuang Tzu does not serve as a 'third species' destined to play the role of analogical mediation, in the manner that light links the visible to sight. His 'vision' or 'light' is not on the order of the perceptible and intelligible as in Plato. It is rather an illumination of the emptied self and non-being. Therefore, it is a 'dimmed light.'

To Chuang Tzu, violence to the unnameable other cannot be terminated by yet another vision or intellectual insight to unveil the location of alterity (as in Derrida) or by bowing down in silent deference to an unnameable Other (as in Levinas). Actually, Chuang Tzu's thought is about conceiving an ethics that does not end up denouncing freedom in return for an irreversible responsibility. It is all and all about freedom. This is because, *although responsibility to the other is what ethics is all about, the other does not emerge only through speech. The other is always mutually implicated in, and interchangeable with, the self. Thus speech will always produce silence as its other. Thereby, to be able to listen to silence is part and parcel of being ethical; and that is what makes ethics unsayable, and the unsayable ethical.* At any rate, to be ethical is not a matter of making everybody hostage to the voice of moral commands from a superlative power (of the other) against the self. It is rather a spontaneous response of the 'emptied but mature self' to abide by the course of nature that always preserves and enables.

The speech that speaks of this ethics is not located in the intersection of the expressible and the inexpressible; still less is it a simple 'identity politics,' that is, a 'revenge' of the inexpressible become expressible; nor is it a simple reversal. In a manner different from the enunciative mode of injunction evidenced in Wittgenstein, Chuang Tzu says, 'he who knows to stop at what he does not know is perfect.'[65] This is not a voice from Hermes, a priest, a judge, a philosopher, or from the place of the professionals in comparative philosophy. He instead asks and answers, 'Who knows the argument that requires no speech for the Tao that cannot be named? If anyone can know, he is called the store of Nature (which embraces all). The store is not full when more things are added and not empty when things are taken out. Yet we don't know where the supply comes from. This is called dimmed light.'[66]

The notion of the store of Nature (*tien-fu*) resembles the Platonic *khora,* which can also receive all and allow itself to be marked or affected by what is inscribed in it while remaining without form and proper determination. However, the *khora* remains an empty place (for God to dwell). If there is no God to dwell there, the place remains empty although it is not an absolute void. Yet, doesn't this suggest at the same time that anyone who tries to speak of it is also playing the role of God? In any case, the *khora* gives possibilities but does not originate. In contrast, the store of Nature does supply; it nurtures; it is originating. It is illuminated not by the intelligible sun of Platonic thought but by dimmed light only. It is also where Chuang Tzu's *ethics of the unsayable* is played out for the myriad possibilities to emerge. The locus of this ethical fecundity is within the human self but not conceived as a particular 'place.'

Can we then deduce that Derrida has remained trapped in metaphysics and Chuang Tzu has transcended Derrida, thus completing a dialectical movement via comparison? Or, is Chuang Tzu therefore non-philosophical while Derrida is still philosophical? The answer should be deferred until we have explored what it means to be 'philosophical' in each historical specificity. At any rate, it lies not in invoking a universalist frame of comparison that masks the will and logic of onto-theological re-appropriation. Rather it lies in acknowledging different ethics or ethics as difference. While Derrida, who justifiably claims that 'I am not simply a philosopher,' is acutely aware of the dilemma of political intervention in a modernity that is always already structured or haunted by the violence of texts or textualized violence, his deconstructive ethics, played out in and out of philosophy, longs for *khora* as an 'alternative'/non-site to speak without being disengaged. Chuang Tzu's life-enhancing ethics entails enabling the emptied but responsive self as the other-than-site for another politics in an increasingly hypocritical world, thus allowing himself to be 'philosophical' if the situation requires. Both are paradoxical ethics and ethics as paradox conceivable philosophically only at the cost of reducing their resistances to a certain kind of theory. Yet their different ethics might remain ethical if their differences are not sublated by the violence of comparative philosophizing.

Comparative philosophy has put these thinkers who lived thousand of years apart side by side. Yet have the dialogues between them truly begun? Although we can produce speech after speech, paper after paper, in the discipline of comparative philosophy, questions about the comparative enterprise persist. What are we indeed comparing? When comparative philosophers remain immersed in digging out the ineffable from the global array of traditions, to what extent are they able to listen to the silence? Richard Rorty made a provocative remark at the Sixth East-West Philosophers' Conference held in 1989 in Honolulu, saying, 'So we have to be careful not to let *this taste* [for the ineffable] seduce us into the presumption that, when it comes to other cultures, only our counterparts, those with tastes similar to *our own,* are reliable sources of information. We should stay alert to the possibility that comparative philosophy not only is not a royal road to intercultural comparison, but also may even be a distraction from such comparison. For it may turn out that we are really comparing nothing more than the adaptations of a *single transcultural character type* to different environments.'[67]

Here, Rorty issues a staunch warning that, although comparative philosophy sets itself the task to hear from the other, it risks the danger of subsuming the other into the familiar same. Nonetheless, while Rorty calls attention to a single 'character type' and a 'taste' of '*our* own,' he cannot escape falling prey to his own cynicism. For I think there is more at stake here — at least more than this tendency to collapse all the 'ineffables' and 'unsayables' into a single category, the type of *our own.* If Rorty is correct in pointing out the danger involved in some characteristic ways of 'comparison for the West,' he is at the same time complicit in reducing to oblivion an important part of comparative studies. Ironically, that part is what Rorty himself claims to prefer to 'philosophy,' namely, historical narratives.

Philosophizing / Aestheticizing Chuang Tzu: Moments of Imperial Violence

Modern philosophy always tends to turn ethics and politics into theory. In attempt to prevent the transformation of this essay into just another philosophical statement about theory, I would like to put these various issues into their related historical context. Accounting for the characteristic readings of Derrida as a nihilist philosopher and a frivolous literary theorist necessitates going back to the trajectory in which North American academic institutions, especially the Yale-School, received his thought. That part of the intellectual history I surely do not need to elaborate here. In contrast, the path in which Chuang Tzu becomes a philosophical and literary figure takes one back to the rise of Sinological Orientalism in the heyday of British imperialism.

According to Girardot, who charts the transformation of Western interest in Chinese Taoism, the growth of interest in reading Chuang Tzu philosophically emerged between the 1870s and the 1890s, concomitant to the institutionalization of a new British-led Sinological scholarship.[68] Rapid Western imperial expansion in the late nineteenth century, and the dominance of positivism and evolutionism, prompted Max Muller in Germany to pursue a scientific study of 'comparative religion' that was 'armed' with the tools and methods of philology. To Max Muller, compiling and controlling the literary heritage of Oriental tradition for 'science' was to be done in the way a museum 'colonizes the past' by collecting, classifying, and displaying the artifacts of history. Echoing Muller, E.J. Eitel, the editor of the then influential Sinological journal *China Review,* said that 'the struggle that is enjoined with Oriental civilizations will be won not by missionary evangelization, not with shot and shell, and not by feats of engineering skill but by the more subtle weapons of Western science, on the battle field of practical, speculative and critical philosophy.'[69] It is in this context that selected texts of Taoism, such as *Tao Te Ching* and *Chuang Tzu* were elevated to the status of 'Taoist Bibles.'

James Legge was the key contributor to Muller's project, *Sacred Books of the East.* His translations became the foundational sources for the Western scholarly interest in Taoism. As a missionary, 'amateur' scholar, and colonial administrator in Hong Kong, James Legge translated the Chinese classics within a variety of traditions. The old French Orientalism still figured prominently in Legge, who was interested in mapping a developmental pattern that distinguished between some original pure system of thought and its eventual superstitious decline. Therefore, he selected Chuang Tzu and Lao Tzu mainly as thinkers dissociated from the magic, alchemy, practices for *hsien* immortality and sect activities, which were relegated the domain of later Taoist superstitions, contaminated by Buddhism. The opposition between 'early/pure' and 'later/corrupt' Taoism also dovetails with Legge's Protestant perspective which perceives the development of religions in China through a narrative comparable to the trajectory in which the pure system of morality and thinking of Christianity was deemed to have gradually grafted onto itself Roman Catholic-like 'monasteries and nunneries.' Legge's idiosyncratic interest in looking for an equivalent concept of a monotheistic God in Chinese traditions also cast a shadow on his efforts to preserve and defend a vision of early Taoism that was composed mainly of pure thinkers who were enlightened by an idea comparable to a monotheistic God.

These complex interplays of narratives and comparative methodologies were all ingredients as well as products of the process of implicating Chuang Tzu and Lao Tzu into the newly arrived 'world of comparison' which is simultaneously a kind of scholarship, (imperial) politics and popular fantasy — Max Muller's original plan for the *Sacred Book* was to teach the general public the superiority of European Civilization. Ironically, the 'foolish enthusiasms' for 'Oriental Wisdom' on behalf of the non-academic public spurred the scholarly apparatus. James Legge, a transitional figure among these forces, nurtured images of Chuang Tzu and Lao Tzu as Taoist thinkers, holding them up against the emerging Sinologists armed with a more overtly combative, suspicious and rationalistic approach, and pleading for a more reverent, sympathetic, 'comparative' method.[70] Ironically, at the height of imperialism, Chinese thought appeared to be most comparable to Western ideas.

The distinctively 'Leggian' conception of Chinese monotheism is now forgotten; it could not survive under the attacks both of the theologically oriented missionaries and the new professional Sinologists. Yet the 'pure and the corrupt' dichotomy still dominates the study of Taoism; it is palpable today. Mainstream academic Sinology after Legge remained content with the image of Chinese culture as characterized by secularity and rationality. With the help of a series of classics compiled by James Legge, Chinese traditions of thought were canonized, with Confucianism occupying the core of the 'Great Tradition' of Chinese civilization, while Taoism was relegated to the margins. Chuang Tzu's image as a distinctly 'philosophical' and 'literary' figure finds confirmation in the general treatment of Taoism as merely 'philosophical, literary or sociological impingement' on Chinese civilization. The thought presented in Taoist 'sacred books' such as *Chuang Tzu* has been, till very recently, received mainly as a philosophical text dissociated from the long history of Taoism as a wide spread, long held and still living set of popular religious, bodily and political practices. As a consequence, while commentators today find it difficult to deal with Chuang Tzu's distinct but historically embedded ethics and engaging politics, they seem readily fascinated by his mysteriously charming rhetoric.

This is not the place to make the case for a full-scale revision of the current Sinological scholarship on Taoism, which is absolutely necessary before thorough research and intellectual interrogation can begin. Nonetheless, readers deserve to be reminded of how much our comparison is always already haunted by our colonial past — a past which is too easily denied in China in light of claims that it has never been fully and formally colonized.[71] Admittedly, even the para-comparative reading I have done above cannot claim to be totally free from those textualities already woven into the history of imperialism and the reality of coloniality. Despite all the differences that may arise from looking back upon Taoism as a complex intellectual, religious and even political phenomenon, it is clear that the image of today's Chuang Tzu, as full of 'sublime mysteries' derived from a purely Eastern thought and as always aesthetically alluring, is actually a contingent product of the juncture of certain theological projection by some Western missionaries, old Orientalist scholarship and emerging Sinological discourses. Traces of these intellectual and political practices are still haunting our reading of Chuang Tzu or Taoism as an important part of Chinese everyday life. Today we do not so much see positivistic, combative Western Sinologists who step forth to challenge the very existence of Taoism as a coherent mythology, or to ask whether book like *Tao Te Ching* is nothing but a forgery, battling with some of their churchmen over whether such popular superstitions are 'comparable' to any Western conception of religion. Rather we see today the same sublime and mysterious image of Chuang Tzu being enthusiastically recuperated, by Western and non-Western writers, through a specific, collaboratively constructed comparative mechanism armed with telescopic lenses of a now paradigmatic but somewhat sundry postmodernism. For some Chuang Tzu is useful for therapy, for others a source of Chinese national pride.

Commenting on the emerging Sinological Orientalism and its constitution of the late-Victorian image of Taoism, Girardot says that, in different ways, both the missionaries and the Sinologists affirmed the total otherness of China with respect to religious traditions. The missionaries thought China too religious yet lacking a monotheistic God, while the Sinologists thought that there were no theism, religion or mythology at all. The two approaches — the more combative, suspicious and rationalistic approach of Sinology and the relatively reverent, sympathetic, and civil approach of Legge's comparative religion — are but different intellectual strategies of representation to control the past. Needless to say, thanks to the rise of nationalism, the terms of comparison have changed dramatically today, as have the stage settings, the costumes, the lighting, as well as who will play the role of the masters in need of controlling the past. The availability of toolkits for 'sciences' is also rapidly changing. Today no one would still conceive the plausibility of a Chinese Sky God, as did James Legge, charged as he was with 'methodological empathy.' There are hundreds of reasons for people to denounce that 'eccentric' idea as nothing but Western hallucination. Nevertheless, there are no signs that the desire for the highest of the highests have stopped, or will stop, haunting the national intellectuals' minds. Zhang Longxi certainly will not be the last and only one to ask, 'Where is our Chinese Logos?'

At present, with the globalization of all aspects of human existence, the 'desire for comparability' has become so pervasive that you don't need Max Muller to give the Chinese a definition of their religiosity, or a missionary like James Legge to make the Hebrew God into the standard measure for Chinese deities, still less an 'amateur Sinologist' like E.J. Eitel to trumpet the 'weapons' of Western sciences. Yet, in a certain way, all of them have become part of a national legacy. What is more, you can find people everywhere, who, without coercion, find solace or astonishment in discovering master words or images that may be copied. They are cheerful in discovering in themselves something 'comparable' to those master words. In this fetish for master words and the mad race for comparability, one might turn to 'universal metaphoricity' in order to domesticate Chuang Tzu. Or, one might have recourse to 'law' or 'principle' to assure the 'comparability' of Chuang Tzu and Derrida. Are we then still able to retrieve the origin of the standard, to establish which mode of comparison privileges the one over the other? In the post-colonial world of comparison, is there any sense in differentiating between original and copy? Who ultimately holds the original?

Paraphrasing Chuang Tzu, we may say there is the original, there is the copy; there is not yet having the original to have the copy; there is not yet having the original to have the original to have the copy... All we know is that, for comparison to take place, a master word, the myth of the original, or the 'global standard' has first to be posited. This is not only true of 'comparisons for the West' but also of 'comparisons for the East.' In light of the daily haunting of master words, what are the conditions of possibility for — paraphrasing Habermas — an 'ideal comparative situation' for dialogue to take place? Within those regimes of comparability, how much more are cultural differences and singularity of human life, as well as sharing and solidarity, rendered unsayable?

Spectrality, Comparison and the Decolonization of Mind

In the recent discussion around Benedict Anderson's *Spectre of Comparison*, Partha Chatterjee accuses Anderson's comparative vision of continuing to hold up the North Atlantic as the yardstick for the ethical legitimacy of nationalism.

He contends that universalism is unevenly available to different people. He says, 'The universalist ideal that belongs to Anderson as part of the same inheritance that allows him to say "my Europe" can continue *to encompass* its others as it moves from older national rigidities to newer cosmopolitan lifestyles. For those who cannot say "my Europe," the choice seems to be to allow oneself *to be encompassed* within global cosmopolitan hybridities or to relapse into hateful ethnic particularities.'[72]

H.D. Harootunian, although he considers Chatterjee's attempt to find sites outside capitalism and colonialism romantic, echoes Chatterjee when he criticizes Anderson's metaphor of the 'inverted telescope,' claiming that it ends up magnifying the West at the expense of the non-West. He characterizes Anderson's strategy of the spectrality of comparison as one that 'works to change the body and flesh into its apparition'; yet, insofar as he presumes it is only Europe's flesh and body that undergo alchemical transubstantiation, Anderson remains unable to distinguish between the apparition and its reality. Under his 'hauntology,' Anderson covertly returns to Western ontology; he is concerned more with how the 'shadow of Europe' stretches across Southeast Asia than with looking genuinely into how Southeast Asia (or the non-Western world), as living bodies, are haunted and terrified by the return of their own pasts. Harootunian then calls for a genuine 'hauntology' based on a 'mapping out' of the domain of spectrality, to find a way for the disappearing past to return, overcoming the separation of history.[73]

While I agree with him on the importance of recognizing the surfacing of the forgotten past for the 'ghostly effect,' which Harootunian would like to form as a critique of the Euro-American modernity, I would wonder if his account risks prematurely exorcising the spectre of colonialism, by 'mapping out' separate domains of the past as 'history.' Clearly, we are still a long way from a clear account of how 'the past' (our non-Euro-American past) has already been haunted by Colonial-Orientalist-Sinological perspectives. I think that Anderson's overtly sociological-determinist tendency initiates an over-reaction, which haunts even his critics who take for granted Anderson's assumption that comparability is the result of the global spread of instrumental rationality. To this effect, Harootunian writes, 'this sense of comparability — the power and necessity of instrumental rationality to grasp knowledge and experience — was, at the same time, made available to precisely all those Asians like Watsuji, Soetomo, and even Chatterjee who took its possibility for granted in constructing their own critical strategies.'[74]

With this caricatured, automatist image of the long march of industrial modernity, we would easily let go of our colonialism. Moreover, Pheng Cheah's call for attention to the 'frame' of comparative vision would not be properly addressed, for comparability cannot simply be reduced to the result of the restless spread of capitalism's energy.[75]

The situation, rather, is one in which coloniality as the spectre of Western modernity has indeed continued to haunt us even when we try to invoke 'other temporalities' to break from the linear/empty one. As Derrida says, 'even an "immemorial past" is still modeled after and dissimulated as a past.' In the *modern* 'world of comparison,' where comparing always prevails over listening, where the past can almost find no presence except through comparison with others, the spectre of colonialism continues haunting us by transfiguring itself into various 'comparative schemas' which render present all the pasts. In that light, where is the line that clearly demarcates the domain of the indigenous past free from colonial control? Does it not re-import the naturalized boundaries of nations uncritically? For example, who is the 'pre-colonial' Chuang Tzu? Even the 'Tao of Pooh' or its Hong Kong counterpart (Choi Chi Chung's comic) are merely reincarnations of the Western/Eastern stereotypes about 'the Chinese,' cooked up by the colonizers and inherited, modified and developed by national intelligentsia. These stereotypes are now inflected back to the West, pointing to the mystic 'truth of the unsayable' while concealing the 'unsayable truth of colonial reality.' The immemorial past of this Chuang Tzu is ironically not their 'own' non-European pre-colonial reality but that of the coloniality, which has always been disavowed.

Therefore, the matter is one of how and in what ways the lens of the comparative telescope is coloured more than whether it has been held inverted, magnifying one side at the expense of the other. It is those colours, inflected against the spectrum as a comparative schema, which determine the visibility and invisibility that allows anyone using the telescope to see things far away and long past. They paint for each brand of nationalism its fantastic image of cosmopolitanism, as a sort of 'portable ontology.' Among the colonized, they result in more than 'restless double-consciousness' (as Anderson describes it). They produce insatiable desires — inconsolable even after death — to seek one's self through the invocation of comparative schemas. This is an instrumentally enhanced impulse to gaze at one's self via the other, rather than an ear to listen to the other.

Therefore, I would venture to say that, before we take Anderson's sociological explanation of the rising technical capability for comparability for granted, what we need to take into account is the psychoanalytic-philosophic formation of this 'desire for comparability.' How has this desire informed the present inter-national configuration of knowledge systems across national boundaries, not so much as a mere shadow of Europe, nor as the fatally forgotten past, but rather as the effect of the long colonial/imperial history on the academic agenda, intellectual horizons and popular imaginations of the colonized hybrids that emerged *as 'nations'*? To what extent does this desire frame the intellectual and political dialogue among and, more importantly, *within* nation(s)? In what ways are different types of 'comparative schema' invented and re-invented out of this desire? How are different missionary, Oriental, imperial, sub-imperial and national narratives borrowed, mixed, shared, transmitted, transfigured, and spectralised, rather than just copied? To what extent have these schemas and narratives been institutionalised, in the form of imperial, national, and even international establishments that are not just 'casting a shadow' on, but actually framing, our present global and different local horizons for intellectual dialogues and popular fantasy — of the self and the other?

If the metaphor of spectrality invoked by Anderson is useful in breaking our cognitive boundaries that stop us from understanding our existence as globalized/colonized/modernized, we have to recognize that nationalism is not just a result of sociological possibilities which are over-determined by material circumstances, but the daily institutionalised haunting of this 'desire for comparability.' In this light, Chatterjee's criticism of Anderson hits the mark, for he questions Anderson's distinction between bound and unbound seriality, as way to mark the difference between potentially liberating politics of 'classical nationalism' and inherently constricting and conflicting ethnic politics. It is naïve to believe that technologies themselves can tell which one belongs to a more progressive politics. More importantly, if serialization is so much bound up with comparison, comparison will no doubt also induce serialization as its embodied form. The abyssal inflection(s) would generate incessantly — and perhaps increasingly — its individuals as well as its 'quotidian universals.' For example, the Olympic Games might be seen as a new seriality emerging beyond the United Nations.

In this regard, Chatterjee and Harootunian as well still greatly underestimate the extent to which it is not just 'the past' but universalism itself that is conjured up. It is not that certain 'universal ideals' can encompass its others, while the others are only waiting to be encompassed, but that they are always products of complicity. Universalism is not the opposite of particularism, nor can one clearly differentiate those who can lay claim to 'my Europe' from those who cannot.[76] So long as unsayable ethics and the politics of everyday life is politically serialized by colonial governmentality, or governmentality as coloniality, and intellectually sublated by onto-theological appropriation disguised as comparativism (be it comparative philology, comparative religion, comparative philosophy, comparative literature), 'Europe' and 'nation' are (rehearsing Chuang Tzu) merely two interchangeable and intersubstitutable terms. Otherwise, what do we make of the endless haunting voice of the comparativist ghost: Where is 'Our Logos'?

Post-script

After rigorous exchanges and rejoinders with each other, Levinas expressed his gratitude and 'pleasure of a contact with Derrida made in the heart of a chiasmus.'[77] The Greek letter X denotes a crossing or interlacing which signifies two lines of thought that are bound to cross. Nevertheless, it is surely true that the dominant practices of contemporary East-West comparative philosophy — which works by isolating and comparing abstract themes (such as the unsayable) from Chuang Tzu, Derrida, or Levinas — never really find points in which the lines of thought can really cross. For the problem is not to find sameness (e.g. the *unsayability*) in these thinkings of the unsayable. Although they do conceive one thing or another hard to speak of, they are writing and speaking to open up respectively different new spaces in which different moments of ethics and/or the unsayable encounters can speak. To bring these unsayable ethics 'on the same footing' is to compare without listening to their differences; it simply re-enacts the drama of the Reason's cunning. Chuang Tzu, Derrida and Levinas would, I think, agree that every claim to comparability is a recuperation that generates its own other — 'the incomparable.' Only when those unsayable murmurs and incomparable others can be listened to in those non-sites occupied by selves always ready to have their flowery words and elusive classification schemes erased can dialogue truly begin to be free from the global violence of modern serialization. Then there will not be a moment of silence, a pause in any 'great music,' but a more heavenly mutual piping; not an intellectual drama staged on the comparative theatre with glamorous 'lighting effects', but an alchemy of wisdoms for life and struggles, which is lit only by a 'dimmed light'.

Notes

1 This paper is dedicated to the late Professor Edward T. Ch'ien, to whom I am deeply indebted. From his most memorable and intellectually challenging evening classes I attended, I learned what difference meticulously close reading can really make for cross-cultural humanities study. The first draft of this paper was actually written in 1994 when I was studying Chinese intellectual history under his supervision; although, given the lapse of time, the focus and argument have been changed substantially now. Thus I am also grateful to Thomas Lamarre, Stephen Muecke and Meaghan Morris for their encouragement and valuable comments. All mistakes and overstatements are, however, my own.

2 Benedict Anderson, *The Spectre of Comparisons : Nationalism, Southeast Asia, and the World* (New York: Verso, 1998).

3 Pheng Cheah, 'Grounds of Comparison' *Diacritic* (1999) 29:4, 11.

4 Lydia H. Liu, 'The Desire for the Sovereign and The Logic of Reciprocity in The Family of Nations' *Diacritic* 29:4 (1999): 150–77.

5 Partha Chatterjee, 'Anderson's Utopia' *Diacritic* (1999) 29:4, 128–34.

6 J. J. Clarke, *Oriental Enlightenment. The Encounter Between Asian and Western Thought* (London: Routledge, 1997).

7 T. W. Organ, *Western Approaches to Eastern Philosophy* (Athens: Ohio University Press, 1975), 7.

8 G. J. Larson and E. Deutsch, eds., *Interpreting Across Boundaries: New Essays in Comparative Philosophy* (Princeton: Princeton University Press, 1998), 18.

9 Richard Rorty, 'Philosophers, Novelists, and Intercultural Comparison: Heidegger, Kundera, and Dickens' in *Culture and Modernity*, ed. E. Deutsch (Honolulu: University of Hawaii Press, 1991), 8.

10 Jacques Derrida, 'Violence and Metaphysics: An Essay on the Thought of Emmanuel Levinas,' in *Writing and Difference* (Chicago: The University of Chicago Press, 1978), 112.

11 Derrida, 'Violence and Metaphysics,' 112.

12 Jacques Derrida, 'How to Avoid Speaking: Denials' in *Languages of the Unsayable*, ed. S. Budick and W. Iser (New York: Columbia University Press, 1989), 4.

13 Jacques Derrida, 'Difference,' in *Margins of Philosophy*, trans. A. Bass (Chicago: University of Chicago Press, 1982), 6.

14 Derrida, 'Difference,' 6. Emphasis is mine.

15 Derrida, 'How to Avoid Speaking: Denials,' 9.

16 Michelle Yeh, 'The Deconstructive Way: A Comparative Study of Derrida and Chuang Tzu,' in *Journal of Chinese Philosophy*, 10 (1983): 95–126.

17 'Way' is another translation of the concept Tao, first used by the French Orientologist Stanislas Julien.

[18] Yeh, 'The Deconstructive Way,' 96.
[19] Yeh, 'The Deconstructive Way,' 105. Emphasis is mine.
[20] Gayatri Spivak, 'Translator's Preface' in Jacques Derrida, *Of Grammatology* (Baltimore: The John Hopkins University Press, 1974).
[21] To this effect, Yeh quotes a sentence from Derrida's article '*Différance*' in which he says '*Différance* is the non-full, non-simple 'origin,' the structured and different origin of differences' (107). Oddly, however, the next sentence — 'The name origin thus is no longer suitable' — does not appear in Yeh's analysis.
[22] On the differences between Lao Tzu and Chuang Tzu, see Zhao Weimin, *Chuang Tzu's Tao* (1998).
[23] Yeh, 'The Deconstructive Way,' 112. Emphasis is mine.
[24] Yeh, 11. Emphasis is mine.
[25] Zhang Longxi, *The Tao and the Logos: Literary Hermeneutics, East and West* (Durham: Duke University Press, 1992).
[26] Derrida, *Of Grammatology*, 92.
[27] Zhang, *The Tao and the Logos*, 26.
[28] Zhang, *The Tao and the Logos*, 26. Emphasis is mine.
[29] Zhang, *The Tao and the Logos*, xi. Emphasis is mine.
[30] Apparently in keeping with this wish for 'equal footing,' the cover design of Zhang's book presents Hermes riding to the left on a flying horse, while Lao Tzu rides to the right on a unicorn; the matched eyelines suggests a wish to talk.
[31] Wu Kuang-ming, *Chuang Tzu: World Philosopher at Play* (New York: Crossroad Publishing Company, 1982), 62.
[32] Wu Kuang-ming, *Chuang Tzu*, 62–63.
[33] Soren Kierkegaard, 'Against Proofs in Religion' in *Classical and Contemporary Readings in Philosophy of Religion*, ed. J. Hick, 3rd ed. (Englewood Cliff, NJ: Prentice Hall, 1990), 167.
[34] Derrida, '*Différance*,' 26.
[35] *The Complete Work of Chuang Tzu,* Burton Watson, trans. (New York: Columbia University Press, 1962), 36–37.
[36] Derrida, '*Différance*,' 22.
[37] Derrida, 'How to Avoid Speaking: Denials,' 15.
[38] Wu Kuang-ming, *Chuang Tzu*, 78.
[39] Wu Kuang-ming, *Chuang Tzu*, 82.
[40] Yeh, 'The Deconstructive Way,' 108.
[41] Derrida, 'How to Avoid Speaking: Denials,' 13.
[42] Derrida, 'How to Avoid Speaking: Denials,' 18.
[43] *A Source Book in Chinese Philosophy,* W.T. Chan, trans., (Princeton, NJ: Princeton University Press, 1963), 182.
[44] W.T. Chan, 186.
[45] W.T. Chan, 186. Translation modified.
[46] Yeh, 'The Deconstructive Way,'113.
[47] Derrida, 'How to Avoid Speaking: Denials,' 19.

48 Chan, 190. Translation modified.
49 H-G Gadamer, *Truth and Method* (London: Sheed & Ward, 1975), 91.
50 Gadamer, *Truth and* Method, 94.
51 Gadamer, *Truth and Method*, 92.
52 Wu Kuang-ming, *Chuang Tzu*, 120.
53 Watson, 303.
54 Chan, 201.
55 Chan, 186–7.
56 Derrida, 'How to Avoid Speaking: Denials,' 8.
57 Derrida, 'How to Avoid Speaking: Denials,'11.
58 Derrida, 'How to Avoid Speaking: Denials,'23.
59 Zhang, *The Tao and the Logos*, 128. Emphasis is mine.
60 Derrida, 'How to Avoid Speaking: Denials,'24.
61 Jacques Derrida, *Limited Inc*, (Evanston, IL: Northwestern University Press, 1988), 152. Emphasis is mine.
62 Derrida, *Limited Inc*, 152–53.
63 T. Foshay, 'Resentment and Apophasis: the Trace of the Other in Levinas, Derrida and Gans,' in *Shadow of Spirit. Postmodernism and Religion*, ed. P. Berry and Andrew Wernick (London: Routledge, 1992), 87.
64 Edward T. Ch'ien, *Chiao Hung and the Restructuring of Neo-Confucianism in the Late Ming* (New York: Columbia University Press, 1986), 161. Edward T. Ch'ien, 'The Conception of Language and the Use of Paradox in Buddhism and Taoism' in *Journal of Chinese Philosophy*, 11 (1984): 375–399.
65 Chan, 187.
66 Chan, 187. Translation modified.
67 Rorty, 'Philosophers, Novelists, and Intercultural Comparison,' 8. Emphasis is mine.
68 N. J. Girardot, ' "Finding the Way": James Legge and the Victorian Invention of Taoism,' *Religion* 29 (1999): 107–121.
69 E. J. Eitel, (1873) 'Amateur Sinology' *China Review* 2 (1873): 1–8. E.J. Eitel, born in Germany, was also an ex-missionary who served for a long time in the colonial government of Hong Kong in various high posts, and had great influence on educational affairs of the colony.
70 Herbert Giles, who served in the British consulate to China, once queried the existence of a coherent text of *Tao Te Ching* and entered into a debate with James Legge, which now has become legendary.
71 One of the effects of the undue canonization of traditions of Chinese thought easily witnessed in many contemporary studies of Chinese intellectual history is the marginalisation of the syncretist tradition reconciling apparent differences among Confucianism, Taoism and Buddhism. An undeservedly ignored study of this tradition, together with many great insights breaking the current nationalist/colonial orthodoxy in the field of Chinese Studies is found in Edward T. Ch'ien's work. For example, see his *Chiao Hung and the Restructuring of Neo-Confucianism in the Late Ming* (New York: Columbia University Press, 1986).

[72] Chatterjee, 'Anderson's Utopia,' 128–34.

[73] H. D. Harootunian, 'Ghostly Comparisons: Anderson's Telescope,' *Diacritic* 29:4 (1999): 135–49.

[74] Harootunian, 'Ghostly Comparisons: Anderson's Telescope,' 144.

[75] Cheah, 'Grounds of Comparison,' 14.

[76] Elsewhere I have discussed the related issues of intellectual complicity and collaborative relationships in colonialism. See W. S. Law, *Collaborative Colonialism: A Genealogy of Competing Chineseness in Hong Kong*, PhD diss., University of Technology, Sydney, 2002.

[77] Emmanuel Levinas, *Otherwise Than Being or Beyond Essence*, trans. Alfonzo Lingis, (Dordrecht: Kluwer Academic Publishers, 1991), 8.

From Mount Baekak to the Han River: A Road to Colonial Modernization

Hong Seong-tae
— *Translated from Korean by Kang Nae-hui*

1. Here I want to think about the modernization of Korea concretely, in terms of the space of its capital city Seoul. More specifically, I want to look at the road from Mount Baekak to the River Han, via a series of streets: Sejong-ro, Taepyung-ro, Namdaemun-ro, and Hangang-ro. The goal is to understand better the ways in which the impacts of colonial modernization continue to dominate the life of people in this city. The 'road' in my title, therefore, should not be taken in its rhetorical sense 'way' or 'method'; it refers concretely to an actual road used daily by people in Seoul.

2. While Modernity is a product of abstraction, modernization refers to the process of historical change. Modernity may well exist as an abstraction, yet, as a historical process, there must be a plurality of modernizations. The many differences and discrepancies that arise between imperial and colonial modernizations indicate that modernization is never a unitary process. The many mistake, then, would be to construe the empire and the colony as fundamentally the same modern society due to some superficial similarities in ways of life. In the colony, unlike the imperial state, the process of modernization results from a series of historical ruptures forced upon it by the destructive and exploitative practices of imperialism. In brief, in the process of global modernization, imperial state and colony are in a relation of perpetrator and victim. Of course certain

Figure 1: Seoul with Mount Baekak in background

kinds of exchange and interpenetration do occur; nevertheless the fundamental picture is consistently one of unevenness.

A city can be seen as a spatial concretization of society. Seoul shows so many traces of 'colonial modernization.' A prime example is the road from Mount Baekak to the River Han, or Hangang-ro. Reconstructed by Japanese imperialists who wanted a direct route to the Kyungbokkung Palace, the political heart of Chosun, the road now stands as an indelible legacy of colonial modernization. It should really be called 'the Road from Hangang to Baekak,' rather than 'the Road from Baekak to Hangang.' For, in its latter days, the Chosun dynasty was not prepared to reach out to the outside world. Japanese imperialism actually reversed the sense of this road.

3. Behind the Kwanghwamun Gate appears a relatively low but very beautiful mountain peak called Baekak, that is, 'white rock.' In traditional geomantic theory, this peak was regarded as the principal mountain for the capital, because of its connection to Bukak, Seoul's ancestral mountain. Below this peak, the Chosun Dynasty constructed as its political center the Kyungbokkung Palace, which was to be destroyed twice in Japanese military invasions.

The first occurred some four hundred years ago, in the year Imjin (1592), when Toyotomi Hideyoshi's army invaded Seoul and destroyed many of the major

Figure 2: Kwanghwamun with Mount Baekak in background

buildings including Kyungbokkung. As devastating as it was, it was not nearly so thorough and systematic as the second military invasion in 1910, the year of Japan's annexation of Korea. The impact of the second invasion on the topography of Seoul was quite different, however. For, the second invasion entailed a process of colonial modernization in which Japanese imperialists undertook a radical transformation of all of Chosun society, in order to dominate it efficiently and effectively. Seoul underwent a process of complete destruction and thorough reconstruction for the first time in its history. The five-hundred-year old city simply disappeared. The imperial annexation of Korea entailed not merely military invasion but a far-reaching transformation of city space.

4. Japanese imperial planners transformed the route from Hangang to Baekak into an urban avenue in order to assure that its army could reach the Kyungbokkung Palace with the least delay. In the guise of 'modernizing' the city infrastructure, they also dismantled the castle walls around Namdaemun (South Gate) and leveled Hwangtomaru, a hill that once stood in the vicinity of present-day Kwanghwamun Crossroad, in order to allow for the broad avenue from Hangang to Baekak. In sum, the modernization of Chosun was inseparable from the domination of Chosun. It was as if to conceal or justify the violence involved in urban reconstruction, that they named the road from Kwanghwamun Crossroad to

Figure 3: Chongdokbu

Namdaemun 'the Great Peace Road,' for in fact the process had been anything but peaceful. Today, however, rows of skyscrapers line the road, and so little evidence remains to testify to the history of invasion and colonization.

After its annexation of Korea with the establishment of an 'invasion road,' the Japanese government erected a government-general building, the massive Chosun Chongdokbu, which was situated squarely in the middle of Kwanghwamun, the Main Gate of Kyungbokkung Palace, and Gunjungjun, the principal edifice of the Palace. The site was calculated to make thoroughly visible the destruction of the former Chosun and the subjugation of the Chosun people. For the building disrupted the prior, traditional relations between the other sites. Fairly recently, the building was dismantled, as part of the policy of 'correcting history' promoted by Kim Young Sam, the first civilian president of South Korea after over thirty years of military dictatorship in the postwar era. Thus Kyungbokkung Palace has recovered some of its former beauty and dignity. Only the dome of the former Chongdokbu building remains, preserved in Independence Memorial Hall.

The story does not end, however, with this 'correction of history,' for such efforts at 'correction' engendered their own political problems. Erased, for instance, were all historical traces of the Chongdokbu, which arguably served as one of the most important reminders of the colonial period. Few cared to think that, to set the record straight, the issue of Korean collaboration — with Japanese imperialism and with the postwar dictatorship — had to be brought to the table. It is essential to make collaborators assume to responsibility for their actions, historically and legally. In the absence of such reckoning, Korean society has not changed in any fundamental way. Erecting Chongdokbu was the political symbol of Japanese imperialism, dismantling it was the political symbol of the Kim Young-sam government. History repeated itself, first as tragedy then as farce. Colonial modernization has entailed a steady intensification of social paranoia and schizophrenia at once. Remedies, naturally, are hard to come by. Kim's government did indeed try to achieve some manner of historical reckoning with its policy of correcting history. Yet it lacked the will and ability to achieve its goal.

On the Taepyung-ro Street now stands Seoul City Hall, originally constructed as the headquarters for the Kyungsung Precinct under Japanese imperialism. West of it once stood the Kyungunkung Palace, and to its right was Wongudan, the altar built by Kojong to inform the heavens of his coronation as ruler of the Daehan Empire (*Daehanjeguk*) in 1897. Emperor Kojong resided in Kyungunkung Palace (subsequently renamed Duksukung under the Japanese) in the last turbulent days of his reign, agonizing over the crisis of Chosun. The construction of Taepyung-ro Street under the Japanese separated Kyungunkung and Wongudan, and the construction of the Kyungsungbu Building between them finished the division and destruction of the royal palace of the Daehan Empire. As with the establishment of the government-general building between Kwanghwamun and Gunjungjun, the Japanese strategically selected this site to make visible both the destruction of Chosun and the dominion of the new rulers.

A hotel now occupies the Wongudan area, and only an attached building, Hwankungu, remains. Ironically, the hotel is called 'Chosun.' Hwankungu stands behind the Chosun Hotel, and its coffee house, renowned for its window seats with views on the rear garden, has become popular for marriage meetings. One can only laugh at this turn of events.

5. Emperor Kojong resided within the main gate of Kyungunkung, called Daehanmun. Today the changing of the guards before the main gate is a daily ritual. While the ritual may recall something of the extinct Chosun, the present condition of the palace makes it difficult for people to get detailed sense of the past. In the vicinity of Kyungunkung, in the Jungdong area, are many reminders of the historical violence involved in the annexation of Chosun to Japan. Because

Figure 4: After dismantling Chongdokbu

the world powers once placed their settlements around the Kyungunkung Palace, today the American, British and Russian Embassies are still located here. Emperor Kojong tried to draw on their authority in order to keep the forces of Japanese imperialism in check, but to no avail. For, as demonstrated by the secret agreement between the United States and Japan (the Taft-Katsura agreement of 1905), the world powers had already agreed to devour Chosun. Apparently, Kojong knew nothing of this agreement, but even if he had, there was little he could do to challenge their move.

In 1895 Japanese renegades murdered Empress Myungsun, and in 1907 the Japanese forced Kojong to abdicate. Since then, Kyungunkung was renamed Duksukung after Kojong's royal name. Within three years Chosun had been reduced to a colony of the Japanese empire.

6. Although today diminished by the broad avenue and tall buildings, the Namdaemun once towered impressively over its vicinity, as the southern gateway into the capital city of Seoul. Castle walls once enclosed the city, crossing from peak to peak on the four surrounding mountains. The systematic destruction of Seoul included these walls, starting with the walls around Namdaemun. A state visit by the Crown Prince of Japan provided the occasion for their destruction, as well as the excuse: the prince was deemed too exalted to pass through that gateway.

Figure 5: Namdaemun

The Koreans who now live in Seoul are scarcely aware of the arbitrary reconstruction of their city under colonial rule. I agree with those who regret the dismantling of the Chongdokbu Building, who insist on the importance of recovering rather than erasing this violent history. Is it not the fate of those who ignore history to repeat it?

7. Further south of Namdaemun is Seoul Station, the main railroad station, modeled after Tokyo Station, which was, in turn, modeled after Amsterdam Station in the Netherlands. While the stations are thus quite similar, the social contexts of their construction are profoundly different. Tokyo Station was part of a process of imperial modernization, while Seoul Station was part of a process of colonial modernization, that is, an imposed modernization.

Seoul Station differs from government buildings such as Chongdokbu in that it is a place of everyday activities. In this respect, it serves as a reminder that Japanese imperialism, imposing modernization, reached into daily life. Under the iron fist of Park Chung-hee (who also bore a Japanese name, Dakaki Masao, for he graduated with honors from two Japanese military academies), Seoul Station became a symbol of subordinate industrialization. With the deterioration of life in the country due to the policy of 'low wage and low grain prices,' hundreds of thousands of young people fled rural areas to live in Seoul. Naturally, they passed through the Station's gate.

Figure 6: Seoul Station

Surely it would be no exaggeration to say that Koreans now inhabit Seoul without thinking about the destruction and distortion wrought by Japanese imperialism. This lack of critical perspective on their environment derives from the people's habituation to the impacts of modernization, for Park Chung-hee, a product of Japanese imperialism, basically furthered its impact in his 'modernization of the fatherland.' Under the rubric of 'modernization' and 'development,' Park constrained Koreans to construct high-rises, highways and streets to be dominated by the automobile. Park, its faithful dog, thus completed the project begun under Japanese rule, that of destroying Seoul.

Thus, even after the Independence of 1945, genuine liberation from the colonial project did not occur. True, some of the political hardships that came of foreign domination and subjection improved, yet economic and cultural domination became more severe. This is part of the ongoing legacy of Japanese imperialism and its impact on the people, institutions and environment of Seoul. To overcome this legacy, the citizens of Seoul would have needed to take control of urban spaces and related institutions after Independence. This has proved impossible, however, due to more than a generation of collaborators occupying the positions of power.

8. Instead of the Korean people assuming responsibility, the United States simply replaced Japanese imperialists. American presence differs from that of Japan. Still, it has undeniably continued the same set of problems insofar as South Korea has become a veritable colony of the United States. So many areas of Seoul testify to this colonizing presence.

9. As the broadest avenue in South Korea, Sejong-ro, the boulevard that originates at Kwanghwamun Gate, is justifiably the symbolic center of Korea's modern history and the site of intersection with its traditions. From the street facing the gate, one sees the traditional grouping of Mount Baekak, Kyungbokkung Palace and Kwanghwamun as well as very modern edifices such as Presidential Residence Chungwadae, the Administration Building, and the King Sejong Cultural Center. Unfortunately, rather than delight in this aesthetic juxtaposition, one becomes more aware of the riot police making their daily inspections of passers-by. After the September 11 bombing, the police even began to carry light machineguns.

The purpose of such inspections is to assure the safety of the nearby U.S. embassy. In Korean, the United States is called *miguk* or 'beautiful country.' The reality of American treatment of South Korea is far from beautiful, however. It is not for nothing that it is often described as an 'ugly country.'

10. Every year since 1999, on Earth Day, automobiles have been barred from Sejong-ro, and people enjoy the streets instead. Yet, even this happy event is marred by the hoards of police who surround the embassy.

When one approaches the embassy, one sees something protruding from the wall that looks like a lamppost. It is not a lamp, however, but a surveillance camera. Even with its entourage of Korean policemen, the United States must still feel uneasy. Yet, to cloak their lack of confidence, they disguise their camera as a lamppost.

Even more absurd is the 'dog collar' on a tree just outside the embassy walls. Clearly designed to prevent intruders from climbing the tree to scale the wall, it nevertheless proved to be illegal. Once it was called to public attention, the embassy was bombarded with criticism and protests, and had to remove it.

Fortunately, the United States has decided to move its embassy to another site in Seoul. With the new plan came new hopes for the old site. One proposal

Figure 7: Sejongro on Earth Day

Figure 8: Surveillance camera outside the Unted States embassy

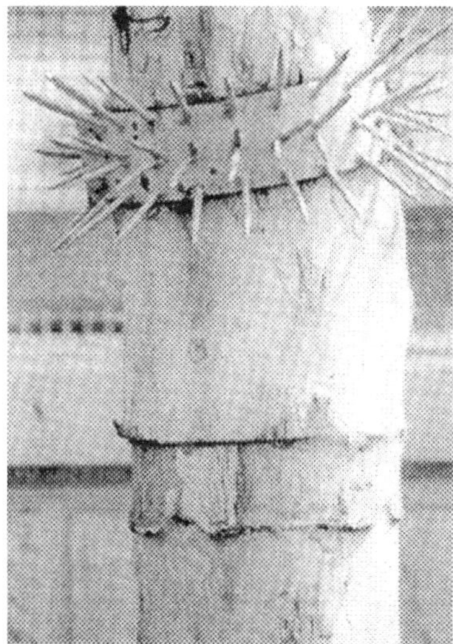

Figure 9: Protective devices on trees outside the United States embassy

involves the transformation of the site from one that evokes foreign domination to one that would allow for the construction of cultural facilities like the Museum of Modern Art.

11. Past Seoul Station and further down toward the Han River, red walls line both sides of the road. This is Yongsan Garrison, the location of the headquarters of the United States Army in Korea. Its total area covers over three million square meters, making it the size of New York's Central Park or double the size of London's Hyde Park. Originally the site for the Japanese army garrison, the Japanese handed it over to the United States at the end of war, a rather literal instance of American imperialism replacing Japanese imperialism in South Korea.

Years ago, the site was on the southern approach to Seoul, on its southern outskirts. Now that Seoul has expanded across the Han River and even farther south, the site of the U.S. Army base now sits at the geographic center of the city. Is it not hard to believe that the troops of foreign army would occupy the center of a nation's capital for over half a century, even though the nations are allies? Their presence signals that the history of colonization has yet to end in South Korea.

Figure 10: Aerial view of Seoul with Yongsan Garrison

As the photograph demonstrates, the Garrison is one of the few green areas left in Seoul. Citizens have asked for the return of this land to create a park, among other things. The U.S. response remains ambiguous, in deliberately overlooking an earlier agreement. In 1991, the United States agreed to return the land yet quickly reneged on their promise, requesting a new site twice the size of the present one. Should the Korean government cede more land to the American army, when the U.S. already has some 90 military bases in South Korea, which occupy 244 million square meters, and when the occupiers regularly violate Korean laws and engender all manner of conflict and strife? Recently, for instance, an American civilian who worked at the Garrison was arrested for dumping toxic waste into the Han River. Korean authorities, including the municipal government, could do little to punish him or to make the Garrison authorities responsible for such environmental crimes (as when the Garrison had an oil leak that polluted the city's ground water). The South Korean government is powerless in face of such flagrant breaches of the law by United States army personnel due to an unequal agreement, SOFA (the ROK-US Agreement on the Status of Forces in Korea). To say that the U.S. military bases in South Korea are 'spaces of injustice' is an understatement.

Traditionally, Yongsan was esteemed as an auspicious site because waters and mountains joined there. Yet the United States has so long occupied this land that for most Koreans it is as if the auspicious site had never existed. Today it symbolizes the U.S. presence in South Korea, a second wave of 'colonial modernization' based on American imperialism.

12. Eventually, in 1991, a portion of the land devoted to the Yongsan Garrison returned to Korea. An area that had formerly been a golf course was slated to become a public park. The Kim Young Sam altered this plan, however, reserving half of the land for the National Museum. Because his government suddenly decided to dismantle the Chongdokbu Building (which had housed the National Museum after the construction of the Administration Building), a new home for the National Museum had to be found. Of course, while some agreed that it was improper to use the former center of Japanese imperial domination as a National Museum, many found it shocking to dismantle the Chongdokbu Building so abruptly. Kim Young Sam's decision earned him a reputation for ignorance where previously he had a reputation for courage.

Figure 11: Near the National Museum

Ironically, signs of colonial domination haunt the new site for the National Museum. Not only is the site difficult to reach (having long been held apart), but also a helicopter field lies just in front of it. This means that as visitors enter or leave the museum U.S. military helicopters, taking off or landing, greet them. What other country in the world has had to build its national museum on a foreign military base, due to a lack of available land? Naturally, the Korean government has made requests for the removal of the helicopter field. Yet, in its characteristic fashion, the United States Army has been slow to comply, making a number of unacceptable stipulations. As a 'space of injustice,' the likes of Yongsan Garrison might be hard to find elsewhere in the world.

13. The modern spatial organization of Seoul began with its occupation and reconstruction by Japanese imperialism. Insofar as the spatial organization of any place has historical and social implications, the occupying and reconstructing of it also implies a profound social and historical reconstruction. This is precisely why those who have dominated Seoul have gone to such lengths to reconstruct Seoul in their own manner — not only the Japanese imperialists but the post-Independence dictators and American occupiers — and to restructure Korean history and society as well.

Figure 12: Protest to reclaim land occupied by United States Army

Over the last hundred years, Korea has thus undergone a series of radical transformations, which were undertaken under the pretext of modernization yet entailed repressive colonial domination. These radical transformations have resulted in the total destruction of history, culture, and nature as they were formerly lived and experienced. Asphalt and cement have now covered over nearly every trace of that prior life and experience, so completely altering the flows of light, wind, and water, and so thoroughly dividing modern Seoul from its past sources of vitality, that today it is but a sickly shadow of its former self.

There are nevertheless various movements to stem the tide of destructive reconstruction, and this is one way in which the power of citizens is now gradually being expressed. One day in June 2001, people braved storms to gather in the middle of the road to Hangang that runs through the Yongsan Garrison. These were ecologically minded citizens who wished to reclaim the occupied land, to preserve some space of nature from the suffocating development that has overtaken Seoul. Among their demands was the reconstruction of the road that once ran from Baekak to Hangang, which would reverse the tide of colonial modernization. I dream, too, of a day when Koreans will all embrace Seoul's history and its nature and culture, when they will together strive to resolve the many problems that remain from the long history of colonial modernization.

Part 2

Speech, Writing and Empire

The Ending *-da* and Linguistic Modernity in Korea

Kang Nae-hui

I

Probably the most important feature of standard Korean today is that most of its sentences end in *-da*. If one surveys the gamut of modern linguistic activity — narration, literary or art criticism, textual analysis, essays, commentaries, newspaper editorials and reports, court sentences, public statements, descriptions of facts, research reports, theoretical argumentation, academic discussions, broadcasting announcements — one finds that the sentences employed in such different circumstances all tend to end in *–da*. To the uninformed observer, the ubiquity of this final syllable might thus appear inherent to the Korean language, insofar as every sentence in Korean — interrogative, imperative, exclamatory, or assertive — has its characteristic final syllable. There are, however, many possible endings, even for a single sentence type. Possible endings for assertive sentences, for instance, include *–ô*, *-o*, *-yo*, *-zyo*, *-ra*, and *-ne*, without taking dialects into account. The dominance of the assertive *-da* derives, therefore, not simply from the inherent nature of the Korean language, but also from social practices through which Koreans have come to accept the usage of *-da* endings as the standard.[1] Over the last half of the century, various social mechanisms and apparatuses have been mobilized to ensure the dominance of *-da*. A prime example is the enforcement of the polite assertive — *pnida* for public speaking among elementary school children. While the disciplinary insistence on *–pnida* has begun lose some of its force — as the recent ascendancy of the spoken assertive *–yo* attests, it still pervades public education. It is surely no coincidence that the military, one of the most important disciplinary apparatuses in Korea, has been actively involved in the obligatory use of *–da*.[2] Not a few men drafted into military service recall having been disciplined for not using the 'dakka' style — that is, the use of the assertive *-da* with the interrogative *-kka*. If the use of *-da* has become the norm for such occasions as lectures, conference papers, or public address, and for news reports, argumentative composition, or commentaries, it is standardization of Korean that results in this mandatory and institutionalized use. In sum, the ubiquity of *-da* is a product of historical construction, and the very fact that all the sentences I have written in the Korean version of this essay have thus far ended in *–da* attests to its dominance.

The prevalence of *–da* is, in fact, a rather recent invention, the result of transformations that took place less than a century ago. This is not to say that *–da* had no prior usage in Korean; one already sees instances in the exclamatory *-roda*, *-doda*, and *-niida* used in documents that date from the time of the invention of the Korean alphabet in the fifteenth century. Moreover, variations on *–da* occur in a number of older texts. For instance, the present impolite *-hada* appears in such sixteenth-century books as *Dongukshin'soksamgang'haengsildo* (The new sequel to the pictures of good conduct in the eastern country) as well as in the eighteenth-century translation guidebooks *Paktongsa* and *Nokôldae*. The present *-nda* and the past *-ôttda* appear in many nineteenth-century documents. The *-da* system of endings, however, never dominated. Until the 1910's, it appeared with far less frequency than *-ra* endings (which included *-ira*, *-nira*, *-nora* and *-dôra*).[3] It was in some of the new modern short stories written around this time that *–da* began to replace the *-ra* system in assertive sentences. Once it came to dominate modern fiction, *-da* started to spread to literary criticism, academic papers, and newspaper editorials in the 1920s. By the late 1920s and early 1930s, it had come to dominate the range of modern discourse.

Needless to say, the construction of this new linguistic system caused a cultural upheaval, dramatically transforming linguistic sensibility and the grounds for expression, thus playing a key role in the formation of linguistic modernity. The formation of the *–da* system produced an effect similar to what Karatani Kōjin some time ago referred to as 'another writing' or 'the new sentence.' He suggested that, in the late nineteenth century, Japanese writing underwent an important transformation, making possible the emergence of 'modern literature' through the 'discovery of landscape' and 'interiority.'[4] Here I argue that in Korea this 'new writing' had to do with the emergence of the *-da* endings, and that without them, expressive modes of comparison, argumentation, assertion, explanation, exposition, discussion, description, narration, and analysis would have taken completely different form. With *-da* inflections, not only the grammatical relations within the sentence and between sentences, but also logical construction and forms of expression changed. It would be no exaggeration to say that the emergence of the *-da* ending system was a linguistic event of enormous importance that continues to have a tremendous impact today.

The *-da* ending did not become dominant in a single stroke. New social conditions were necessary, such as the waning of traditional literary culture, the emergence of modern discourses with their new producers, and a new linguistic sensibility. This process was not without conflicts, but, as is common knowledge, the winners were those modernists who tended to valorize such modern standards as truth, certainty, objectivity, and legitimacy, as well as the factuality of facts, knowledge, and discourses. Modernity formed only with violence and shuddering, for, as Naoki Sakai has pointed out, 'Modernity is inconceivable unless there are occasions where many regions, people, industries, and polities are in contact with one another despite geographic, cultural, and social distances.'[5] Indeed, Korea's linguistic modernity formed at a time when colonial expansion and imperial interests forcibly 'opened' the 'hermit kingdom.' The turmoil that surrounded the formation of linguistic modernity, however, stemmed not only from contact with distant cultures but also from new relations emerging within Korea. Linguistic audiences changed substantially as pre-modern forms of expression, and the situations of enunciation that enabled them, were excluded. Even though linguistic modernity would have been inconceivable without the forcible introduction of foreign cultures, it is also true that linguistic modernity was part of an ideological and disciplinary process, in which Korean society, while resisting colonization by Japan, came to address dialect speakers in such a way as to summon them into a modern standard language. The emergence of linguistic modernity in Korea could be seen as a process of 'primitive accumulation' through which a new linguistic public came into being.

II

It took over a quarter of a century for the changes in sentence endings to reach completion. Historically, the Gap'o Reform of 1894 provided the initial impetus, with its new policy of writing public documents in *gukmun* or national language and including *gukmun* in the civil service exams. The adoption of this policy forced profound changes in the linguistic and cultural lives of the residents of the Korean peninsula. The very use of the term *gukmun* implied a radical change in literary culture. *Gukmun* replaced such disparate writing practices as *ônmun* (vulgar letters), *banjôl* (half letters), and *amkûl* (women's letters), all of which had formerly been regarded as inferior to *za* (letters), *munza* (written letters), and *jinsô* (real letters). With the introduction of *gukmun, jinsô* became *hanmun* (Chinese letters), undermining the prior authority of *jinsô*. The adoption of the word *hanmun* reinforced a new awareness that what had been previously regarded as 'real letters' were actually 'Chinese letters,' that is, foreign letters. Thus, as the opposition between *gukmun* and *hanmun* replaced that between *ônmun* and *jinsô*, the status of *gukmun* improved, enabling policies for an independent language.

This is not to say that there had been no prior awareness of national language. The creation of *hunminjungûm* as a phonetic or 'alphabetic' writing system, one distinctive from Chinese characters, in the late fifteenth century showed awareness on the part of Koreans that their national language differed from Chinese. The creation of the new Korean alphabet soon led to the proliferation of *ônhae*, that is, translations of seminal Chinese texts into Korean. As usage of the newly invented *hunminjungûm* — also styled *ônmun* — spread to such literary genres as *gasa* (songs), *naebang gasa* (the female epistles), *sijo* (poems) and *sosôl* (minor stories), the practice of writing in Korean became relatively widespread. Due to the restriction of its usage to *ônhae, gasa,* and *sosôl*, however, *ônmun* could not become central to literary culture. *Ônhae* were confined to the translation of *jinsô* into *ônmun* in order to 'civilize' people, epistolary styles of *gasa* were used for personal communication, and *sosôl* were deemed inferior to *daesôl* (major stories or canons). Indeed, terms such as *onmun, amkûl,* and *banjôl* were contemptuous expressions for the indigenous alphabet. *Hangûl*, the name now almost universally accepted, did not appear until the 1910s.[6] The marginal and secondary position of *gukmun* is made abundantly clear by the fact that, until the late nineteenth century, Korean intellectuals used Chinese solely and exclusively for public discourse and in intellectual pursuits.

There is no need to insist that the adoption of the national language in official documents through the transformation of *ônmun* into *gukmun*, and *jinsô* into *hanmun*, had an enormous cultural significance. What bears close attention, however, is the new possibility for agreement between the spoken language and the dominant system of writing. This agreement between speech and writing was historically novel. The age-old custom by which intellectuals wrote almost exclusively in Chinese began to disappear as a consequence. To be sure, it did not vanish overnight; certain compromises were made: while 'all the edicts should be written in *gukmun*, *hanmun* can be added or the mixed style of *gukmun* and *hanmun* is allowed.'[7] Because such compromises allowed for a mixed style that was practically Chinese, many intellectuals still felt entitled to argue for Chinese over *gukmun* writing. The Minister of Education Shin Ghi-sun thus argued that it was 'not right to write in *gukmun*, to abandon Ching letters,' for '*gukmun* writing would turn people into beasts.'[8] Nevertheless, with the introduction of *gukmun* into public documentation, Chinese gradually lost its former status as the means of public communication. True, some intellectuals like Hwang Hyun, who committed suicide to protest Chosôn's absorption into the Japanese Empire in 1910, wrote in Chinese until their death. Yet the career of Shin Chae-ho is more representative of the times: he transformed himself from a traditional scholar into a nationalist intellectual, deploying the mixed style. As a result, by the 1920s, those Confucian scholars who continued to write classical Chinese were not even considered intellectuals at all.[9]

This movement to bring about an agreement of speech and writing through the adoption *gukmun* was not a simple reconciliation of oral and written styles. It was not a matter of writing in a colloquial style but rather, as Karatani Kôjin had pointed out in the context of the 'unification of speech and writing' (*genbun'itchi*) in Japan, a matter of abolishing *hanmun*.[10] His remarks may seem counter-intuitive insofar as the usage of Chinese expressions persists in both Japanese and Korean today. Yet, if we think in terms of *hanmun* (Chinese sentences) rather than *hanza* (Chinese letters), his comments are insightful. For the revolutionary nature of the Gap'o Reform is to be found not only in its promotion of *gukmun* but also in its exclusion of *hanmun*. That the movement was, in a very real sense, based on the exclusion of *hanmun* is reinforced by the observation that, after the end of the nineteenth century, public debates raged over the usage of Korean styles versus mixed styles (not *hanmun*). For instance, a newspaper like *Doknip Shinmun* (Independence News), expressed its hopes for 'all men and women, regardless of their birthrights and classes, to read' and 'to easily understand' its reportage, deployed the Korean style.[11] On the other hand, *Hwangsung Shinmun* (Imperial City News) utilized the mixed style, for which Emperor Kojong had made allowances. Rather than a simple battle over styles, this was a sort of 'culture war' between pro-Enlightenment modernizers, who wished to follow the cultural currents from Japan and the West, against conservatives, who wished to retain something of continental Chinese culture. Although, as is well known, the modernizers gained the upper hand, the debates over Korean writing continued throughout most of the twentieth century, and persist today. What I wish to underscore here is that the exclusion of Chinese became a matter of fact. The agreement of speech and writing, to 'naturalize' the Korean language, had to exclude *hanmun*. This occurred by making *hanmun* appear equivalent to *hanza*. Thus, in the twentieth century, Chinese usage in Korean was gradually restricted to Chinese-derived expressions, now naturalized or assimilated within the 'natural' Korean grammar.

If the movement of intellectuals against *hanmun* had important cultural ramifications, it was in part because the course of events made such movements inevitable. To continue to write in Chinese styles was tantamount to isolation, both from the newly emerging readership as well as from fellow intellectuals. The adoption of *gukmun* effected a 'deterritorialization' of the prior terrain of written expression, which involved separation and independence from China on the one hand, and on the other hand, the collapse of the forms of cultural hegemony that informed the previous power formation. When Shin Ghi-sun stated that 'to write in *gukmun* is to transform people into beasts,' he clearly felt that the elites were 'people' while the masses were 'beasts.' Yet such comments make it equally evident that the situation was such that the ruling elites could no longer disregard the latter. By the end of the nineteenth century, Chosôn's established order had begun to dissolve irreversibly: the dynastic regime proved unable to suppress the peasant revolution of 1894, and drew on support from Japanese and Chinese forces. In fact, it was the Japanese, who, after ousting the Chinese, imposed reform policies such as *gukmun* writing.

It is said that when Prime Minister Kim Hong-jip received Kojong's permission for the reforms, he apologized to the king, saying 'It is with deepest regret and sorrow that we have changed our five-hundred-year-old culture.' Then, as Kim Byung-si said, 'having insulted your majesty, we all deserve death,' the king and all the present burst into tears.[12] Nevertheless, under pressure from Japan, the adoption of *gukmun* was inevitable. Having witnessed the Japanese defeat the Ching Empire's forces, King Kojong had no choice but to make the best of an untenable situation. He became an exemplary modernizer, taking the symbolic lead by becoming the first to lop off his traditional locks. The adoption of *gukmun* was one of many such measures like the haircut ordinance and the introduction of the solar calendar, which served to 'free' Korea from its customs and traditions, launching the country on a path to autonomous modernization that could only meet with failure.

III

The adoption of *gukmun* presupposed a new audience. As even the conservative newspaper *Hwangsung Shinmun* had to admit, it was much easier to learn than Chinese.[13] Contrary to *hanmun* or *jinsô,* which enabled the elites to preside over the public sphere, *gukmun* potentially enabled the masses to express themselves. While *gukmun* constituted an effort by the elites to mobilize the masses, this effort produced unpredictable and uncontrollable effects. The ruling elites needed popular support in order to fight off foreign incursions, yet, as the peasant revolution of 1894 attested, the masses had already begun to mobilize themselves, in the form of an anti-feudal movement — whence the Chosôn government's self-defeating decision: to rely on Japan and the Ching empire, and to uphold, albeit reluctantly, the tenants of the Gap'o Reform.

The Era of Patriotic Enlightenment is often used to designate the period between the Gap'o Reform (1894) and Japan's colonization of Chosôn (1910). Millions of Koreans left home at this time. Those who joined in the peasant uprising against the domestic feudal regime or took action against modern foreign forces were unable to return to, or remain in, Korea. Many had to migrate to places like Manchuria to escape poverty and oppression at home. Much as Homi Bhabha has indicated, these diasporic movements gave rise to new forms of gathering.[14] Associations like Doknip Hyup'hö (Independence Association) and Hwangguk Hyup'hö (Imperial Association) formed during this period, and new social spaces like Christian churches, schools, public halls began to appear. These new spaces afforded the masses new opportunities for public discussions and for speeches, and it became 'very fashionable for people regardless of their status and age, from seven-year-old child to young ladies and woodcutters, to present public speeches everywhere on the streets.'[15] There was every sign of a national crisis, about which people wanted to express their opinion. 'Not only policemen, soldiers, and merchants, but also women and servants began reading the *Jeguk Shinmun* (Empire News) and came to understand the losses and gains in the realms of international affairs, politics, and industrial development.'[16] The formation of the General Assembly (*manmingongdong'hö*) Doknip Hyup'hö in 1898 dramatically demonstrated the new importance of public discourse. Thousands of people gathered to criticize the corruption of the imperial regime and foreign intervention into public affairs, in what became the first street demonstration in modern Korean history. Protestors demanded an end to concessions to foreign powers, calling for autonomous administration by the empire.

It is crucial to note, however, that (what were now construed as) premodern forms of expression had not yet disappeared at this time. As mentioned previously, unlike *Hwangguk shinmun, Doknip shinmun* strove for a universally accessible writing style, an exclusively Korean style, which meant the suppression of the Chinese-influenced style that deployed characters, expressions and diction derived from Chinese.[17] At the level of sentences, however, the story is different. In terms of its sentence structure and inflections, *Doknip Shinmun* did not at all differ from *Hwangguk Shinmun*. The bulk of sentences in both newspapers ended in *-ira, -nira, -dôra, -nora, -roda,* or *-doda*. Such inflections presuppose a set of hierarchical relations between speaker and listener, evoking traditional sensibilities and linguistic hierarchies. They make the performative dimension of linguistic address apparent, signaling exclamations and positions that speakers adopted in order to enlighten or discipline their listeners, often condescendingly. While the inflections *-roda* and *-doda* belong to the *–da* system, they have fallen out of common usage due to their tendency to impart a sense of the speaker's (superior) positioning.

The radical transformation of inflections gained momentum in *shinsosôl* (the new novel).[18] The 'new novel' initiated new forms of description and narration by increasing the frequency of the present tense inflection *-nda*. The inflection

-dôra that dominated the 'old novel' tended to place the event and the situation being narrated into the background. The inflection *-nda* foregrounded them, calling attention to the very scene of the narrated event. The second sentence of Yi Injik's *Hyôl ûi nu* (Bloody Tears) is exemplary in this respect:

> ...a lady some thirty years old, whose complexion, so white as if covered with face powder, becoming red as a cherry in the remorseless light of the sun, is in a great hurry, with such a flurry of steps — skirts pulled down, nearly baring her breasts, and hem trailing on the ground — that she cannot make any progress in spite of her every effort to move forward.[19]

Despite the novelty of its narrative style, however, the 'new novel' did not bring about the stylistic revolution of linguistic modernity insofar as it remained dominated by the *-ra* ending system.[20] Linguistic modernity demanded the establishment of a new system, the *-da* system, as the dominant inflection. I would argue that the establishment of agreement between speech and writing was not sufficient to effect a 'modernization' of the Korean language. While the adoption of *gukmun* was necessary for the establishment of a new literary and cultural ground, it did not suffice for the historical emergence of modern Korean.

This does not mean, of course, that the agreement of speech and writing was of no great consequence. One crucial consequence was the complete separation of the audience for classical Chinese and that for *ônmun*, which allowed people simultaneously to use the premodern *-ra* and the modern but still incomplete *-da* system. This mixture makes sense historically in light of the necessity for mobilizing people in order to promote patriotism and enlightenment. In their pursuit of an autonomous course of modernization (even under Japanese imperial rule), people enthusiastically took part in public discussions in the newly created sites of gathering such as schools, churches, meeting halls, and new organizations as well as in the streets and at public rallies. The continued use of *–ra* inflections makes sense in light of such public forums for persuasion. Likewise in the instance of the novel, as Im Hwa has pointed out: 'Even the best and newest contents could not have been disseminated had they not adopted their forms of expression from the "old novel."'[21] The success of discourses of patriotism and enlightenment depended on their capacity to persuade as many people as possible. Even though the linguistic forms were undergoing a process of transformation that would ultimately sever them from traditional interests, forms of knowledge and lifestyles, the public had not yet acquired a new language of its own. For a speaker to attract public attention, he or she could not necessarily rule out or disregard established practices. While speakers and writers had to discourse on new problems, they did not necessarily have to deliver them in a completely new way, as Im Hwa remarks. Most important was to impart a sense of the seriousness of these matters, to create a sense of national crisis, in order to persuade people to participate in the movement to expel foreign forces and to construct an independent and modern society. Although inflections such as *-ira, -nira, -nora, -roda,* and *-doda* implied hierarchies of address, intellectuals who wished to justify and propagate enlightenment and patriotism were able to employ them with audiences familiar with older styles. Conversely, for those people who had finally found a means to speak out due to the agreement between speech and writing, the hierarchies implicit in older styles positioned them to new advantage. In view of the highly complicated system of honorific expressions in Korean that positions speakers in accordance to their social status, to speak and write publicly in the *–ra* style was a potentially empowering experience — whence the trend for 'people, regardless of their status and age... to make public speeches everywhere in the streets.'

Additional changes occurred in the 1900s. Not only did usage of the present *–nda* increase, but also *–dôra* became the most frequently used *–ra* inflection in newspapers.[22] This inflection, in contrast to *–nira, -nora* or *–roda,* gives the impression of recounting an event or story factually. The increasing frequency of *–dôra* inflections in newspapers marks a new emphasis on objective reporting rather than civilizing or instructing the people. The standard of objectivity in reporting surely resulted, at least in part, from the tightening of Japanese censorship, calculated to regulate the public formation of opinions. In sum, the power of Korean discourses on enlightenment lay in 'their capacity for dynamic mutation derived from oral culture' and their ability 'to mix so-called "literary" and "non-literary" arguments and narratives, and description and narration.'[23] After Annexation, however, the freedom of expression that arose in the era of Patriotic Enlightenment waned. The emphasis on objectivity in reportage led to the suppression of potentially subversive forms of expression such as satire, parody, as hyperbole, as well as those 'excessive' forms of expression used traditional hierarchical address liberally, thus overturning them. The widespread use of *–dôra* thus coincided with a period of transition toward the *–da* system, which began to dominate a decade later, in the 1920s.

IV

Wisdom has it that Kim Dong-in's short story 'Yakhan ja ûi sûlpûm' (Sorrow of the weak, 1919) inaugurated usage of the modern *–da* style.[24] Kim Dong-in openly expressed his dissatisfaction with Yi Kwang-su's use of inflections, and consciously attempted a style radically different from his. In particular, he took issue with Yi's use of such endings as *–dôra* and *–ira*, which he considered too evocative of written styles. Kim thought the spoken style superior to written style for fictional narration. His argument should not be taken at face value, however. The spoken style, as used in everyday speech, is impossible to adapt for fictional narration. The problem is primarily one of honorific endings used in daily speech, which do not allow for a neutral narratorial position. Moreover, even with the now standard 'dakka' style, such problems remain. In other words, Kim did not really use the spoken style; he invented one with *-da* inflections. He surely objected to *-ira* and *-dôra* (assertive inflections that no longer exist) because they sounded too 'premodern.' For Kim, Yi Kwang-su's style still bore traces of the pre-modern style that ought to be eliminated. In his 'Yakhan ja ûi sûlpûm,' appear neither *-ra* nor the ancient *-roda* still used occasionally in Yi. Yet he also objected to present tense inflections such as *-handa*, *-ira*, and *ida* that occur frequently in Yi. He disliked them because 'they cannot express the keen psyche and emotion of the modern man,' and because they do not make for clear 'distinctions between subject and object.'[25] This is the hallmark of a distinctly modern linguistic sensibility. Ultimately, Kim's solution was to put his sentences in the past tense, for he thought that Yi's failure stemmed from the predominance of present inflections. This passage from Yi Kwang-su's *Mujông* (Heartless) shows, however, that present inflections did not dominate.

> Indeed, it has already been more than ten years now. There was a man named Pak Jinsa who lived in a neighborhood three miles south of Anju in the Province of Pyung'an Namdo. He had been a scholar for over forty years, and so there was no one who had not heard of him. Members of his clan had originally belonged to the nobility and had enjoyed considerable fortune and influence, comprising several tens of households; but, branded as traitors in the rebellion of the year Shinmyo, most of them had been put to death, horribly, while only Pak Jinsa's immediate family had survived. Fifteen or sixteen years ago, he had traveled to the land of Ching and returned with new books published in Shanghai. Learning in detail about the West

> and Japan, understanding that Chosôn would not remain as it was, he was about to embark on a new civilization movement.[26]

All the sentences in this passage end in the past tense *–da* inflections, except the first one. Given this evidence to the contrary, how could Kim Dong-in possibly argue that Yi utilized only the present tense? Was this a deliberate distortion? Or, did Yi's use of *–da* inflections somehow fail to convey the modern linguistic sensibility that Kim sought? In the above passage, the hero Hyung-sik meets with the heroine Yong-chae (whom he has not seen since childhood) and recalls their early years together. From the standpoint of the narrative present, 'it has already been more than ten years now,' and Kim might have thought it too obvious for Yi to employ the past inflection *-ôttda*. True, *-ôttda* sounds more modern than *–dôra*, an inflection that frequently appeared in both 'old' and 'new' novels, and an inflection that Yi Kwang-su himself frequently used. Yet, as will become clear in the context of Kim's writing, the inflection *–ôttda* only imparted this modern sensibility — a kind of monologue style that reveals the narrator's inner world — when used in specific ways. If Yi's novel (even his use of *–ôttda*) fails to achieve such stylistic effects, it is because his *–ôttda* inflections appear alongside premodern forms like *–roda* and *–dôra*, thus calling attention to the enunciator's positioning within social hierarchies. In effect, Yi retained the unstable, dynamic, mixed style of the era of Patriotic Enlightenment, envisioning his novel as a form of enlightenment.

Kim Dong-in's use of the past *-da* produces a radically different effect. The following is a passage cited by Kim himself in order to explain the difference between past and present tense styles:

> The pleasurable feeling of the fan's cool breeze and his gooseflesh made (makes) him sleepy. He was (is) adrift between sleeping and waking, on clouds rising into the sky. He did (does) not know how many hours pass. The mellow day turns to showers. The day, so hot, now cooled (cools) with the rain. Moisture permeates the room. The mist from raindrops as they splash to the ground enters the room. He abruptly opened (opens) his eyes.[27]

Kim puts present tense verbs in parentheses in order to compare the effect produced by the use of the present instead of the past tense. He submits that the use of present tense *–da* inflections would result in an anarchic confusion of the character's subjective world with the objective world around him. The past tense, however, allowed for 'a completely consistent distinction' between them.[28] Kwon Bodrae has pointed out that 'the -*ôttda* style is better suited to maintaining distance between the characters and the narrator, the characters and the reader.' She argues that, had Kim used the present tense *handa* instead of the past tense *hayôttda,* and *ittda* instead of *issôttda,* 'the reader would have remained confined to the very spot where the narrated action occurs.'[29] The past –*da* inflections (that is, -*ôttda*), however, remind the reader of both 'the time of the narrated event and that of narration,' thus rendering the event as it happened in the past, and simultaneously reviving it 'in the present as a past' by calling attention to the experience of narration.[30]

Kim Dong-in prided himself on achieving two stylistic reforms. First, he introduced the pronoun *gû* into Korean; second, he completely shifted writing from the 'traditional present tense' into 'the past tense.' Kwon Bodrae agrees, maintaining that Kim Dong-in inaugurated the –*ôttda* style, that –*ôttda* (that is, the past –*da*) had never been used before him.[31] These claims, however, do not hold up to close scrutiny. Kim was neither the first to use the past –*da,* nor did he rely exclusively on past –*da* inflections. Not only had Yi Kwang-su already used the past –*da* but also it occasionally occurs in nineteenth century texts of the *gasa* type. As evidenced in the above example with its instances of the present tense ('turns to showers' and 'enters the room'), Kim himself did not rely exclusively on the past –*da*. This is not to deny Kim's importance as a stylistic reformer but to suggest that his real innovation lay elsewhere. I would argue that it was not his use of the past –*da* that enabled Kim to 'revive the past in the present of narration.' Rather, his success stemmed from his use of them with the modern –*da,* thus eliminating the premodern –*ra* and –*da* inflections. His stylistic revolution then derived from his consistent and exclusive use of the –*da* system. The use of –*da* inflections had increased from the 1910s, from the time when Yi In-jik had began to write 'new novels.' The frequency of their use continued to increase in Yi Kwang-su's *Mujông*. Yet, until Kim Dong-in's work, -*da* inflections still appeared alongside –*ra* inflections. Kim's innovation lay in his consistent use of –*da* in assertive sentences, which inaugurated a modern linguistic sensibility in Korean.

As for his introduction of the pronoun *gû,* Kim thought that it functioned like the third person 'he' and 'she' in English. He took pride in this choice, later stating that 'even now when I think about it, it was a splendid decision.'[32] Kwon comments that, in a language in which 'a fully developed third-person pronoun was not available,' the introduction of *gû* was certainly a great change, one that affected the fictional world as much as 'I.' For *gû* made it 'materially possible to depict the third person's inner world much as did 'I.'[33] While I agree, I also wish to stress that the emergence of *gû* coincided with the formation of the *-da* system. Yet this was no coincidence, not fortuitous, as it were. It was part of a new linguistic sensibility, a new territory of expression, or, to use Karatani's terms, a new 'landscape,' which the formation of the *–da* system made possible. Next I wish to consider some of the changes that it produced.

V

As *–da* inflections came to dominate assertive sentences, they lost much of their musicality due to the exclusion of *–ra* inflections, which stemmed in part from the decline of the practice of 'book singing.' Traditionally, one recited books, to facilitate the memorization of Chinese texts. The *–da* style, however, is meant to be read silently. It calls attention to what is signified rather than to the phatic dimension of communication. Naturally, the *–da* is not completely devoid of musicality; one can read it aloud, and individual styles suggest different rhythms and accentuations. Still, rhythmic homogeneity is a basic feature of the *–da* style, insofar as phonetic writing assures a greater homogeneity in the pronunciation of syllables. As a consequence, modern Korean writing, with its homogeneous syllabic structure, is well suited to silent reading.

The use of the *–da* style also encouraged shorter sentences. Premodern inflections such as *–ni* and *–ra* function in the manner of conjunctions, allowing sentences to ramble on indefinitely. While *-ra* sentences easily reached a length of some five or six hundred syllables, *-da* sentences only rarely exceed one hundred and fifty syllables.[34] Significantly, the use of conjunctions necessarily became more common. As longer sentences became divided into a number of shorter sentences, the relations between them had to be specified. Moreover, complex sentences began to appear, in part due to a new emphasis on the subjunctive mode, which came in response to the attention accorded to the statement made rather than to the enunciating position. This situation made new kinds of logical connection between sentences necessary. In sum, the rise of the *–da* style had a tremendous impact on the musicality and the length of sentences as well as their logical relations.

The most crucial feature of *–da*, however, is the positive and assertive tone that it imparts to sentences. Because *–da* tends to mask the position of the speaker, it does not impart any sense of the hierarchical attitude (such as the domineering or patronizing tone that characterizes some premodern forms of address). With *–ra*, on the contrary, it is difficult to erase the sense of the speaker being present, talking to you. The *–da* inflections minimize the writer-speaker's presence, thus highlighting content. This is because they derive from the copulative, which transforms a sentence into a proposition. With *–da*, diverse kinds of statements impart the same sense of assertiveness, regardless of their truth value. 'He is a bad person' (*gû nûn nappûn saram ida*) is much the same as 'A tree is a plant' (*namu nûn sikmul ida*). They create the effect of making a proposition by minimizing the writer-speaker's presence, resulting in a sense of neutral, factual, truthful description, narration, explanation, argumentation and so forth.

Thus the *–da* style serves to make the content of the sentence appear truthful and factual, encouraging the reader to focus his or her attention only on what is enunciated. Take, for instance, this passage Yi Ghi-young's '*Mincho'* (The country village) published in 1921.

> The waters flowed down from Taejobong Valley, and skirting Hyanggyomal Village, ran through the willow forest below the village, while the narrow road to Dongmak-gol Valley climbed the mountain ridge, meandering through rice paddies and dry fields, traversing the brook.[35]

One cannot deny the presence of a narrator in this passage, in that the place names imply knowledge only available to someone familiar with the site. Nevertheless, his presence is not intrusive, for he only states those facts necessary to this description of world. Thus we imagine the water running down through the valley, and the road climbing up the mountain. Naturally, it is the narration that allows for this concretization or objectivization. Yet the sort of intrusive narration that comes with *–ra* is greatly diminished. The reader attends to the story rather than the act of enunciating or story telling, and the diminishment of the narrator encourages the reader to complete the narration herself. The reader is thus invited to appropriate the story world as her own. I would argue that *–da* inflections are essential in this process, since they permit the reader to speak to herself as she (silently) reads. The use of *–da* inflections foregrounds the enunciated rather than enunciation making the landscape appear as a reality into which the reader may enter.

This 'landscape effect' is not limited to fictional narration, as will attest this piece of criticism written by Kim Ki-jin in 1924.

> Today's movement for tomorrow is for the sake of tomorrow. Insofar as literature, regardless of its participation in this movement, has no innate value, we are willing to utilize it as a weapon for today's movement. As such, this literature is useful for today and has a *raison d'etre.*[36]

Such writing presents a sensibility completely different from that typically found in the editorial statements of the Patriotic Enlightenment period. The sentences are assertive, carrying that sense of directly presenting fact, reality, or truth itself. Even if one opposes Kim's argument that 'literature does not possess its own innate value,' the sense of factuality remains, for the opposing statement also takes on the aura of presenting a *fait accompli,* something that is truth as soon as pronounced. It makes little difference if the sentence in question is a fictive proposition like *'gû nûn ki ga kûn namu chôrûm kôttda'* (He was as tall as a tree). Written in *-da,* the sentence has the same construction as a scientific proposition like *'mul ûn suso du gae wa sanso han gae ro iru'ôjinda'* (Water consists of two hydrogens and an oxygen). Its message thus passes for fact, regardless of its truthfulness or falsity. Now the problem is one of whether there is any way to avoid such 'reality effects.' Probably there is not. As soon as you begin to read such sentences, you are in the grips of their logic. By making the enunciated appear as fact, they let you enter the landscape or 'story-time' of the statement. One important result of this 'contemporarization' is to summon the linguistic public to participate in the stated content of the *-da* sentences. You tend to emphasize and identify with the enunciated, and thus you become its contemporary. This is basically the same with narration, academic argumentation, or the 'truth' of news reports.

Oddly, *-nda* and *-ôttda,* basic to the *–da* style, were formerly regarded as impolite inflections. Given the highly developed system of honorific expression in Korean, the ascendancy of impolite forms for narration, criticism, and reportage comes as something of a shock. Yet it was precisely the adoption of such a shocking leveling of the prior system that made it possible to produce an agreement between objective and subjective worlds, between the story world of the characters and the reader's experience of it — contemporizing them — precisely due to the way in which *–da* sentences allowed for 'the way one addresses oneself.'[37] While this mechanism of foregrounding the narrative rather than the narrating would not be effective in the complete absence of a narrator, it is nevertheless true that *–da* inflections allows the narrator to present himself privately, as if addressing himself. This in turn allows the reader to take the place of the silent narrator, appropriating the story as his or her own.

How could such a private form of address become a general, normative way of addressing unspecified multitudes? Herein lies the importance of the third person pronoun *gû*, mentioned above. This pronoun had the capacity to function as 'a third person with interiority in proportion to the "I."' In conjunction with *–da* inflections, *gû* helped constitute the modern landscape in which the interior world becomes presented as an objective reality. *Gû* does not function as a mere object for the 'I' but becomes a subject in its own right, with its own inner world. Thus *–da* sentences, ostensibly in the third, can operate like an internal monologue. They easily become the reader's own phrases, as he harkens to his own voice as he silently reads. As a consequence, the reader is constantly aware of the 'truth' or 'reality' of what is enunciated. The overall effect of this listening to oneself is one of agreement rather than coercion. Maybe this is why unspecified multitudes can participate in *–da* sentences and enter into an ideological process of identification with their content and message.

VI.

In the 1920s, usage of the *–da* style gradually spread, and it became the dominant narrative style. Newspapers proved indispensable, because most of the first modern novels appeared in serial form. Below is an example, a passage from Min Woo-bo's 'Bupyôngcho' (Duckweed), serialized in *Donga Ilbo*, the day following the newspaper's inauguration on April 1, 1920. (No punctuation marks appear in the original.)

> Until the age of nine I thought that my mother was with me If I cried someone immediately would come to calm me holding me until the tears dried Never had I gone to sleep without a kiss and when cold snows of winter blew she would sing lullabies hugging me close to her chest and warming my cold feet The songs are still in my ears[38]

As this passage attests, from the outset of journalism, novels occupied a unique position, for no other forms of expression in the newspaper used *–da* inflections consistently. The editorials in *Donga Ilbo*, for instance, deployed the older *-roda, -doda, -jiôda, -nira,* and *–nora,* and *–dôra* dominated the reporting and other sections. That all the sentences in Min Woo-bo's story ended in *-da* must have struck readers, for it was the only section among editorials, official notices, miscellanies, and advertisements that used the *–da* style. The use of illustrations in serialized novels only served to enhance its novelty, and these illustrations also differed profoundly from their premodern counterparts. These early exemplars of modern visual culture situated human figures in such a way that they appeared to be conversing with each other with a proximity unimaginable in earlier forms of illustration.[39] Much as in advertisements for haberdasheries whose shoes and hats had begun to appear regularly in the papers, this new visual style created the impression that figures were closer to the reader's eyes, riveting his or her attention to them.

In sum, the *–da* style came to dominate through the medium of newspapers, which entailed a series of transformations that focused attention on the interiority of the narrated world. Gradually, from the early 1920s, the *-da* style began to migrate into other forms of expression in *Donga Ilbo* and *Chosôn Ilbo* such as literary criticism and scholarly essays. It had spread to reporting by the late 1920s.

Much of the 'modern feel' of the *–da* style lay in its strangeness and novelty, its foreignness. Kim Dong-in, who is credited with its invention, studied in Japan in his youth; apparently he conceived his novels in Japanese and subsequently translated them into Korean. In effect, the Korean *–da* bears a certain resemblance to Japanese *–ta* inflections. Not surprisingly, Yi In-jik, the writer credited as the first to use the present tense *–nda* in a modern way, also learned Japanese. Naturally, although writers who had studied Japanese introduced and perfected the modern *–da* style, this does not mean that *–da* endings were adopted from Japanese; there are premodern precedents for the Korean *–da*. Moreover, the affinities between the Japanese *–ta* and the Korean *–da* cannot be explained by the observation that both languages belong to the Ural-Altaic family. Rather, writers in both languages were responding to an analogous problem, that of constructing a mode of writing that felt modern. Initially, this style could only have looked and sounded outlandish and exotic.

Although newspapers played a crucial role in propagating the new style, this new medium did not determine its success. Other conditions were necessary, too. For instance, the importance of the new linguistic public merits consideration.

Recall that the premodern *–da* was considered an impolite expression. The leveling effect of *–da* becomes clearer when one turns to contemporary newspaper accounts that deploy the older endings, with their authoritative tones and hierarchical implications. What kind of linguistic public would approve of this new, leveling style of address? It would surely appeal to those who were, or who wished to be, free from the traditional forms of discrimination such as social status and gender. In this context, access to *–da* sentences appears to have provided Koreans with a new means of self-expression, which also empowered them in a way that *–ra* endings had not. Impolite yet private, *-da* inflections enabled the portrayal of the interior landscape of the speaker's mind as an objective reality. As a result, the reader or writer of the *–da* style does not register the impoliteness of its usage but rather gains access to the landscape itself. Silently reading, the reader participates in that landscape.

The emergence of this new linguistic public also had to do with Korea being under colonial rule. The rise of the *–da* style would not have been possible without the destruction of older social hierarchies that came with Japanese colonialism. It comes as no surprise then that the *–da* style was used primarily with modern discourses and discourses on the modern. Its ability to delineate the narrated content, the described world, and thus objects of knowledge, the style was ideally suited to making fictional constructions appear as reality. This new reality together with this new linguistic public formed the conditions under which the *–da* style could dominate. The sections of the newspaper that quickly followed the novelist *–da* style included essays on natural science, scholarly commentaries, literary criticism, and editorials, whose writers were the novelists, doctors, scholars, essayists and scientists involved in the formation of colonial modernity. Interestingly enough, reporters joined this group rather belatedly. This was not only due to their dependence on the *–dôra* style. More importantly, the attitudes prevalent in the period of Patriotic Enlightenment persisted far longer in journalist circles, as the newspapers strove to sustain their hold on the new public sphere.[40]

This is not to imply that the *–da* style enabled a better system of representation and expression. It allowed for a very specific form of expression, predicated on the *–da* style appropriation of the domain formerly occupied by *–ra*. Thus *–ida* replaced *-ira* and *–nira*, and *-ra handa* replaced *-dôra*. Moreover, the *–da* system itself underwent significant changes. While the impolite *-nda, -hada, -ida, -ôttda* became common, exclamatory endings like *-doda,* and *-roda* disappeared. New expressions appeared, such as the present progressive *-go ittda,* the future *–ûl gôssida* and the perfect past *-ôtt'ssôttda.* Thus modern Korean proved capable of generating all assertive sentences with *-da* inflections.

VII

According to Karatani, 'Landscape is an epistemological framework, and as soon as a landscape is created, its origin is occulted.'[41] With this observation, Karatani criticizes Japanese literary critics for their inability to recognize the historicity of the landscape of modern Japanese literature, due to their absorption into it. Surely such 'occultation of origins' is not automatic but demands continued efforts to sustain it. Karatani suggests that, once you become absorbed in landscape, you only come out of it with great difficulty. For Karatani, it was the novelist Natsume Sôseki, schooled in both Chinese and English literature, who refused to belong to modernity even as he dwelled in it. People like Sôseki were probably rare in modernity's early days. In our postmodern age, however, not a few Koreans feel discontent over the landscape of the *–da* style, notably those who tend to abbreviate words, to create emocons on their computers, and who rarely use established inflections, manifesting a strong antipathy for the dominant features of modern Korean.[42] They are not the first, however, to express their discomfort with *–da.* The poet Kim Ji-ha, for instance, once complained about the 'refrigerated style' generated with hangul sentences.[43]

The problem with *-da* sentences comes of their imposition of a certain closure on what is written. Reading them, you cannot but feel an emphasis on completing sentences. The *–da* marks a definite end to the sentence. When *–da* appears at the end of each sentence, you cannot escape the feeling that each sentence attains closure. While sentences enter into relations with one another, each one remains a world onto itself. Hence the impression that each *–da* sentence stands apart from the others, demanding conjunctions, demonstrative pronouns and other pronouns to link them. The use of *–da* not only constructs a sort of territorial closure around them but also serves to stabilize and consolidate sentences. Moreover, unlike the older *–ra, -da* sentences lack much variation with respect to accentuation and intonation, appearing rather rigid and monotonous. The effect arises in part from the way in which they tend to coagulate into assertive public discourses. It is not only poets like Kim Ji-ha who find this feature of modern Korean unsatisfactory. Others feel that most communication in Korean, whether academic, communicational, creative, critical or judicial, has become standardized and stereotyped, with all discourses producing the same impression of a 'solid fortress.'[44] I have argued that this solidity, rigidity and tendency toward stereotyping came with the dominance of *–da* in declarative sentences.

Part of the sense of closure created by the *–da* style comes of its autonomy from the spoken language. Even though inflections like *-ôtta* and *–nda* derive from impolite spoken forms, and even though writers like Kim Dong-in claimed that 'whatever remained of the written style was totally transformed into spoken language in our hands,'[45] there exists nonetheless a profound gap between spoken Korean and the *–da* style. In particular, as discussed above, there is the way in which the *–da* style introduces new relations between sentences as autonomous entities as well as a sense of the subordination of words to the sentence. The *–da* style thus imparts a feeling radically different from that produced with other inflections.

Nonetheless, the landscape discovered through *–da* is not given once and for all. It must be repeatedly naturalized, which entails a historically conditioned disciplinary process, related to colonial modernity. It is crucial to call attention to the historicity of modernity as a process, to the heterogeneous historical forces that come into conflict, that thus produce different kinds of impacts. Surely this is why the 'landscape effect' must be constantly occulted. The discovery must be repeated if it is to appear natural. Likewise, modernity must be continually remade and renewed, which is why resistance to it continually reappears, as with the bombings of September 11, 2001. To become and to remain modern is to be hailed, forcibly and incessantly. Because this summoning is a process of interpellation of subjects as modern individuals, it constitutes everyday life and forms our sense of ourselves.

In early March of 1960, as a third grader, I attended outdoors class in which my teacher talked about the presidential election to be held in mid March. He gave some explanation — which I don't recall — as to why certain candidates should be chosen as the next president and vice president. After his lecture, he wanted to see how well students had learned his lesson. To my shock and dismay, he picked me to provide the answer his question. The discomfort was not that I did not know the 'correct' answer (that the next president and vice-president ought to be Rhee Syngman and Yi Ki-bung). It was not only that I felt pressured to support candidates whom others around me saw as dictators. Rather the discomfort was because I had to reply in a language still foreign to me. Born in Kyongsang Province, I spoke (and am still speaking) in a regional dialect. Speaking standard Korean involved the construction of sentences with *–da* inflections. I don't recall my response but distinctly remember my heart pounding with fear as I tried to speak a foreign language.

Today, some forty years later, I compose *–da* sentences without difficulty. I share this ability with the majority of Koreans due to formal education and military service. Yet, to become expert, one needs more than the basics. The ability to write *–da* sentences is thus tantamount to the exercise of a particular kind of power. It allows one to forecast weather, broadcast news, deliver lectures, write novels or criticism, or compose an essay or research paper. In sum, the ability to compose in the *–da* style allows one to discern the factuality of facts, which is the domain of professionals and experts.

Partha Chatterjee has argued that Indian nationalists created the private and spiritual sphere of national culture in opposition to the public sphere of the British colonial state. He thus sees national culture as modern despite claims for its primordial status, for it formed in response to British colonial rule, posing an Indian modernity as an alternative to British modernity.[46] Similarly, Korean nationalists have gone to great lengths to establish the *–da* style, a Korean modernity, under Japanese colonial rule; some of the early national linguists risked imprisonment and even death at the hand of the Japanese, in order to pursue the scientific study of Korean.[47] This raises questions about how one assesses one's relation to the founders of linguistic modernity. Should I be grateful? Has the experience of modern Korean enriched lives and produced happiness? On the one hand, I appreciate the skills I have acquired for stating fact, narrating stories, analyzing problems, and presenting positions. On the other hand, I cannot help feeling some of the discomfort I felt some forty years ago when I attempted to speak *–da* sentences publicly for the first time. With the *–da* style, I still feel myself uncomfortably positioned between the premodern space-time (that I have been disciplined to discard) and the newly opened space-time of modernity. I still find myself far from the expressive domain that I hope to create. The *–da* system allows me to write an essay such as this, yet it forecloses other possibilities.

While retaining the accents of my native dialect, I have become a speaker of modern standard Korean. Yet, this entrance into linguistic modernity can never erase the impact of disciplinary interpellation.

Notes

1 The *-da* endings include such variations as the root inflection *-da*, the present tense *-ida* and *-nda*, the present progressive *-go ittda*, the past *-ôttda*, the perfect past *-ôtt'ssôtda*, and the future — *ûlgôsida*. In this paper, I alternately refer to them as '*-da* endings,' '*-da* system,' or '*-da* style.'

2 Recall, in this context, that Park Chunghee's military coup was responsible for initiating 'dependent modernization' in South Korea.

3 Even in newspapers, the modern medium par excellence, *-ra* endings predominated. For instance, among about 800 endings used in the issues 1 to 7, 23, 30, 31, 88, 200 of *Mansebo* in 1906, there were some 630 *-ra* endings. See Saigusa Sikatsu, 'Izung pyogi wa kûndaejôk munchae ûi hyôngsong: Yi In-jik shinmun yônjae *Hyôl ûi nu* ûi kyông'u' (Double inscription and the formation of a modern style: the case of Yi In-jik's serialized novel *Hyôl ûi nu*), in *Hanguk kûndae munhak e natanan ilbon chehôm* (The experience of Japan in modern Korean literature) (Seoul: The proceedings of the 54th symposium for Society of Korean Literary Studies, 19 Aug 2000), 63.

4 Karatani Kojin, *Ilbon kûndae munhak ûi kiwôn* (The Origins of Modern Japanese Literature), trans. Park Yu-ha (Seoul: Minumsa, 1997), 104, 155.

5 Naoki Sakai, 'Introduction,' *Traces: A Multicultural Journal of Cultural Theory and Translation* 1 (2001), viii-ix.

6 *Hangûl* was first used in 1913 to denote the Korean alphabet. *Han* derives from the *han* in *Daehanjeguk* and refers to the ancestral Hans. *Han* in Korean also means 'great.'

7 Cited in Yi Eung-ho, *Kaehwaghi ûi hangûl undongsa* (A history of the *hangûl* movement in the period of civilization-enlightenment) (Seoul: Sungchungsa, 1975), 118.

8 Cited in Yi Eung-ho, 247

9 Yu Sun-young, *Hanguk daejung munhwa ûi kûndaejôk kusông kwajông e daehan yônggu* (A study of the modern construction of Korean mass culture), Korea University Ph.D. dissertation (1992), 229.

10 See Karatani, 62-77.

11 Quoted in Yi Eung-ho, op. cit., 232.

12 Yi Eung-ho, op. cit. 102.

13 'As *banjôl* letters are so easy that even ordinary men and women can learn them within a period of roughly ten days, some eight or nine out of ten people can overcome their illiteracy... *Banjôl* letters are the easiest and simplest letters in the world, so that the general social opinion is that the *banjôl* of Daehan (Great Han) should lead the literary world.' Cited in Yi Eung-ho, 222.

14 Homi K. Bhabha, 'DissemiNation: time, narrative, and the margins of the modern nation,' in *Nation and Narration*, ed. Homi K. Bhabha (London and New York: Routledge, 1990), 291.

15 Ko Mi-suk, '*Gyemongi ûi damron, gyemongûi susahak*' (The discourse of enlightenment, the rhetoric of enlightenment), *MunhwaKwahak* 23 (Fall 2000), 206.

16 Pak Eun-shik, *Pak Eun-shik jônjip, jung* (The complete writings of Pak Eun-shik, the middle volume) (Seoul: Danguk University Center for Asian Studies, 1975), 17; cited in Choi Ghi-young, *Daehan jeguk shiggi shinmun yôngu* (A Study of the newspapers in the era of the Daehan Empire) (Seoul: Ilchogak, 1991), 12.

17 'Chinese-influenced style' here refers to the Korean writing style that includes expressions derived from Chinese. Although it utilizes Chinese characters, expressions, and idioms, it is, in effect, Korean insofar as it operates on the grammatical basis of Korean.

18 The 'new novel' or *shinsosôl* is distinguished by its tendency to deal with contemporary affairs and to present narratives in a transhistorical or supernatural fashion. The new novel emerged in opposition to the traditional novel (now called 'old novel' or *gusosôl*).

19 Yi In-jik, *Hyôl ûi nu*, (Seoul: Ulyumunhwasa, 1994), 1.

20 See note 3 above.

21 Im Hwa, *Shinmunhaksa* (A history of new literature) (Seoul: Han'ghilsa, 1993), 166-67; cited in Han Ghi-hyung, 54.

22 According to Saigusa Toshikatsu, of the 630 *-ra* inflections mentioned in note 3, 530 were *-dôra* inflections.

23 Ko Mi-suk, op. cit., 204, 207.

24 This may not be true, for Yang Kun-shik's *Sûlpûn mosun* (A sad contradiction), published in *Bando siron* in 1918, was also written exclusively with *-da* endings. See 'Appendix 2' in Han Ghi-hyung, op. cit.

25 Kim Dong-in, 'Chosôn kûndae sosôl go' (On the modern novel in Chosôn), *Chosôn Ilbo*, July 28 — Aug. 16, 1929; reprinted in *Hanguk ûi kûndae sosôl I: 1906-1930* (The modern novel of Korea I: 1906-1930), revised edition, ed. Chun Kwang-yong (Seoul: Minumsa, 1990), 292.

26 Yi Kwang-su, 'Mujông,' in *Hanguk ûi kûndae sosôl I: 1906-1930*, ed Chun Kwang-yong (Seoul: Minumsa, 1985), 146-47. Translation of this passage is particularly difficult, given conventions of tenses in English. The first sentence ends with *–iroda*, which is not a temporal marker but an exclamation. I have used 'indeed' in English to convey the exclamation, and the conventions of English tenses suggested to me a sense of the past ('it has already been') that is present ('now'). Moreover, the past of this present past is then conveyed with the pluperfect (had been), rather more concisely in temporal terms in English than in the Korean used by Yi.

27 Kim Dong-in, op. cit., 292.

28 Ibid., 293.

29 Kwon Bodrae, *Hanguk kûndae sosôl ûi kiwôn* (The origin of the Korean modern novel) (Seoul: Somyungchulpansa, 2000), 253.

30 Ibid., 254.

31 Ibid., 253.

32 Kim Dong-in, op. cit., 291.

33 Kwon Bodrae, ibid., 250.

[34] The use of the *-da* endings did not automatically lead to a shortening sentences. The early modern novel 'Yeojangbu' (The heroine) which appeared in 1922 in the *Donga Ilbo* shows that *-da* sentences can also continue indefinitely. This was an unusual case, however.

[35] Yi Ghi-young, 'Minchon,' in Chun Chang-yong, op. cit., 225.

[36] Kim Ki-jin, 'Kûm'il ûi munhak, myông'il ûi munhak' (Literature for today, literature for tomorrow), in Chun Chang-yong, op. cit., 411.

[37] Kwon Bodrae, op. cit., 249.

[38] *The Donga Ilbo*, 2 April, 1920.

[39] Kang Nae-hui, 'Kûndaesông ûi "chunggyôk" gwa hanguk kûndaesông nonûi munje' (The 'impact' of modernity and the problems in the discourse of modernity in Korea), *Munhwa Kwahak* 25, (Spring 2001), 203-219.

[40] In this context, we may recall that by the 1930s 'A good journalist was expected to be one who had public-spirited passion, insight, principled position and a talent for writing, and only articles fighting for rightful causes were considered good.' Yu Sun-young, op. cit., 307.

[41] Karatani, op. cit., 32.

[42] Not surprisingly, most guk'ô hakja, or 'scholars of the national language,' vehemently oppose this as a 'deterioration of our language.'

[43] I could not find the exact source of this remark, but when I met him in October 2001, Kim affirmed that he once indeed said so.

[44] Ko Mi-suk, op. cit., 203.

[45] Kim Dong-in, op. cit., 201.

[46] Partha Chatterjee, 'Whose Imagined Community?' in *Mapping the Nation*, ed. Gopal Balakrishnan (London: Verso, 1996), 214-25.

[47] In 1942, over thirty nationalist linguists were arrested and sentenced to prison terms, and two of them, Yi Yun-jae and Han Jing died of tortures. It is not clear, though, whether this attempt to establish the national language influenced the dominance of *-da* endings.

Ethnomusicology's Ambivalence; or, Writing and the Imperium's Construction of Ethnic Objects

Ethan Nasreddin-Longo

Dualisms generate enormous conceptual universes. They rely on an apparently freewheeling interaction of terms, but in order to describe and contain a potentially infinite spectrum of differences with their dualist framework. In ethnomusicology, as in the related and 'senior' discipline of anthropology, dualisms have long been at the epistemological heart of all matters. One might well argue that, historically, the 'prime duality' of such disciplines has been an 'us/them' divide that establishes the conditions of possibility for anthropological and hence ethnomusicological knowledge. Indeed it has been persuasively argued in any number of contexts that this divisive effect is as much an episteme as a discipline. In this sense, us/them functions as a text upon which one can inscribe many other qualities that may in turn function in certain contexts as elucidations of the prime duality. The us/them dualism can thus become 'here/there' — and, depending upon the kind of historical framework that is mobilised, it becomes 'primitive/modern,' or 'ethnically-neutral/ethnically-marked,' or 'Euro-American/ non Euro-American,' to give some obvious examples.

What interests me is how these dualisms are related palimpsestically, by which I mean how they are inscribed upon the prime duality in any number of ways and in any number of configurations. This palimpsestism is such that, as time passes, the invocation of one dualism invokes many others. Clearly, the idea of this palimpsestism allows for all sorts of conceptual slippage, and invites a provoking set of questions. Under what conditions does us/them come inevitably to evoke, say, 'literate/non-literate'? Must us/them always lead one to mobilise a specific series of other binary pairs, always leading to something other than itself, and turning back again? These are, of course, enormous questions involving careful considerations of politics and history, which are beyond the scope of this paper. For my intent is not to critique and probingly analyze each linkage, but simply to sketch a set of relations and thereby provide a starting point from which an in-depth critique might proceed. My aims are of necessity much more modest — I am interested in two aspects of what might be dubbed the ethnomusicological episteme.

First, I am fascinated by the fact of slippage itself, the palimpsestical effects that arise when knowledge wheels around the us/them dualism. Second, I am concerned that the dualism is not inert, that the pairs are not equal partners. There is a profound unevenness in ethnomusicology's prime duality. To anticipate my argument, I find that the us/them dualism is founded upon, and grounded in, a specific kind of subject/object relation, one that might be thought of as modern. For it is a subject/object relation in which the subject always stands over (and, in a sense, under and before) the object. This entails a constant 'subjection of the object' in which the subject is continually in search of new objects to subjectify, in which the subject must incessantly produce and consume new objects. Not surprisingly, I see in this subjection of the object an imperious and even imperialist process, one that coalesces in ethnomusicology around a discourse on writing.

Imperium. The significant definition of the term, as found in the second college edition of the *American Heritage Dictionary* is 'A sphere of power or dominion; empire.'[1] In this instance, I am thinking of the admittedly nebulous, yet nevertheless definable area of the art music-culture of Europe and North America, a music-culture which includes such people and organizations as the musical thinker Charles Seeger, the singer Arlene Auger, the Kronos Quartet, Haydn, Tania Leon, Toru Takemitsu, many if not all symphony orchestras, the nineteenth-century violinist Joachim, and of course many traditional scholastic musicians. This list is woefully short, laughably incomplete, and downright eccentric in its inflections — it must be, given the expanse of the music-culture. In such a list, there is no possibility of comprehensiveness, and consistency would flatten the texture of the music-culture. My intent is simply to demonstrate that what is called the 'Western art-music culture' is not limited to the confines of one nation-state (or to a single historical epoch), but has a cultural power very much characterized by the idea of 'a sphere of power or dominion;' thus I use the term 'imperium.' I do not use the term 'empire,' given that that term suggests both a particular historical moment and also a very particular kind of international and national social order. Even so, of course, 'imperium' does not preclude the possibility of 'empire' — it merely expands the notion of 'imperiality' into times and places in which traditional notions of empire are contested (periods in which, for example, people can use a self-descriptive term such as 'post-colonial'). These are perhaps transitional moments whereat empire may be in a period of reformulation or perhaps even dissolution, but still moments at which imperial machinations are still very much in evidence. In short, given globalization and the profound interconnectedness which it implies along with the extraordinary blurring of class and ethnic distinctions, I wish to speak of an 'imperium' that operates through and beyond any particular 'empire.'

Writing is a much more familiar term, yet its use in a paper about music requires some explanation. I will speak about writing in two senses: not only that writing that consists of theoretical construction and explication, but also that writing that comprises the actual graphic act and mark themselves. In other words, I see writing as both discourse and inscription. When one looks at writing as both discourse and inscription, one discovers an eerie complicity between ethnomusicological theory and Western practices of musical inscription. Basically, ethnomusicological discourse defines writing in a very narrow way in order to establish the existence of musical cultures without writing — that is, those cultural contexts are construed as unconcerned with musical notation, this mark-making or inscription. A profound confusion arises about the status of writing, which proves productive for ethnomusicology in constructing its others.

The confusion centres on the materiality of writing. The music of those cultures that do not make marks is construed as somehow immediate or unmediated and maybe immaterial. Which is to say, writing is linked to materiality, but it is a kind of 'fallen' materiality. Sound without marks is linked, albeit vaguely, to something like immateriality. But it is definitively linked to some order of being which is fundamentally different from the one concerned with making of marks, with writing music. Is 'non-graphed' sound (for lack of a better term) truly immaterial? Likely not, but the nature of the materiality of such sound is not the point of this tract. Clearly, one could speak, in the manner of Derrida, of 'writing before the letter,' and show how non-graphed sounds, or non-written music, is full of stops and starts, breaks and cuts, that are not entirely other to writing. Yet what concerns me here is how ethnomusicology constructs its others on the basis of musical inscription, thus implicitly adopting the disciplinary, imperious norms of Western art-music, even as it longs and claims to be outside them. It is to this end that I draw attention to graphing, and how ethnomusicology theorizes the act of graphing.

In the world which ethnomusicology seeks to describe, and which, in the process of description, it actually constructs, a variously defined and fundamental duality between the imperium and its others is actualized. This conceptual and praxical foundation is of course an historical legacy, in so far as the conditions of possibility of the field itself are rooted in the nineteenth century's mainstream musical privileging of central European art-music canons, and the concomitant denigration or complete lack of awareness of non-art-musical expressions. These disciplinary conditions of possibility lead to several conclusions and observations. First, the prime duality between us and them is, obviously, an epistemological tool of imperial origin and usefulness, for it allows the imperium to construct its others. Second, this duality remains operative to the extent that, in ethnomusicological practice at the end of the second millennium, it is still seen as disciplinarily incorrect to study the art-musics of the imperium. In brief, the flow is one way. The imperium cannot be taken as an object of knowledge; it serves only as the subject of knowledge.

The injunction against turning the tables and studying the imperium as an ethnomusicological other serves as a reminder that the series of dichotomies that coalesce around the prime duality of us/them always entail a subjection of one term to the other. For instance, to name a few of the frequently actualized dualities that flavour ethnomusicological discourse, one often contends with dualities such as text/praxis, artifact/process or written/oral (or written/aural). These are in many respects place-holders for other dualities formerly employed but now held to be out of political favour, but more clearly linked to imperial categorization, dualities such as modern/primitive, literate/non-literate, and so forth. Needless to say, those who are modern and literate are the subjects of knowledge.

It is important to note that the subject of this knowledge takes the guise of passion, of passionate interest. Ethnomusicology's dichotomies usually entail passion for that music that is not written. The operative notion is that the non-written must have been transmitted through a romantic and intense experience of immediacy, which is then apotheosized as — paradoxically — divinely human. In a gesture that echoes such complexly paradisiacal and primitivist narratives such as *Robinson Crusoe, South Pacific*, or indeed the Judeo-Christian myth of the Garden of Eden, ethnomusicology prefers to construct its objects and spaces as ones unsullied by the trappings of modern Western culture, which usually includes writing.

What is written then is not the province of ethnomusicological thinking, because writing lifts one from the romance of then, there, and them, and seemingly forces one to return to one's prosaic and fallen present, perhaps sadly reminding one of one's assumed ontological complicity in Original Sin. The mixed metaphor that asserts that writing 'lifts' one to a 'fallen' state shows the profound confusion that reigns over the status of materiality in ethnomusicology. Moreover, it signals the very mixed feelings that attend the ascription and construction of identity. The ethnomusicologist wants the other but can never become the other. So it is that, in ethnomusicological practice, what is ethnic is what is not high-art; and what is ethnic certainly is not European or North American.

In other words, there is conceptual slippage across various dichotomies, and thus an association is forced between non-written musics, non-literate or oral cultures, and the exotic other. Temporal and spatial elements, as Johannes Fabian tells us, are also folded into the mix.[2] As a consequence, the non-literate (or 'primitive') remains then and there, whereas the modern and literate always become here and now. It should be noted that this passion for the other's music and culture ultimately serves to protect the ethnomusicologist's status as the subject of knowledge. Writing music has been made to be about identity, and as we will see, about race or ethnos.

The basic point then, is that ethnomusicology is practiced in a traditional modernist and imperial framework. This is true even in the present when its surface concerns seem to be congruent with radical practice. This imperious modernism is most evident in the field's tacit reliance upon consuetudinary — and significantly dichotomous — epistemological practices. One might in this case go so far as to claim that dichotomy is evidence of the imperium — and vice versa. This is because ethnomusicology's dichotomous epistemology is always predicated upon an asymmetry between subject and object in which the object is subjected, subjugated.

Now, because the prime duality is protean, it is essential to discuss it in some of its other guises — for instance, that of primitivism and modernism. The anxiety that currently attends usage of these temporal notions (because they so obviously which represent a very fundamental dichotomy in colonial discourse) should also be extended to the duality of literate/non-literate. In ethnomusicological discourse, a formation that tends to sustain the imperium's status as subject of knowledge, the privileged objectival forms have been constructed as non-literate. There thus remains in ethnomusicology a disciplinary and epistemological fascination with literacy and its opposite. Literacy is preferable to the primitivism of its other, yet the desired modernity threatens to destroy ontological romanticism and original (and probably godly) purity. Thus writing becomes an onto-theological condition. That is to say, the existence of musical notation is taken as evidence of literacy, and literacy is linked to the modern and ultimately with the Western. As a result, written Western art-music traditions must be excluded from ethnomusicological consideration. This exclusion is clearly a marker of imperious thinking, insofar as it slips between us/them and literate/non-literate on the basis of unexamined (and probably unexaminable) assumptions that yoke history and geography in a teleological destiny.

In order to shake the field of ethnomusicology from its reliance upon imperial habits of cognition, it seems important to make some form of intervention, as overused as the concept may be in the poststructuralist world. Such an intervention could be made around ethnomusicology's mistrust of writing — a basic fear of, and fascination with, Western practices of musical notation, which I will call 'graphophobia' — for it is clear that ideas about writing are integral to these habits of thought. Disciplinarily and practically, such an intervention might be located in investigations of the art-music of the imperium, the unchallenged subject or 'prime determinant' from which the enormous and unwieldy category of non-Western music is constrained to derive whatever meaning it can. Such work, while challenging ethnomusicology's historically inculcated graphophobia, also begins the related process of confounding the subject/object relation that is so much a part of ethnomusicological authority. Briefly and simplistically, subjects tend to write, while objects do not. Counter-ethnomusicological work, by focusing on the art-music of the imperium, may begin to critique these traditional habits of thought. In any event, it is crucial to speak of writing in a musical context, as well as Euro-American attitudes towards writing. In this context, I would like to map out the relations central to such an investigation, which must begin with a look at the graphophobic discursive formation itself, for graphophobia defines the field of ethnomusicology.

Many commentators have tussled with constructing and/or refining definitions of ethnomusicology. Indeed, in 1964, Bruno Nettl himself commented, 'Like most young disciplines, ethnomusicology has engaged in a good deal of self-criticism and self-introspection.'[3] Nettl then describes three parameters that work objectively to define the scope of the field as it appeared to one of its major practitioners in the nineteen-sixties: (1) the music of 'non-literate' societies; (2) the music — partially or totally written and/or theorized — of cultures seen to be analogous to the art-music culture of the imperium; and (3) folk music. Of course, the field has expanded in some significant ways, and to add to Nettl's definitional work regarding the scope of the field, it is important to note the current concern with what are called popular musics, a concern which has come to play a delightful and increasingly fundamental role in the field of ethnomusicology.

To concentrate solely upon objects defined by ethnomusicology, however, is to misrepresent both the character and force of ethnomusicology. One of the most important contributions that ethnomusicology has made to the study of human expression is the linking of the social and/or praxical with the musical, or even more radically, the defining of the musical as inherently praxical. This is a gesture with multiple implications that might potentially challenge ethnomusicology's hegemonically situated eye (or ear). It is clearly a broadly-conceived field, and Nettl for one feels that most ethnomusicologists 'are prepared to include all cultures of the world, including Western civilization, but they recognize the greater importance to themselves of non-Western and folk music.'[4]

The inclusivity that Nettl extends to both the West and the Rest is quite attractive, but it should be noted that including the West as an object is fraught with a certain amount of discomfort. The existence of the field is quite frankly predicated upon certain differences (in both object and interrogative approach) between musics found and used in what Nettl calls 'Western civilization' and those found and used elsewhere. The prefix 'ethno' is used as a marker of such differences. The occasional attempts to reformulate the notion of musicology to include the study of all musical phenomena have not worked, and any irony that now attends the phrase 'the West and the Rest' is lost in practice. The West and the Rest becomes a statement of doctrinal fact. Classically, traditionally, a split in musical scholarship has been defined. On the one hand, there are those who work in the various fields that are considered to be musical scholarship proper. Apparently, it is unnecessary to mark the music, music theory, history, musicology, and literature of the West as Western. It is simply music, music theory, history, musicology, and literature. On the other hand, research on any aspects of other music-cultures must bear the weight of the ethnic. It is broadly referred to as 'ethnomusicological.' The implication of this split, or at the very least its effect, and perhaps even the underlying belief, is that the imperium has no ethnicity. The imperium is structurally normative, while everything and everyone else is clearly marked due to their differences. This disciplinary divide entails asymmetry and unevenness, an imposition of ethnicity on them by a hegemonic authority. And the term 'ethnic' and its related prefix 'ethno' must be seen as distancing devices that establish hegemony of the Western subject over its others. The term 'ethno' comes from the Greek 'ethnos,' meaning 'people.' Yet it has come to imply something akin to 'identity.' In its strict, practice-bound sense, it is interesting to note that 'people' (the ethnos) seem to be coloured and/or situated in other ways in other spaces and places, while those who represent the imperium are not, strictly, people. One can then ask, with extreme trepidation, what in fact the practitioners of the imperium are. 'We' might be bacteria, 'we' may be gods, but clearly we are the subjects of knowledge.

Despite the foregoing attempt to sketch a set of relations, it is not my intention to describe the field of ethnomusicology *in toto* — others such as Bruno Nettl have already done important work in this regard. I focus mainly upon how ethnomusicology's others are constructed as objects — music-cultures and not theoretical ruminations — largely on the basis of an injunction against including the art-music culture of the imperium within the field of ethnomusicology, an injunction in force regardless of the actual methodological approaches used to isolate and examine objects. The crux of the problem is the reliance upon the action of a 'master term,' which ends up reifying relations within simplistic hierarchisms (us over them; subjection of the object), rather than inviting thinking through relational fields of power. It simply confirms imperialistic interaction even when — and perhaps especially when — an inversion of the master term takes place. A carnival is inaugurated on a disciplinary scale, but one that betrays all Bakhtinian hopes.

As the master term, the art-music culture of the imperium is figured as a silence. Yet it is, in its silence, powerful insofar as it defines an entire world simply by the force of its silent presence, without theorization and without question. As long as this 'silence which acts' is actualized, a silence which, when acting, 'ethnicizes' some while it 'de-ethnicizes' hegemonic others, it will not be possible to move away from hierarchisms and the colonial repetitions which they mark. While the epistemological unevenness sustained by this duality is not *ipso facto* racist, there is no doubt that it comes to the service of very traditional racialist strategies of thought. This ethno-based thinking, particularly at this historical moment whereat the ascription of ethnicity is of paramount and politically sensitive importance, can easily be made part of both passive and active racist projects and epistemologies.

I have moved away from describing the graphophobia with which the field of ethnomusicology is riven, as outlined above. My concern for ethnomusicology's graphophobia emerged, metonymically and almost ineluctably, from my exploration of what I've referred to as the ethnomusicological prime duality. The key to this silent, seemingly inevitable connection is the body of palimpsestic relations between associated dualities, which rely on yet conceal an essential connective mechanism — an ambivalence about written music, which entails a longing for the non-written accompanied by a pronounced fear that others may be writing. The palimpsestic relations allow one — and indeed, by way of a form of conceptual shorthand, invite and even force one — to say one thing and mean yet a host of others. Thus, in any discussion of the imperium and its others, one also invokes, say, literate/non-literate, or any number of other dichotomous attributes. Yet, it is typically writing or literacy that becomes a mask for other markers of identity, spinning deftly into other, less subtle and consequently more telling dualities such as 'racinated/non-racinated' ones that seem ineluctably to appear around the question of writing. Such connections need not be articulated overtly, and often cannot be. They have become, through historical practice, always-already-performed investigative/constitutive acts, whose noncommittal nature must then be emphasized. This certainly says something about hegemonic thought processes and their connectedness to dichotomous thinking. It further speaks to the reliance of that style of cognition upon what might be called, following post-structuralist conceptualizations, the 'essential silencing' of alterity.

As a consequence, it is crucial to insist that writing is not a value-free phenomenon, without any relation to identity formation. Writing has a very Euro-American mien, particularly in the realm of musical notation that is the site wherein all of ethnomusicology's fears and anxieties tend to focus. Some forms of musical writing that lie outside the imperium have entered the province of ethnomusicological thinking — Javanese chain notation, simplified Asian notation, or the system of notation used in Shape-Note hymnody. Nonetheless, these kinds of writing are then mapped along a continuum, located somewhere between the graphic systems of the imperium, and the putative orality of all those other music cultures that were usually called, at least in former days, non-literate. Even though some of the other forms of musical writing are mapped into the centre of this continuum, they are conceptually allied more with orality than they are with literacy or graphics. (To repeat, in ethnomusicology, there is a tendency to define writing and literacy in extremely narrow terms in order to allow such freewheeling associations as script = literacy.) Even when not thoroughly exoticized, these graphical systems are nevertheless marked as different, as other, regardless of their capacity to denotate music. In this way, to the extent that they remain representative of a 'them over there,' they tend to be marked as ethnic. And 'ethnic,' as I've said previously, is a term that serves merely to mark distance from the imperium. It is not surprising then that it is also the prefix which has come to define the field that studies other systems — ethnomusicology.

Ultimately, it matters little to ethnomusicology that what Nettl calls 'Asian and North African high cultures' write music, and write extensively. For ethnomusicology, what counts is that they do so differently from Euro-Americans. It is surely contentious to insist on this point, but the upshot of this particular quest for differences is that the other's writing is not allowed to be writing as the imperium defines it. This difference is most evident in the different disciplinary approaches that are used, and apparently needed, to examine those music cultures that use writing yet are considered to be other — as is the case with the examples previously cited — Javanese chain notation, simplified Asian notation, or the system of notation used in Shape-Note hymnody. Theirs is always writing of a different order and kind. In an ethnomusicological context, the temptation is to call non-Western graphical systems 'oral writing' in order to emphasize their conceptual and sometimes practical connection with vocalization. Yet it is a bad abstraction insofar as all graphical systems have some connections to vocality. It would make better sense to think of writing — ours and others' — and to look at differences in practice and reception.

Nettl's evocation of non-Western 'high cultures' suggests the possibility of something other but not inferior to the imperium. Yet, somehow, probably because the norm for 'high culture' is writing, the same dualisms remain operative. Rather a simple matter of the existence of other forms of musical notation, analysis invariably turns to different attitudes towards writing and its existence (bordering on a study of mentalities, as it were). The duality involved is almost always the prime duality, and secondarily those dichotomous reveries attendant upon it. As a consequence, the existence of other writings is a source of ambivalence. Where there is seemingly no writing (that is, writing in the narrowest sense of inscription), one finds a palpable romanticization of the oral and the aural. Yet, where some form of writing is in evidence, its existence tends to inspire a gamut of conflicting feelings that centre on the problem of modernization, of Westernization, of native purity versus foreign corruption, or foreign invasion, or cultural imperialism. In sum, there is a host of binarisms invoked to sustain the possibility of pure outside to the imperium. There is a sort of Edenic narrative about the garden and its fall.

In sum, the writing that exists in those sites marked as ethnic must ultimately be disavowed: it is taken as evidence of some manner of 'fall' — penetration of a virginal polity by a corrupt and corrupting, modern, Euro-American, and masculinist presence. These riotously metonymic connections between gender, identity, and power are impressive, for they tend to use language that evokes something like cultural rape, or, at the very least, of an ill-conceived coupling rooted in cultural inequality. Oddly, this ambivalence about the rape or fall of the ethnic other is not itself seen as evidence of violation or unevenness, even though it should constitute such evidence. In sum, writing becomes the scene of an ambivalence toward the other through which the others' subjection is then disavowed, as merely part of the general narrative of an unhappy fall, rather than an epistemological power play. This is because ambivalence and disavowal are rooted in the epistemic practices of ethnomusicology, and are thus bestowed with a provisional and immediate invisibility. Nevertheless, should we not take the insistence upon metaphors of rape as evidence of a subjection of the object? For, ultimately, it demands that the colonized behave as colonial to allow for the apparently a priori and necessary performative repetition of colonial tropes.

From an epistemological and disciplinary point of view, writing is as central to ethnomusicological constructions of identity as race is. It simply has been less theorized in ethnomusicological frames, possibly because of the ever vaunted, overdetermined and extremely culturally specific notion that music entails non-materiality. These are ascribed qualities that made Hegel and others swoon with delight, and that caused Kant to mistrust the sonic arts.[5] However, if one shifts the focus (as I have attempted) to writing and its connections to identity (the palimpsestism made possible by reinscribing the norm of the imperium's writing in multiple registers of analysis), then writing always already means race, modernity, masculinity, presence and 'presentness'; and evokes a matrix of related terms. Even though the connections between these terms may seem oblique and sometimes vague, palimpsestism works thusly: when one writes, one is the modern subject, one located in an Euro-American frame. One then produces artifacts or musical objects, and thus removes (albeit only in a deeply illusory way) musical activity from the supposed realm of praxis. In the end, to say that Western art music is artifact, written, modern, Euro-American, graphic, scripted, and so forth, is in one sense to say the same thing. What 'the same thing' is remains productively veiled, and any clarity one can find is ultimately located in a tightly bound definition: it is imperial music.

In other words, all attempts to define the imperium's music border on tautology, which serves as a reminder of just how closed the epistemological system is. Despite its incessant dualisms, the second term is always subjected to the first; and a third, or fourth, or fifth is always foreclosed. This is the description of hegemony, of the 'silence that acts.' It is the subject. Its object is the ethnos, or ethnic other. The other, of course, is thought to have a very fraught relation to writing, and by extension, to the privileged terms of other, related dualities. Writing is a process inextricably meshed with the subjugation of the other. Because, in ethnomusicology, writing remains reserved for the imperium and continues to be denied to the ethnos, it becomes imperative to undertake an investigation of writing, its conceptualization, and its reception. These offer three possible sites for intervention into the imperious practices of ethnomusicology. Most specifically, attention must be paid to graphophobia, to the ambivalence and consequent disavowal that underlie ethnomusicology's fear of writing.

All in all, dualisms play a fundamental role in organizing the episteme of the imperium, and all of the dualities of which I've heretofore spoken are deeply embedded in the maintenance of its social and political orders. They are evidence of a frankly colonial residue in an age that is frequently characterized as 'post-colonial.' While dualism is the condition of possibility for the scope and range ethnomusicological inquiry, it is the subjection of the object that assures the authority of that knowledge. Dualities have never been simple because they are at once reductive simplifications and expansive generalizations. Yet, given their aggressive actualization and deployment, it is important to work with them in order to begin to undermine the ways in which they impose and sustain unevenness. In a world such as ours, one described in another context by Trinh T. Minh-ha as having elements of the Third World in the First (and vice versa), dualities and their attendant hierarchisms must not remain uncontested, precisely because their mechanisms of ambivalence and disavowal remain so potent. For this reason, it remains important to confound ethnomusicology's subject/object relations, and one way to do this is to open questions about the status of writing in ethnomusicological contexts. This might help to rethink 'white' as 'coloured' (to invoke a brutish duality which lurks behind so much late-second-millennium cultural work), to confound a traditional and poisonous racialism, one which perniciously mimics a value-free cognitive preference. Such an intervention also moves one away from Manichean ascriptions that allow one to view some forms as sinister, and others as pure.

I'd like to close by invoking Gayatri Spivak's important question — 'Can the subaltern speak?'[6] a question inextricably wedded to issues of longing and silencing, to ambivalence and disavowal. Her conclusion, in the end, is that the subaltern cannot speak, at least at this juncture. I'd like to suggest then, given this state of affairs, that one try to make the non-subaltern speak, at least ethnomusicologically, against its own dominance by examining it as one examines and has examined the subaltern. By doing so, one ascribes peoplehood (which is to say, its status of ethnos) to the imperium's activity and production, thus placing its work 'in relation.'

Notes

1. *American Heritage Dictionary* Rev. Ed. (Boston, New York: Houghton Mifflin Company, 1991), 645.
2. Johannes Fabian, *Time and the Other: How Anthropology Makes Its Object* (New York: Columbia University Press, 1990).
3. Bruno Nettl, *Theory and Method in Ethnomusicology* (New York: Free Press of Glencoe, 1964).
4. Nettl, *Theory and Method in Ethnomusicology*, 8.
5. G.W.F. Hegel, *Philosophy of Fine Art* [1807], trans. F.P.B. Osmaston (G. Bell and Sons,

1920; reprint, New York: Hacker Art Books, 1977). Immanuel Kant, *Critique of Judgment* [1790], trans. Werner S. Pluhar (Indianapolis: Hackett Publishing Company, 1987).

6 Spivak, Gayatri Chakravorty, 'Can the Subaltern Speak?' in *Marxism and The Interpretation of Culture*, ed. Cary Nelson and Lawrence Grossberg (London: Macmillan, 1988), 271–313.

Colonial Ambivalence and the Modern *Shôsetsu*: *Shôsetsu shinzui* and De-Asianization

Atsuko Ueda

This paper inquires into several historical manifestations that coincidentally intersected in the mid-1880s Japan: the publication of Tsubouchi Shôyô's *Shôsetsu shinzui* (*The Essence of the Novel*), a critical work that designated 'civilized emotions' as the primary theme of the modern novel; the decline of the People's Rights Movement, allegedly the first democratic political movement in modern Japan; the forces of de-Asianization, which are clearly manifest in Fukuzawa Yukichi's article appropriately entitled 'Datsu-a ron' (De-Asianization, 1885); and finally, the reconstitution of *gakumon* (commonly translated as 'knowledge' or 'learning') as a space to develop the 'national spirit' (*kokumin no seishin*). The main objective of the paper is to bring to the fore the historicity and the politicality of Shôyô's modern *shôsetsu* by examining the way in which the People's Rights Movement, de-Asianization, and the reconfiguration of the realm of knowledge intertwine and engage with the production of the modern *shôsetsu*. In so doing, I seek to derive the ideological foundation that shapes the institution of modern Japanese literature that even now designates *Shôsetsu shinzui* as its own origin and Shôyô as its founder.

The standard narrative of modern Japanese literature characterizes *The Essence of the Novel* as a text that produced the modern Japanese novel by imitating the 'Western novel.' However, we must keep in mind that, despite its title, this text by no means describes the 'essence' of a pre-existing entity called the 'novel.' As I will explain in more detail later in this paper, within the discursive site of *Shôsetsu shinzui*'s production, the 'Western novel' was an amorphous figure, and the term *shôsetsu* was yet to be standardized as a translation of the 'novel.' In short, '*shôsetsu*=novel,' a formula now naturalized within Japanese literary criticism, had yet to gain its later recognition.

Furthermore, it is important to note that the discursive space within which Tsubouchi Shôyô wrote this seminal work was in a state of chaos, which was, in part, a result of a dramatic increase of writings that found their way to Japan subsequent to Meiji Japan's encounter with the West. In order to accommodate the newly imported writings, Meiji translators created new words and neologisms, but also had to rely on existing signifiers to take on new signifieds. The boundaries of the existent system of signification thus needed to be stretched; and this inevitably led to a transformation of the discursive system as a whole. In short, it is vital to situate *Shôsetsu shinzui* as a text that attempted to produce a medium appropriate for the designation 'modern *shôsetsu*' by negotiating with the transforming and unstable system of signification that constitutes itself. With this in mind, this paper will specifically focus on the manner in which the equation *shôsetsu*=novel was produced and attempt to identify and critically examine the multi-faceted effects that issued forth in its production, as well as analyze the varying and ever-transforming discursive domains with which it intersected.

'The Autonomy of Knowledge': Knowledge vs. Politics

In the years 1882-3, around the time Shôyô began writing *Shôsetsu shinzui*, 'the autonomy of knowledge' (*gakumon no dokuritsu*) became one of the maxims linked to nation building. To identify the underlying drive that shaped the call for 'the autonomy of knowledge,' let us look at a passage from Ono Azusa's speech, which he gave at the founding ceremony of Tokyo senmon gakkô (Tokyo specialized school, the present-day Waseda University), a school with which Shôyô was affiliated.

> This is what I wish to demand from this school. By continuing to reform our school for ten or more years, we should commit ourselves to developing the school that teaches our youth in our language (*hôgo*) and bring about the autonomy of our knowledge (*hôgakumon*). (Hear, hear, huge applause). The autonomy of the nation depends on the autonomy of its people, and the autonomy of the people is rooted in the autonomy of their spirit (*seishin*).

> (Hear, hear, applause). The autonomy of the spirit is, in fact, based on the autonomy of knowledge, and thus, if one desires the nation to achieve autonomy, its people must first attain autonomy. (Huge applause). If one desires for its people to achieve autonomy, the spirit must first attain autonomy. And thus if one desires for the spirit to achieve autonomy, knowledge must first attain autonomy. (Huge applause).[1]

What Ono promoted in the name of 'the autonomy of knowledge' was not a claim for the objectivity or universality of knowledge, but the autonomy of '*our* knowledge,' which was, in his view, inextricably linked to the act of 'teaching' in 'our language' (*hôgo*). He continues, 'Teaching our youths in foreign languages through foreign books, as if knowledge is not lofty or wise enough otherwise, is only a hindrance in teaching and is certainly not the way to bring about autonomy of knowledge.'[2] The argument he puts forth can, in fact, be read as a direct criticism of Tokyo University, whose courses were taught by 'hired-foreigners' (*oyatoi gaijin*) using 'Western textbooks.'[3] Ono's argument for 'the autonomy of knowledge,' therefore, was a call to 'liberate' themselves from Western books and languages. Such, according to Ono, was necessary to achieve the 'autonomy of national spirit,' which in turn was a prerequisite for the 'autonomy of the nation' itself.

Yet we must not jump to the conclusion that Tokyo senmon gakkô limited its textbooks to materials originally produced in Japanese or by Japanese thinkers. The 'table of textbooks and references' which lists the primary texts that Tokyo senmon gakkô used in its classes consists of works by Alexander Bain, Herbert Spencer, and John Stuart Mill, among other 'Western' writers.[4] It is clear, therefore, that 'our knowledge' did not signify texts produced in Japan, nor texts written in the Japanese language. Instead, it referred to a body of works that was endorsed as 'knowledge' necessary in the path toward modernization, and that were translated into a language to which the readership had access, even though originally written in a foreign language (primarily in Western languages); these texts were then distributed extensively, to the extent that a certain level of familiarity was achieved, a familiarity that granted them the status of '*our* knowledge.' Furthermore, in order to fulfill what Ono promoted as the 'autonomy of knowledge,' the texts had to be commented on and talked about in 'our language.' Such practice, according to Ono, was ultimately linked to the 'autonomy of the national spirit.'

Reserving a more detailed discussion for later, it is worthwhile to note here that, in the process through which 'foreign (Western) knowledge' becomes '*our* knowledge,' the subject 'we' is posited as one that *possesses* such knowledge. In effect, this body of knowledge—the very means of modernization—becomes that which belongs to 'us.' As we shall see later, Japan as the possessor of 'modern knowledge' is essentialized when Japan discovers the 'less-civilized peoples,' thereby defining itself as an agent of enlightenment that leads them in the path toward modernization. The mechanism of 'mimicry' that can be identified in this process intersects with the figure of a '*gakusha*' (the knowing subject) that is mobilized in defining Japan's relationship with the 'less-civilized' Asia.[5]

Just three months after Ono gave his speech, Fukuzawa Yukichi, who had in fact attended the ceremony during which Ono spoke, published *Gakumon no dokuritsu* (*The Autonomy of Knowledge*).[6] Fukuzawa clearly subscribed to the same maxim, but the focal point of his call for 'the autonomy of knowledge' was 'severing the connection between knowledge and politics.' He states, 'Since severing the connection between knowledge and politics is important for a nation, I pray that Japanese knowledge (*nihon no gakumon*) will be separated from Japanese politics.'[7] Nonetheless, as Fukuzawa himself acknowledges, the line between politics and 'knowledge' could not be clearly drawn at this moment in time. It goes without saying that 'knowledge' is ideologically and historically bound, and at the time, 'knowledge' was yet to be firmly defined. In other words, the forms of knowledge (e.g., the principles by which to govern the nation, the constitution, etc) that were endorsed among the members of the intelligentsia varied in accordance with their political agendas. Criticizing the intimate connection between the two, Fukuzawa posited 'knowledge' as a realm completely independent of politics and political parties.

> Fundamentally, 'knowledge' is comparable to martial arts and fine arts in that it has no inherent relationship with politics. Regardless of a person's political inclinations, he should be qualified as a teacher if he has the ability to teach. To inquire into his political inclinations and to evaluate the good and bad of his political views in the process of hiring him has grave consequences. Of course, people may simply overlook it for now, but it is an augury of great disorder and chaos. I imagine the ways of the world in years to come and gravely worry that, if Japanese knowledge remains connected to politics, the degree of calamity may follow the disastrous precedents of the Song dynasty or the former Mito province.[8]

Fukuzawa thus deems the 'connection' between politics and knowledge as 'an augury of disorder and chaos' and argues that it is for the good of the nation to sever 'knowledge' from a realm in which a political stance determines its validity. In other words, while Fukuzawa, like Ono, links national independence with the autonomy of Japanese knowledge, he differentiates himself by claiming that 'autonomy of knowledge' rests upon its severance from politics. This can be read as a direct criticism against Tokyo senmon gakkô, a school that had a strong affiliation with the Kaishintô political party. Tokyo senmon gakkô tried to downplay its connection with Kaishintô, but given that its founder was Ôkuma Shigenobu, the former Minister of Finance, who left the cabinet after the Meiji 14 Incident and founded Kaishintô, it could not escape the criticism that it was founded specifically to produce Kaishintô supporters.[9] Fukuzawa's criticism, however, extends to other schools as well, many of which were founded after the Meiji 14 Incident, when the parliament was set to convene in ten years. *Minken* activists, therefore, were eager to produce their supporters/voters through their schools. In effect, Fukuzawa's criticism was directed at the entire educational scene where mustering political supporters was the primary objective for those involved.

Let us examine Fukuzawa's linguistic operation from a slightly different angle and ask: What are the rhetorical effects of positing the opposition between politics and knowledge? When we examine his argument from this perspective, we find that 'knowledge' is a rhetorical figure that consolidates a community divided by different political agendas. In other words, the opposition is ultimately a means to postulate 'a unified nation.' This would further explain the rhetorical link between 'the autonomy of the nation' and 'autonomy of knowledge.' And ultimately, by claiming that 'for a *gakusha* who is responsible for our youth's education to be involved in politics is devastating for national well-being,' he rejected Ono's version of the 'national spirit' and constructed a figure of the '*gakusha*' (the knowing subject) who would embody an entirely different 'national spirit' from the one posited by Ono.[10] Let us further examine Fukuzawa's *gakusha* by exploring its link to his famous maxim, *fuhen futô*, or 'no-prejudice, non-party affiliation.'

In 1882 (Meiji 15), the very year Tokyo senmon gakkô was founded, Fukuzawa began producing *Jiji shinpô*, a newspaper that began its circulation with the motto, 'no-prejudice, non-party affiliation.'[11] It became the main medium for the '*gakusha*-Fukuzawa' to disseminate his thoughts, all the while retaining a position 'outside' of politics. The logic inscribed in 'no-prejudice, non-party affiliation' thus aligns itself with his notion of 'the autonomy of knowledge.' The connection between the two becomes more than apparent in the events *Jiji shinpô* covered (or, more accurately, did not cover) in the years between 1882 and 1885, when the People's Rights Movement began to lose steam. During these years, numerous *minken*-led uprisings were carried out across the nation, beginning with the Fukushima Incident, followed by Incidents in Takada, Gunma, Kabasan, Chichibu, Iida, and Osaka. While other *minken* newspapers displayed their political stance in reporting the uprisings, *Jiji shinpô* remained practically silent on the issue. Instead, its primary concern centered on Japan's relationship vis-à-vis Qing China and Korea. In other words, 'no-prejudice, non-party affiliation' is a twofold rhetorical strategy that limits its textual engagement to 'foreign' relationships that allows 'Japan' to represent/constitute itself as a single unified nation, while, at the same time, evades and conceals the domestic division that clearly was manifest in the uprisings. Fukuzawa may have retained the position of *gakusha* (allegedly a position dissociated with politics), but his linguistic endeavors, which continued to engage with nation building, were political through and through. I seek to identify the politicality inherent in the realm of knowledge; and to do so, it is necessary to perform a rigorous examination of the 'autonomy of nation' that intersects with the maxim 'no-prejudice, non-party affiliation' –hence invariably with the autonomy of knowledge—focusing especially on Japan's position vis-à-vis Asia.

'The National Spirit' as a Vehicle of Teleological Shift: From 'Asia' to the 'West'

On March 16, 1885, Fukuzawa published 'Datsu-a ron' ('De-Asianization') in *Jiji shinpô*. Written amidst the anxiety caused by the Kôshin Incident, a coup d'état carried out by the pro-Japanese activists in Korea in December 1884, 'De-Asianization' is a well known piece in which Fukuzawa claimed, 'In my heart, I sever my ties with the evil people of East Asia.'[12] In order to explore the full implication of this work, the narrative of progress and advancement that shapes 'Datsu-a ron,' which is evident in the following passage, must be placed under rigorous scrutiny: 'Japan is geographically on the Eastern end of Asia, but in terms of our national spirit, we have left the old confines of Asia and have joined Western civilization.'[13]

In order to see the significance of this passage, we must keep in mind that 'Asia,' 'Japan,' and the 'West' were yet to cohere as fixed entities and were yet to have a stable place within the geopolitical dynamic of the time. In the quote above, 'Asia,' 'Japan,' and the 'West' all appear to be fixed, but it is through a certain linguistic strategy that they constitute themselves *as units* on the textual surface. And at the core of this linguistic strategy is the figure of 'the national spirit.'

Needless to say, 'the national spirit' is without form. But precisely because of this, the figure conceals the instability and ambivalence that intervenes in Japan's formation as a unified subject. By positing 'the national spirit' as a criterion by which to narrativize Japan's 'progress,' Fukuzawa absorbs all the existent imbalance and instability and posits 'Japan' as a stable evolutionary subject, as if 'Japan' is already a fully-constituted subject. Japan's constitution as a subject is, in effect, entirely dependent upon the *unifying* figure of 'the national spirit.' 'The spirit,' then, is a rhetorical figure that consolidates and stabilizes 'Japan' as a single national unit. As we shall see shortly, however, this national spirit, a figure upon which 'Japan' relies for its stability, is ambivalent in more ways than one.

The narrative that Fukuzawa puts forth in 'De-Asianization' clearly intersects with the idea of 'the ages of civilization' (*bunmei no yowai*), which he discusses in his earlier work called *Bunmeiron no gairyaku* (*An Outline of a Theory of Civilization*), published in 1875. In it, he divides the stages of civilization into three categories, namely *mikai* (uncivilized), *hankai* (half-civilized), and *bunmei* (civilized), and situates Japan among the half-civilized. He claims that 'in civilization' there is 'both a visible exterior and its inner spirit.' And in order to move toward civilization, they must not only adopt the 'externals of civilization,' such as 'clothing food, shelter, and government decrees and laws,' but must also 'pursue the spirit of civilization.' To do so, Fukuzawa upholds 'European civilization as its goal.'[14]

According to *An Outline of a Theory of Civilization*, then, the 'spirit of civilization' is clearly 'European.' However, on the other hand, Fukuzawa also claims that 'the spirit' is 'people's spiritual makeup,' which 'permeates among the people' and posits the spirit as that which already exists among the people.[15] In other words, while the spirit belongs to Europe, it is also one that represents the specificity of a nation (in this case Japan). Precisely because of this ambivalence inscribed in the national spirit, it can be mobilized to differentiate Japan from

Asia, while also being used to narrativize the manner in which Japan, with its own 'spiritual makeup,' joins the West, as evident in the quote from 'Datsu-a ron': 'in terms of our national spirit, we have left the confines of Asia and have joined Western civilization.'

This is not the only ambivalence inscribed in the signifier 'the spirit.' The spirit, supposedly shared by a given community, can only be produced through the multiple logic of exclusion—the mobilized logic, of course, shifts in accordance with each specific instance. In Fukuzawa's time, moreover, the criteria by which to identify 'the national spirit of Japan' were neither stabilized nor standardized and hence in the process of being sought; and precisely because of that, the signifier 'spirit' could only float in flux. Depending on the logic of exclusion that is mobilized at a given moment, the 'spirit' thus changes its appearance.

Despite this ambivalence and instability (or precisely because of it), 'national spirit' was a figure that was mobilized for Japan to constitute itself as a subject. At the core of Fukuzawa's 'Datsu-a ron,' therefore, is the varying and multi-faceted forces specific to its time, all of which is inscribed in the signifier, 'the spirit.' In effect, while the spirit-as-telos was posited as one that belongs to Europe, Fukuzawa sought to produce a spirit specific to Japan within a discursive space in which the term was mobilized to consolidate the nation itself.

Ultimately, we can identify Japanese colonial ambivalence at work. In order to embody the illusion of progress, 'Japan' continually seeks to differentiate itself from 'Asia,' while simultaneously desiring to become the West; the signifier 'spirit,' with all its ambivalence, accommodates this desire and hence can be mobilized in the act of differentiating itself from Asia and in longing to become the West. Yet the desire is never fully realized. To *become* the West, Japan internalizes (and hence colonizes itself with) the logic of the West such as the International Law of Sovereign States, all the while seeking the 'less-civilized' nations in Asia against which to act like the West. This is what the literary critic Komori Yôichi calls 'self-internal colonization.'[16] This psychological structure by which Japan longs for the identity of a civilized nation, Komori contends, is the Japanese colonial unconscious.

There is another facet to this ambivalent signifier, 'the spirit,' that must also be addressed. 'Spirit' is inextricably connected to the 'half-civilized' position attributed to 'Japan.' In fact, it may be more accurate to say that the multiple ambivalences inscribed in 'the spirit' constantly re-constitute Japan as a half-civilized nation. I cannot emphasize enough that 'Asia,' 'Japan,' and the 'West' were yet to cohere as fixed units or to attain stable positions within the geopolitical map of the time; the varying forces that shape the signifying processes continually (re)defined and (re)positioned 'Asia,' 'Japan,' and the 'West.' The stability, which was nowhere existent, was forcefully produced through the signifier 'spirit,' which needed to be reconstituted and reconfigured when attached to 'Asia,' 'Japan,' and the 'West.' However, despite the fact that 'Asia,' 'Japan,' and the 'West' are continually reconstituted and re-distributed within the geopolitical map, the threefold structure that situates the West as the telos of civilization, Asia as the uncivilized, and Japan as the half-civilized is never de-polarized. In short, the relative standards by which they are situated remains, and the tri-polar structure is retained each and every time they are reconfigured. Japan appears 'in between' Asia and the West, embodying and hence persistently reproducing the colonial ambivalence that continues to foster the desire to be the colonizer while being colonized itself.

Fukuzawa knew perfectly well that the 'national spirit' was yet to exist and that it needed to be produced. This is more than apparent in *An Outline of a Theory of Civilization,* in which he describes the 'order of enlightenment' and argues that, in order to bring about enlightenment, it is necessary to first reform 'the mind of the people' (*jinshin*) before adopting 'the externals of civilization.' In effect, he seeks to first develop 'the mind,' producing the commonality of a community through 'the mind,' and then build the nation through communal identification with 'the national spirit.' This is nothing but a form of nation building via ideological manipulation. And, as we saw earlier, 'knowledge' was chosen as the means to develop the national spirit in the mid-1880s. Ultimately, 'knowledge' was selected as a space in which ideological manipulation was to take place. This choice is invariably connected with the process through which the figure of the *gakusha* (the knowing subject) is mobilized as an agent of enlightenment, one that leads the 'less-civilized Asia' toward modernization. I wish now to turn to Fukuzawa's perception of Asia in order to further examine the manner in which the production of 'Japanese knowledge' engages with the ambivalence inscribed in the national spirit, a figure that is mobilized and utilized multifariously to postulate 'Japan.'

The *Gakusha* and the Colonial Ambivalence: Shifting Views on Korea and China

It goes without saying that, in order to posit a national entity, it is necessary to locate a foreign other from which to differentiate it. From here, I wish to focus my narrative around Fukuzawa's shifting perspectives on China and Korea, while also providing a brief narrative on foreign policies over Korea and China advocated by the People's Rights activists. I will then move on to a specific analysis of Fukuzawa's 'Datsu-a ron.'

By 1881 or so, there was a rhetorically agreed notion that Japan was the most civilized nation in Asia, a sentiment that had gained widespread acceptance among the *minken* newspapers;[17] I say 'rhetorically' agreed because it had to be insisted upon over and over again for it to be believed. This rhetoric became a polarizing force by which varying types of de-Asianization and pan-Asianism (*kôaron*) were narrativized.[18] Around this time, Fukuzawa promoted the unification of Asia by emphasizing the possibility of 'Western invasion,' as evident in his article, '*Chôsen no kôsai o ronzu*' ('On the Relationship with Korea'). Here, he argued that it was 'Japan's responsibility' to 'help the neighboring countries' achieve enlightenment to protect them against Western invasion. To this end, he advocated direct interference, which, at this point, included 'the use of force.'[19]

In July 1882, 4 months after his publication of 'On the Relationship with Korea,' the Imo mutiny erupted in Korea. As a result, the tension between Japan and China intensified drastically. Anti-Chinese sentiment grew in the *minken* newspapers, but aside from the rhetorically agreed notion that situated Japan as the 'leader of Eastern civilization,' the reaction to the Imo Mutiny varied. For example, *Chôya shinbun* argued for immediate military intervention to bring about 'enlightenment' in Korea, while *Tokyo nichi nichi shinbun* criticized the aggressive policies advocated by several newspapers such as *Chôya shinbun* and *Hôchi shinbun* and stated that diplomatic negotiation was the most appropriate solution.[20] Among these articles, we also find ones that praise China's 'swift response' to the coup, thus showing a relatively favorable view of China.[21] In short, despite the common and overt colonialist trope that situated Japan as the most advanced nation in Asia, *minken* newspapers were divided in the action they promoted. China remained a palpable threat and a competitor with Meiji Japan, but anti-Chinese sentiments had yet to galvanize the *minken* activists as forcefully as they would three years later, in the aftermath of the Kôshin Incident, carried out by the pro-Japanese activists in Korea.

Fukuzawa, who had openly advocated the use of force in order to bring about 'enlightenment' in Korea, began to promote indirect interference after the Imo Mutiny. In 'Gyûba Takuzô Goes to Korea' ('Gyûba Takuzô-kun Chôsen ni iku'), an article published from December 1882 to January of the following year, he argues for the 'reform of the mind' (*jinshin no kaikaku*) and identifies Gyûba's role in Korea in the following manner: 'You must neither carelessly interject in their politics nor demand their customs to be destroyed. The primary objective is to transmit the teachings of Western knowledge (*yôgaku*) that you have learned and have their wise upper-class men voluntarily enlighten themselves.'[22] We thus see a clear shift from a call for direct military intervention to indirect 'internal' reform. Inscribed in Fukuzawa's argument, then, is his idea in *An Outline of a Theory of Civilization* that I discussed earlier, namely the conceptual formation of an 'enlightened' nation through ideological manipulation.

We must not, however, jump to the conclusion that Fukuzawa gave up military intervention altogether; far from it. This is clear from the fact that he was secretly involved with the Kôshin Incident that occurred in December 1884.[23] One of the reasons he began to advocate indirect interference was to differentiate Japan from China by situating China as a country that is still caught up with the 'old-fashioned custom' of 'directly interfering with domestic and foreign policies.' Fukuzawa claims that the only 'wisdom' Korea would get out of China is 'the trifling teachings of old Confucian thought' and links the acts of intervention to 'Confucianism.'[24] To further differentiate Japan from 'Confucian-driven' China, Fukuzawa states that it is Japan's responsibility as the leader of Asia to bring about enlightenment in Korea by transmitting 'knowledge of modern civilization possessed by Japanese upper-class men.'[25] It is noteworthy that the 'knowledge of modern civilization' (*kinji bunmei no shisô*) which was earlier labeled 'Western knowledge' (*yôgaku*) is now renamed as 'knowledge of modern civilization possessed by Japanese upper-class men.'[26] This convenient shift must be elaborated by examining the manner in which the figure of the '*gakusha*' (knowing subject) is mobilized in Japan's relationship vis-à-vis Korea and Qing China.

Until Japan's victory in the Sino-Japanese War in 1895, which substantiated Japan's claim for being the most powerful country in Asia, Japan's superiority over Qing China had to be repeated rhetorically in one way or another. The rhetorical link between 'Japan' and 'the leader of Asia' is produced through the figure of the *gakusha*. Fukuzawa claims that 'the role of *gakusha*' is 'to discipline the Koreans' and 'to set right the wrongs of the mind [*kokoro*] and let them by themselves clear the mist of confusion.' In order to do so, he says, it is necessary to 'transmit to the Koreans the Western knowledge he [Gyûba] has learned, and let them voluntarily reach enlightenment.' Fukuzawa's logic here aligns itself with 'the autonomy of knowledge,' because it is the role of a *gakusha* that 'reforms the mind,' and not that of a politician. And this *gakusha* embodies the shift I mentioned earlier, namely the shift from one who is identified as a medium to transmit *Western* knowledge to one that embodies 'the knowledge of modern civilization, possessed by Japanese upper-class men.' What we see is the mechanism of mimicry at work: the act of 'enlightening the Koreans' attributes 'the knowledge of modern civilization' to the Japanese, as if it is *possessed* by the Japanese.

Let me elaborate. The *gakusha*, who, on the one hand, needed to colonize himself with 'Western knowledge,' becomes an agent of enlightenment as he discovers the 'less-civilized' other, in this case Koreans. In the process—specifically in the act of enlightening the 'barbarians'—the Western knowledge he absorbed *becomes* 'Japanese knowledge' and he, the *gakusha*, an embodiment of such knowledge. Colonial ambivalence is clearly foregrounded in the figure of the *gakusha* here. By having the 'barbaric' other access not Western texts, but translated Japanese texts, the Japanese *gakusha* begins to *act* as the colonizer. Accordingly, the subject 'Japan' as an agent that *possesses* the knowledge of modern civilization comes into being. This is the subject of mimicry, a subject that owns 'Japanese knowledge.'[27]

Furthermore, when Fukuzawa claims that 'Japanese knowledge' brings about enlightenment indirectly, 'knowledge' is given legitimacy and validity in and of itself; in effect, he logically exempts the *gakusha*'s involvement in the process. In this logic, the *gakusha* as an arbiter is unnecessary for the 'reform of the mind' because knowledge *automatically* enlightens its receiver. Accordingly, the *gakusha* manages to 'keep his hands clean' and hence is the exact opposite of the politicians, who directly interfere with domestic and foreign policies. Posited in opposition to politicians whose act of direct interference is linked to Confucianism, the figure of *gakusha*, who transmits (and hence embodies) Western/Japanese knowledge, is given a 'neutral' position in this conceptual scheme. We find two binaries constructing this logic, namely Confucianism/Western (Japanese) knowledge and politican/*gakusha* that align themselves with each other. I will later return to these binaries and the neutrality of the *gakusha* as I discuss the privileged subject of the modern *shôsetsu*.

Civilized Emotions vs. The Use of Force

In sharp contrast to the varying reactions to the Imo Mutiny, the *minken* activists were practically united in their anti-Chinese, anti-Korean stance in the aftermath of the Kôshin Incident in December 1884. The Kôshin incident, it should be recalled, was an event that prompted Fukuzawa to write his 'Datsu-a ron.' Numerous *minken* newspapers called for a military confrontation, some arguing for the immediate dispatch of forces to Korea, and others for an alliance with France. *Jiyû shinbun* even claimed that 'this is a great opportunity to display the strength of Japan's military power and surprise the conceited white race.'[28] Why were their reactions now so different from those during Imo Mutiny, which had occurred less than three years before? In part, it was the second time that Japan's rhetorical claim as the leader of Asia was questioned. Yet perhaps the more significant factor was the Sino-Franco War (1884-5), which erupted in between the two coups over competing claims to Annam (present-day Vietnam). The outcome was disastrous for China, and by extension for Japan. Annam was taken as a French colony, which increased Euro-American presence in Asia, and its threat became more immediate and palpable. China was Japan's main competitor in its claim as 'the leader of Asia,' but China, which had supposedly equipped itself with modern weaponry with its Yong wu movement, suffered a devastating loss to France, a country that had, ten years before, suffered a huge loss to Prussia in the Franco-Prussian War. In effect, the Kôshin Incident showed, among other things, that Qing China proved to be militarily stronger than Japan despite its loss to France (a second-rate European country). Japan's self-definition as 'the leader of Asia' was completely undermined, and the fear of Euro-American power reached its peak. The aggressive rhetoric of the *minken* activists, all in favor of immediate military attack, should be read not as a means to protect its position as the 'leader of Asia,' but as a way to substantiate the claim itself.

The Meiji government, however, decided to solve the tension diplomatically. While France secretly offered to form an alliance with Japan, the government signed the Tientsin Treaty with Qing China. This decision was, in part, a result of Japan's status vis-à-vis Euro-America: Japan had yet to successfully renegotiate the unequal treaties. Still subjected to the treaties it signed in 1858, Japan was yet to be categorized as a 'civilized' nation by Euro-America, and though it could rhetorically represent itself as a civilized nation, it could not act with such agency. Perhaps it is more accurate to say that precisely because they could not *act* like a 'civilized' nation, they repeatedly represented themselves as such rhetorically. It is not a coincidence that, ten years later in 1894, Japan entered the Sino-Japanese War immediately after its successful renegotiation with Great Britain.

One other factor needs to be considered in order to understand the Meiji government's decision to take diplomatic measures so as to ease the tension with Qing China. Immediately after the Imo Mutiny in 1882, a future confrontation with Qing China began to appear unavoidable. The Meiji government thus saw the need to strengthen its national army and devised an eight-year long plan, beginning with the issuance of *gunjin chokuyu* (the Imperial Rescript of Soldiers and Sailors) of 1882. However, when the Kôshin Incident occurred in Korea, it was only the second year of the devised plan, and to make matters worse, the nation was in repression because of the Matsukata deflation policy instituted specifically to increase military spending. Japan was in no position to go to war, militarily or financially. Tokutomi Sohô, who was among the few to write against the immediate use of force (nothing to be valorized as an anti-war campaign, however), claimed, 'people already suffer from the hardship imposed on them by taxes, unable to eat day by day. From what pool are we going to pay for the war?'[29] The *minken*-supported uprisings that were carried out across the nation were primarily because of financial hardships. The 'rich nation, strong army' (*fukoku kyôhei*) was clearly in the process of being developed.

Japan, however, could certainly not rid itself of its self-defined status as 'the leader of Asia.' It had to do everything in its power to protect its position as the first in the path toward civilization. Yet Japan could neither realistically act out its claim, nor accept the emptiness of its rhetoric. This was the condition in which Fukuzawa published his 'Datsu-a ron.' After repeating the clichéd narrative of how Japan embraced modern civilization and left the backward confines of Asia, Fukuzawa continues in the following manner.

> The most unfortunate is the existence of the two neighboring countries, one called China, and the other Korea. . . . Men of these nations know nothing of progress or development, whether it be of an individual or of a nation. In this age of travel and mobility, it is not that they have not seen the things of civilizations, but what they see and hear is not enough to move their hearts. Their emotions simply choose to long for the old-fashioned ways, and they are no different from a hundred, a thousand years ago. . . . From the Westerners' perspective, the three countries are close in proximity; and because of that it is not without ground that the Westerners see the same in us, and evaluate us as they do China and Korea.[30]

Here Fukuzawa produces the Westerners' gaze and claims that, despite the fact that Japan had left the backward confines of Asia, it is prone, because of geographical proximity, to be categorized among nations like China and Korea that 'long for the old-fashioned way' and are not 'moved' by the ways of civilization. And to make his point, Fukuzawa states that if (and when) 'Koreans show cruelty in punishing their own people, the Japanese would also be considered to be lacking in compassion.' In this example, it is clear that he is referring to the manner in which the pro-Japanese activists who led the coup were executed in the aftermath of the Kôshin Incident. Let us further inquire into this example by turning to another narrative Fukuzawa wrote on the execution.

A month prior to the publication of 'Datsua-ron,' Fukuzawa published an article entitled 'On the Execution of Independence Party in Korea' ('Chôsen dokuritsutô no shokei'), in which he described the execution in grueling detail. The execution, from his perspective, was utterly barbaric and inhumane because not only the leaders but also their family members were executed. He claims, 'From the perspective of one with civilized emotions, the cruelty displayed makes me shatter with fear, as I feel compassion for the ill-fated people.'[31] Emphasizing that he belongs among the civilized people in his emotions, he situates the use of force as 'barbaric.' He continues,

> Observing the emotions of those in Korea, it appears that, just like the Chinese, they are combative and hostile in nature, many of which are beyond our comprehension. I believe that we are equal by official treaty. But with regards to their emotions, if they do not leave the confines of the Chinese and learn the right way of civilization, and further attain the condition in which we could relate to each other without being completely surprised, we can only categorize the Koreans among the Chinese.[32]

In this narrative scheme, the rhetorical strategy that identifies the use of force as 'barbaric' aligns itself with the evolutionary narrative of emotions. It is further transposed onto Japan, using Saigô Tsugumichi as an example. Fukuzawa claims that, despite the fact that Saigô Takamori was a 'rebel against the nation' for bringing about the Seinan war, his brother Saigô Tsugumichi had been able to occupy a central place in the Meiji government. The following sentence sums up his argument: 'Once equipped with the power to kill, there is no need to kill. This is the strength of civilization.'[33] The use of force, while necessary for any nation, should be controlled, and the ability to control it is equated with 'the strength of enlightenment.' In Fukuzawa's rhetorical scheme, 'barbaric emotions' are rendered visible in the use of force, while civilized emotions are represented by refraining from the use of force. Japan, which in reality does not have the means to use force, becomes a collective that possesses a heart and a mind of civilized men.

In short, Fukuzawa's scheme produced both the civilized emotions/interiority that controls the use of force, as well as the barbaric 'Asian' emotions that allegedly appear in the very use of force. And by 'Asian' he meant the value system that constitutes Confucian thought:

> In this age of enlightenment, they [Koreans and Chinese] uphold Confucianism for their education, and 'compassion, righteousness, courtesy, and wisdom' (*jingi reichi*) as school doctrines, and only focus on the externals of things. Yet, in reality, not only are they ignorant of fundamental rules but are morally corrupt and display tremendous cruelty, all the while showing no sense of remorse.[34]

Just as Fukuzawa attributed China's inclination to interfere with Korean 'domestic and foreign policies' to Confucian doctrines, so too are the Asian emotions that appear in their use of force attributed to the value system upheld by Confucianism such as 'compassion, righteousness, courtesy, and wisdom.' And, according to Fukuzawa, precisely because of their longing for the 'old-fashioned ways' of Confucianism, Koreans 'lost the autonomy of the spirit.'

Datsua-ron ends in the following manner:

> To go about [our foreign relations], therefore, we have no time to wait for the neighboring countries to achieve enlightenment to develop Asia together. If anything, we need to transcend them and be with Euro-America in our

> endeavor. In dealing with China and Korea, no special consideration is necessary just because they are our neighbors. We should treat them the way Westerners would. If we affiliate ourselves with bad people, we cannot avoid bad names. In my heart/mind (*kokoro*), I sever the ties with the evil people of East Asia.[35]

Inherent in the figure of '*kokoro*' (heart/mind) is the linguistic strategy I discussed earlier. 'We' will join Euro-America in the endeavor, because 'we' are equal to them in our emotions that are 'civilized' enough to control the use of force and sever ties with the 'evil people,' the barbarians who use that very force. By the conceptual figure '*kokoro*,' then, Fukuzawa differentiates Japan from China and Korea, thereby securing the identity of 'the most civilized nation in Asia.' With this rhetorical operation, Fukuzawa is able to produce a position that acts like Euro-America 'internally,' or 'in [his] heart,' and the Japanese will 'internally' treat Koreans and Chinese as Euro-Americans do. Positing the use of force as the act of a barbarian, Fukuzawa manages to conceal the reality Japan faced, namely the inability to take military action as a 'civilized' country.

It goes without saying that, if Japan were to *internally* 'sever its ties with the evil people' and join the 'civilized countries of the West,' it would be exempted from proving its 'civilized' state by any type of action. Concealing the geopolitical reality in which Japan found itself, Fukuzawa's narrative succeeds in making the rhetorical link between 'the leader of Asia' and 'Japan.'

It is now necessary to foreground the manner in which this narrative engages with the logic of 'no-prejudice, non-party affiliation' (*fuhen futô*), one of the maxims Fukuzawa promoted, in order to examine the effects of his rhetorical operation. As I suggested earlier, Fukuzawa's textual engagement in *Jiji shinpô* was limited to foreign relations, but with large domestic implications. Inherent in the logical paradigm of 'Datsu-a ron' is the effort to consolidate the nation that is divided by the numerous uprisings supported by various *minken* activists. As we have seen, 'Datsu-a ron' identifies the use of force as a barbaric act; this logic not only restrained the call for the immediate attack against China and Korea, but also situated the *minken* activists who supported the anti-government uprisings as those who had been driven to them by 'barbaric Asian sentiments.' In an indirect reference to the Osaka Incident, the last of the uprisings in 1885, Fukuzawa situates the leaders as 'outlaws.'[36]

The Osaka Incident was a failed uprising by a group of liberal party members who plotted to bring about another coup in Korea with the intention of bringing down the central (Meiji) government. It occurred in December 1885, and the leaders were caught in Osaka where the plot was discovered before it was carried out. Tokutomi Sohô, who was among the very few to voice his anti-war stance in the aftermath of the Kôshin Incident, joined Fukuzawa in criticizing the leaders of the Osaka Incident and described it as 'a deliberate act to stage *The Water Margin* in present-day Japan.'[37] In Tokutomi and Fukuzawa's linguistic paradigm, the leaders of the Osaka Incident were merely 'outlaws' who were driven by 'Asian' emotions indicative of *The Water Margin*. Inscribed in de-Asianization, therefore, was not only a rejection of Asia per se, but also a rejection of the political subject that was upheld by the *minken* activists. 'Weak men simply act out revenge by taking advantage of an opportune moment. And fearing the consequences, they create a disastrous scene as they try to get rid of the root cause immediately.'[38] This is a statement made by Fukuzawa describing the aftermath of the Kôshin Incident, but this could easily apply to the leaders of domestic uprisings.

Shôsetsu shinzui and De-Asianization

I have taken a great deal of time and space to discuss the logic of de-Asianization prevalent at the time of *Shôsetsu shinzui*'s production. We must now turn to *Shôsetsu shinzui* itself and identify the way in which Shôyô's modern *shôsetsu* specifically engages with the linguistic strategy we identified in Fukuzawa's 'Datsu-a ron.' The examination will also extend to the privileged subject of the *gakusha*, a figural embodiment of the realm of knowledge of which the modern *shôsetsu* becomes a part. But before we proceed, I must once again emphasize that the modern *shôsetsu* itself was not yet existent at the time. In order to foreground the specific ways in which the logic of de-Asianization engages with the modern *shôsetsu*, we must pay attention to the process by which Shôyô establishes the boundaries of the *shôsetsu*. To do so, it is necessary to focus, not so much on what he positively identifies as the defining characteristics of the *shôsetsu*, but on what he negates as 'inappropriate' for this medium. Let us begin our inquiry with the following passage that is most often quoted to show that Shôyô advocated the 'realistic portrayal of human emotions.'

> The writer of *shôsetsu* should concentrate on human psychology. Although the characters may be his own creation, he must not design them based on his ideas of good and bad or virtue and vice (*zen'aku jasei*). Instead, he must simply observe (*bôkan*) and copy (*mosha*) them as they are (*ari no mama*).[39]

Let us for a moment suspend the notion that *bôkan* (to observe), *mosha* (to copy), and *ari no mama* (realistic, or literally 'as it is' or 'as things are') signify realism or mimesis. When we focus on what is negated in the passage above, we find that *bôkan* and *ari no mama* are, in fact, posited in opposition to '*zen'aku jasei*' (good and bad, virtue and vice). Shôyô elsewhere claims that *zen'aku jasei* are 'superficial emotions,' inappropriate for the 'modern men' whose emotions are more complex. And the quintessential writer of such emotions was, for Shôyô, Takizawa (Kyokutei) Bakin (1767-1848), a writer of historical fiction, often adaptations of Chinese *hakuwa shôsetsu* (*baihua xiaoshuo* in Chinese) that embodied the linguistic tradition of the Chinese classics:

> Let me give an example. The eight heroes of Bakin's masterpiece *Hakkenden* are monsters of eight virtues (*jingi hakkô*). They cannot, surely, be described as human beings. Bakin's intention from the outset was to write a *shôsetsu* in which virtues would be represented in human form and to describe his characters as perfect beings using the theme of *kanzen chôaku* (encourage virtue, castigate vice).[40]

In the name of realism, what Shôyô rejected was a value system such as *zen'aku jasei* and *jingi hakkô*, the didactic/linguistic system that constituted works such as *The Water Margin* and *Epoch of the Three Kingdoms*. This was a system that was disseminated by writers like Bakin through adaptations of *hakuwa shôsetsu*. What Shôyô rejected, therefore, was the very 'barbaric' and 'Asian' emotions that allegedly appear in the use of force as Fukuzawa discussed in his 'Datsu-a ron.'

The rejection of this 'Asian' linguistic system appears most tellingly in the formula *shôsetsu*=novel that is established by *Shôsetsu shinzui*. As mentioned previously, the title of this seminal text, *Shôsetsu shinzui*, is rather misleading. It is not a descriptive piece in which the 'essence' of a pre-existing entity called '*shôsetsu*' is described. Rather, it is a prescriptive piece in which it sought to produce a new medium, defined by the formula *shôsetsu*=novel. In the standard narrative of modern Japanese literature, *Shôsetsu shinzui* is situated as a text that imitated the Western novel, but this is one that takes the formula for granted.[41] What I wish to focus on here is the choice of the term '*shôsetsu*' as a translation of the 'novel.'

The formula, *shôsetsu*=novel, was far from standardized at the time. In early-Meiji, terms like '*haishi*' and '*haikan shôsetsu*' were used to translate 'the novel,' while *shôsetsu* was used as an equivalent of 'fable' by Nishi Amane in his *Hyaku gaku renkan* (*Encyclopedia*, 1870), as well as a translation for 'old romance' by Kikuchi Dairoku's *Shûji oyobi kabun* (1880; a translation of Robert Chambers, 'Rhetoric and Belles-Lettres,' 1857).[42] Nakae Chômin translated Eugene Veron's *L'esthetique* (*Aesthetics*, 1878; published in Japanese as *Ishi bigaku*, 1883), in which he introduced a variety of literary genres including the novel, but he never used the term '*shôsetsu*.' '*Shôsetsu*' is now a standard translation of the 'novel' but the formula was produced by the valorized position *Shôsetsu shinzui* occupies in the institution of modern Japanese literature. Even *Kôjien, the* standard Japanese dictionary, cites *Shôsetsu shinzui* as a reference to define *shôsetsu*.

The sinified compound '*shôsetsu*' precedes its coupling with the novel, and, accordingly, it had its own signifieds. A dictionary entry often quotes the following passage from *Kanjô* (*Han shu*, or *History of the Han Dynasty*) to provide the first meaning of the term[43] : '*Shôsetsu* writers and *haikan* officials collected the gossip of the local area by listening to rumors on the streets.' *Shôsetsu* was thus a collection of 'small talk,' which derived from events occurring in the local community. The category of *shôsetsu* began to change in the Edo period as *hakuwa shôsetsu* such as *Epoch of the Three Kingdoms* and *The Water Margin* began to be imported from China and its adaptations were disseminated among the readership by writers like Bakin. In other words, *shôsetsu* referred to none other than the texts shaped by linguistic/value systems of *zen'aku jasei, jingi reichi,* and *jingi hakkô*, the very linguistic system that Fukuzawa and Shôyô rejected as 'Asian' and 'barbaric.' The theme that was chosen for the modern *shôsetsu*, which designated the Western novel as its telos, was the 'complex emotions' of 'civilized' beings, incidentally posited against the 'superficial' and 'Asian' emotions. De-Asianization thus clearly plays itself out in the newly established formula, *shôsetsu*=novel.[44]

Furthermore, in the opening passage of *Shôsetsu shinzui*, Shôyô describes and criticizes the proliferation of writings whose central theme is didacticism.

His main criticism against these early-Meiji writings is that they 'simply display cruelty,' and that they are 'blood-thirsty *shôsetsu*' that are produced 'to cater to the taste of the time.'[45] The manner in which didacticism is indirectly linked to cruelty and bloodthirsty characteristics coincides with Fukuzawa's description of the Korean execution. And just as Fukuzawa's linguistic strategy was directed, not only to Koreans and Chinese, but to the 'outlaws' within Japan, Shôyô's criticism is also twofold. This is marked in the absence of *seiji shôsetsu* (political *shôsetsu*), written by the advocates of the People's Rights Movement, from the genealogy of *shôsetsu* that he produces in the opening passage of *Shôsetsu shinzui*. Despite the fact that Shôyô claims that the modern *shôsetsu* should satisfy the eyes of '*gakusha* and adults,' he filters out from his genealogy the very literary works that were popular among them. *Seiji shôsetsu* generally displayed the political stance of the party to which the writers belonged. Accordingly, they were unfit as a medium to consolidate and hence produce the national community. In effect, in this filtering process, we can identify the logic that was inherent in Fukuzawa's 'autonomy of knowledge' and *fuhen futô* (no-prejudice, non-party affiliation). It is the logic of positing a single, unified nation by evading the division evident in the political arena. It is thus not a coincidence that Shôyô's criticism of 'cruelty' and the 'bloodthirsty' features of early-Meiji writings (whether this criticism is a legitimate one or not is not an issue here) coincides with his deliberate omission of the *seiji shôsetsu*.

The language Shôyô described as 'cruel' and 'bloodthirsty' should further be linked to his criticism of the People's Rights Movement, specifically with the political activists associated with the numerous uprisings. Kimura Naoe, in her book entitled, *The Birth of the Youth* (*Seinen no tanjô*), inquires into the way in which the radical activists called *sôshi* were associated with this language of *hifun kôgai*. Kimura claims that the logic of *hifun kôgai* was shaped by a 'language that clearly defined good-evil, right-wrong.' Examining numerous instances of *hifun kôgai*, she draws the conclusion that the sinified style of *hifun kôgai* composed of words 'associated with *Epoch of Three Kingdoms* and *The Water Margin* can only lead to didacticism.'[46] It is worthwhile recalling Tokutomi Sohô's description of the Osaka Incident here: 'a deliberate attempt to stage *The Water Margin* in present-day Japan.' In effect, the linguistic system that shaped (or was shaped by) a didacticism linked to the radical activists of the People's Rights Movement was the very linguistic system that Shôyô rejected in the name of *bôkan* or *ari no mama*. It is thus not a coincidence that we find both the rejection of *seiji shôsetsu* and the rejection of 'superficial' Asian emotions in Shôyô's definition of the modern *shôsetsu*.[47] This new medium, moreover, is inextricably connected to the logic of the autonomy of knowledge in that the figure it seeks to valorize is the *gakusha*, which is, as it may be expected, posited in opposition to a political subject.

Let us now consider the implication of such a medium becoming endorsed as a form of 'modern knowledge.' Despite the fact that *Shôsetsu shinzui* rejected the *shôsetsu*'s practical use by defining it as a form of art, it by no means denied its educational value. Shôyô, in fact, included a chapter entitled '*Shôsetsu no hieki*' ('the Benefits of *Shôsetsu*') in *Shôsetsu shinzui*, in which he claims that the *shôsetsu* 'makes people's character lofty' and 'appeals to man's sensibilities, arousing his finer feelings, gradually driving out lust and luring his thoughts outside the everyday world, and leading him to an awareness of a subtler kind of beauty, then he will be uplifted and made lofty.'[48] The argument he presents here coincides with one in '*Shôsetsu sôron*' ('The Comprehensive Theory of the *Shôsetsu*') where he discusses the indirect value of art forms. In effect, he situates the *shôsetsu* as a means to 'elevate' the mind of the people, or perhaps more specifically, as a means of sentimental education in the formation of the national subject.

When we examine Shôyô's fervent rejection of 'the writer's design' (*sakusha no ishô*), we will be able to see how the modern *shôsetsu* engages with the autonomy of knowledge promoted by Fukuzawa. Shôyô repeatedly claims that a writer creates 'emotions of good-evil, virtue-vice' when he uses his 'design' and thus does not portray things 'as they are.' The Asian linguistic system that embodies (and/or is constituted by) didacticism is thus linked to the writer's design in *Shôsetu shinzui*. In this logic, 'the writer's design' is identified *behind* the narrative structure of didacticism. In effect, the writer's direct manipulation is rendered visible through the 'Asian' linguistic system of didacticism. The modern *shôsetsu*, in contrast, is supposedly free of the 'writer's design,' and the readers' mind is elevated because of the value inherent in the medium (i.e., the modern *shôsetsu*) itself.[49] Let us recall Fukuzawa's argument against direct interference here. He criticized China's direct interference, an act that was specifically attributed to the Confucian system of thought, and gave validity and legitimacy to Western (Japanese) knowledge as an indirect means of enlightenment. Similarly, when the 'emotions' are liberated from the Asian linguistic system of didacticism, and are reconstituted within a new linguistic system as 'complex, civilized emotions,' the modern *shôsetsu* for the first time gains the claim to 'modern knowledge,' that is, as a form of sentimental education.

The new linguistic system that was chosen to portray the 'complex civilized emotions' was the discourse of psychology in *Shôsetsu shinzui*: 'A writer is like a psychologist. He must create his characters based on the principles of psychology.'[50] This psychology to which he refers is nothing like the psychology we have now. In discussing the methodology by which to portray characters, Shôyô claims that a writer 'must study the principles of psychology, as well as those of physiognomy and phrenology.'[51] As is evident from this passage, psychology in Shôyô's day was affiliated with disciplines of Social Darwinism such as physiognomy and phrenology, and thus formed a field of study that attempted to make the interior accessible through examination of physical features, such as nerves, bodily movements, facial features, bone structures, etc. In effect, the characters of the modern *shôsetsu* were to embody Social Darwinian discourse, an authorized 'Science' of the West (this, of course, is also 'Japanese knowledge' given that it had been translated into Japanese and gained widespread acceptance among the readership). The idealized subject of the modern *shôsetsu* thus embodies not only the severance from the Asian linguistic system of Confucianism but also embraces the Western (Japanese) knowledge of modernity. Inscribed in this idealized subject, which is ultimately posited as that which consolidates and embodies the Japanese national spirit, is the mechanism of mimicry—mimicking the colonizer while it itself is colonized.

It is of no coincidence that this idealized subject has another label, namely that of a *gakusha*. Komachida Sanji, the protagonist of Shôyô's experimental novel, entitled *Tôsei shosei katagi* (*The Character of Modern Students*, 1885), in which Shôyô tried to actualize his theory presented in *Shôsetsu shinzui*, chooses the position of a *gakusha* over becoming a politician, the institutionalized path toward success. He claims,

> There is no merit in joining a political party; in fact, only harm is done by it. One would look upon theories lightly, become an empty talker, and would not be able to play up to the role required of a *gakusha*, which is to influence public opinion.[52]

The *gakusha* that Komachida posits here is one that is positioned in direct opposition to any political party, one that sways public opinion without becoming involved in politics; it must now be clear that this figure of the *gakusha* aligns itself with Fukuzawa's autonomy of knowledge. Moreover, the renunciation of the political subject, a subject position that was rejected along with the 'Asian' linguistic system and its 'barbaric emotions,' is clearly inscribed in this scheme as well. It is thus not a coincidence that the *gakusha* in *Tôsei shosei katagi* takes a neutral position, a stance that does not 'directly' interfere.[53]

We have seen the complex ways in which the modern *shôsetsu* engages with a multitude of discursive domains, all, in one way or another, mobilized in the formation of a national subject. The manner in which the autonomy of nation and the autonomy of knowledge were mediated by the ambivalent signifier 'the spirit' decisively shaped the production of the *shôsetsu* as a form of modern knowledge. Within this medium, the instituted idealized subject was a *gakusha*, one that embodies and disseminates colonial ambivalence. In effect, this medium continues to replicate the tri-polar structure of 'Asia,' 'Japan,' and the 'West,' producing and reproducing the gaze of contempt toward Asia and that of longing for the West.

Notes

1 Ono Azusa, 'Shuku kaikô' compiled in *Waseda daigaku hyakunen shi*, vol. 1, edited by Waseda daigaku daigakushi henshûjo (Tokyo: Waseda daigaku shuppan bu, 1978), 462. All translations from the Japanese are mine, unless otherwise noted.

2 Ono, 'Shuku kaikô,' 463.

3 In 1883, he writes the following in his diary: 'I have heard that Tokyo University decided to imitate our school and begin teaching in our own language. This is something to be commended, and it is our school's victory.'

4 'Eigaku kyôkasho hyô' and 'Sankôsho hyô' compiled in *Waseda daigaku hyakunen shi*, 437-439.

5 On the concept of mimicry, see Homi K. Bhabha, *The Location of Culture* (New York: Routledge, 1994).

6 A serial entitled 'On the Separation of Politics and Knowledge' ('Gakumon to seiji o bunri subeshi') appeared in *Jiji shinpô* from January 20 to February 5, 1883. In February 1883, they were compiled and published in a book form under the title *The Autonomy of Knowledge* (*Gakumon no dokuritsu*).

7 Fukuzawa Yukichi, *Gakumon no dokuritsu* compiled in *Fukuzawa Yukichi zenshû* vol. 5 (Tokyo: Iwanami shoten, 1959), 370.

8 Fukuzawa, *Gakumon no dokuritsu*, 377.

[9] In order to avoid this criticism and downplay his connection to Tokyo senmon gakkô, Ôkuma did not attend the founding ceremony.

[10] Fukuzawa, *Gakumon no dokuritsu*, 372.

[11] Most newspapers in circulation, especially *ôshinbun* (literally 'large newspapers'), were affiliated with political parties and factions.

[12] Fukuzawa Yukichi, 'Datsu-a ron' compiled in *Fukuzawa Yukichi zenshû* vol.10 (Tokyo: Iwanami shoten, 1960), 240.

[13] Fukuzawa, 'Datsu-a ron,' 239.

[14] Fukuzawa Yukichi, *Bunmeiron no gairyaku*, compiled in *Fukuzawa Yukichi zenshû* vol. 4 (Tokyo: Iwanami shoten, 1959), 19-21. See David A. Dilworth and G Cameron Hurst trans. *An Outline of a Theory of Civilization* (Tokyo: Sophia University Press, 1973).

[15] Fukuzawa, *Bunmeiron no gairyaku*, 20.

[16] See Komori Yôichi, *Nihongo no kindai* (Tokyo: Iwanami shoten, 2000) and Komori Yôichi, *Postokoroniaru* (Tokyo: Iwanami shoten, 2001)

[17] Shibahara Takuji 'Taigaikan to nashonarizumu,' compiled in *Taigaikan, Nihon kindai shisô taikei* vol. 12 (Tokyo: Iwanami shoten, 1988), 504.

[18] For example, in 1881, when the threat of Russian forces moving south to Korea became palpable, *Tokyo nichi nichi shinbun* claimed that Japan must 'stop Russian forces on behalf of Korea,' calling for the use of force to 'protect' Korea in order to become Korea's new suzerain state in order to display Japan's 'civilized' status (February 22 and 23, 1881). However, at this time, there were newspaper columns that criticized Japan's over-confidence in its military power, such as *Tokyo mainichi shinbun*, which asked 'what do we do about the fact that our military power is not like that of England?' (February 27 and March 2, 1881).

[19] Fukuzawa Yukichi, 'Chôsen no kôsai o ronzu,' *Jiji shinpô* (March 11, 1882) compiled in *Fukuzawa Yukichi zenshû* vol.8 (Tokyo: Iwanami shoten, 1960), 30. Yasukawa Jun'nosuke, in his 'Nisshin sensô to ajia besshi shisô—nihon kindaishi zô no minaoshi' states that Fukuzawa's aggressive stance was criticized as 'an act of plunder' even by his contemporaries. The article is compiled in *Sabetsu to sensô—ningen keiseishi no kansei* (Tokyo: Akashi shoten, 1999), 171-172.

[20] 'Chôsen sajôka no ran,' *Chôya shinbun* (August 8, 1882), 'Chôsen hatashite museifu naru ka,' *Tokyo nichi nichi shinbun* (August 8, 1882).

[21] 'Kan shin no kankei ron,' *Hôchi shinbun* (August 26, 1882).

[22] Fukuzawa Yukichi, 'Gyûba Takuzô kun Chôsen ni iku' *Jiji shinpô* (January 12-13, 1883) compiled in *Fukuzawa Yukichi zenshû* vol.8 (Tokyo: Iwanami shoten, 1960), 502.

[23] As Shô rô makes apparent in his 'Datsu a nyû ô mezasu kindai nihon no ajia ninshiki,' Fukuzawa continued to support military confrontation vis-à-vis China. Shô rô, 'Datsu a nyû ô mezasu kindai nihon no ajia ninshiki' compiled in *Sabetsu to sensô—ningen keiseishi no kansei* (Tokyo: Akashi shoten, 1999), 224-225.

[24] Shô rô also makes clear that 'de-Asianization' meant 'de-Confucianism.'

[25] Fukuzawa, 'Gyûba Takuzô kun Chôsen ni iku,' 504.

[26] The Japanese term for what I render in English as 'possessed' here is *koyû*, which in present-day usage means 'specific to X.'

[27] In discussing this shift from *'yôgaku'* (Western knowledge) to *'nihon no gakumon'* (Japanese knowledge), I wish to underscore the fact that I am by no means suggesting that Japan merely imported and imitated the pre-established 'Western knowledge.' It is not possible for me to delve into the details of this shift that is clearly mediated by different paradigms of 'translation;' suffice it to say that words such as 'import' or 'imitate' that appear to invoke modernization theory can claim validity only when 'translation' is deemed transparent. The process of mimicry I have discussed above cannot be narrativized in such terms but must be examined in reference to the varying and unstable representations of the 'West,' 'Japan,' and 'Asia.' On different paradigms of 'translation,' see Sakai Naoki, 'Jobun' *Traces* (Tokyo: Iwanami shoten, 1999) and Naoki Sakai, *Translation and Subjectivity—On 'Japan' and Cultural Nationalism* (Minneapolis: University of Minnesota Press, 1997). See Komori Yôichi, *Nihongo no kindai* for how 'Japanese language' was mediated by and was produced through a variety of 'translations' from early- to mid-Meiji. See also, Lee Yeounsuk, *'Kokugo' to iu shisô—kindai nihon no gengo ninshiki* (Tokyo: Iwanami shoten, 1996), Yasuda Toshiaki, *Teikoku nihon no gengo hensei* (Tokyo: Seori shobô, 1997), and Osa Shizue, *Kindai nihon to kokugo nashonarizumu* (Tokyo: Yoshikawa kôbunkan, 1998).

[28] 'Nihonhei no buryoku o unai ni shimesu beshi' *Jiyû shinbun* (December 27, 1884).

[29] Tokutomi Sohô, 'Nisshikan jiken ni kansuru no iken' compiled in *Taigaikan*, 413.

[30] Fukuzawa, 'Datsu-a ron,' 239-240.

[31] Fukuzawa Yukichi, 'Chôsen dokuritsutô no shokei' compiled in *Fukuzawa Yukichi zenshû* vol.10 (Tokyo: Iwanami shoten, 1960), 225.

[32] Fukuzawa, 'Chôsen dokuritsutô no shokei,' 226.

[33] Fukuzawa, 'Chôsen dokuritsutô no shokei,' 222-223.

[34] Fukuzawa, 'Datsua-ron,' 239.

[35] Fukuzawa, 'Datsu-a ron,' 240.

[36] Fukuzawa Yukichi, 'Chôsen no taji' compiled in *Fukuzawa Yukichi zenshû* vol.10 (Tokyo: Iwanami shoten, 1960), 498.

[37] On Tokutomi Sohô and *Kokumin no tomo*'s view on uprisings led by the *minken* activits, see Kimura Naoe, *'Seinen' no tanjô—Meiji nihon ni okeru seijiteki jissen no tenkan* (Tokyo: Shinyôsha, 1998).

[38] Fukuzawa, 'Chôsen dokuritsutô no shokei,' 222.

[39] Tsubouchi Shôyô, *Shôsetsu shinzui* compiled in *Tsubouchi Shôyôshû Nihon kindai bungaku taikei* vol. 3 (Tokyo: Kadokawa shoten, 1974), 71. In translating *Shôsetsu shinzui*, I consulted Nanette Twine's translation, *The Essence of the Novel* Occasional Papers #11 (University of Queensland). I often quote her directly, but I have also made changes where I thought appropriate.

[40] Tsubouchi Shôyô, *Shôsetsu shinzui*, 70.

[41] Kamei Hideo, in his *'Shôsetsu' ron—Shôsetsu shinzui to kindai* (Tokyo: Iwanami shoten, 1999), criticizes the manner in which the previous research on *Shôsetsu shinzui* had been governed by the model of influence, Europe invariably being the agent of in influence and Japan the receiver of influence. Providing a new perspective by which to examine the production of *shôsetsu*, Kamei analyzes Shôyô's *'shôsetsu'* in reference to the contemporaneous views of language, history, and art.

42 Nishi Amane, *Hyakugaku renkan* compiled in *Nishi Amane zenshû* vol. 4 (Tokyo: Munetaka shobô, 1981) and *Shûji oyobi kabun* compiled in Sugaya Hiromi *Shûji oyobi kabun no kenkyû* vol. 20 of Kenkyû sensho series, (Tokyo: Kyôiku shuppan sentâ, 1978).

43 The second meaning, incidentally, is the novel, and this is where dictionaries cite *Shôsetsu shinzui* as its reference.

44 On the multiple signifieds attached to the term shôsetsu, see Fujii Sadakazu, *Nihon 'shôsetsu' genshi* (Tokyo: Taishûkan shoten, 1995) and Komori Yôichi, 'Shôsetsu wa itsu umareta no ka,' compiled in Kanai Keiko et al. *Bungaku ga motto omoshiroku naru* (Tokyo: Daiamondo sha, 1998).

45 Shôyô here also criticizes obscene and 'pornographic' works.

46 Kimura Naoe, *Seinen no tanjô*, 89.

47 Of course, *seiji shôsetsu* were not at all homogeneous; they displayed different political agendas depending on the party to which the writers belonged. Shôyô clearly rejected 'Asian' emotions that were, as we have seen, associated with the radical leftists of the Jiyûtô party. How Shôyô perceived the different *seiji shôsetsu* is, unfortunately, beyond the scope of this paper. However, given the absence of *seiji shôsetsu* from the opening passage where he creates a genealogy of the modern *shôsetsu*, it is safe to assume that he did not endorse *seiji shôsetsu* as a form of modern *shôsetsu* he aspired to create.

48 Tsubouchi Shôyô, *Shôsetsu shinzui*, 85.

49 It goes without saying that, even if the modern *shôsetsu* becomes free of the 'writer's design' associated with didacticism, it by no means becomes free of 'design' *per se*. It requires a new 'design,' perhaps one that conceals itself.

50 Tsubouchi Shôyô, *Shôsetsu shinzui*, 70.

51 Tsubouchi Shôyô, *Shôsetsu shinzui*, 163.

52 Tsubouchi Shôyô, *Tôsei shosei katagi* compiled in *Tsubouchi Shôyôshû Nihon kindai bungaku taikei* vol. 3 (Tokyo: Kadokawa shoten, 1974), 343.

53 The privileged figure of the *gakusha* embodies a complex set of issues inextricably linked to the manner in which it becomes a central figure thematized in subsequent canonical works of Japanese fiction. For a detailed analysis of this figure, see Atsuko Ueda 'Meiji Literary Historiography: The Production of "Modern Japanese Literature"' Ph. D. Dissertation, University of Michigan, 1999). What I would like to underscore here is the fact that Komachida's figure of the *gakusha* could only be a conceptual/linguistic figure at the time of *Tôsei shosei katagi*'s production. As mentioned previously, the educational domain had become a space for political battle, especially after the parliament was set to convene in 1890 in the aftermath of the Meiji 14 Incident. Accordingly, advocates of the People's Rights Movement established political parties and attempted to muster support among the voters by founding schools in which to train their supporters. At the same time, government officials began to organize the public educational system with the Imperial universities at the top in an effort to institute a system in which only the graduates of the Imperial universities would gain access to government positions, thereby institutionally excluding those educated in private schools. In 1884, for example, a private school named Shiritsu shôhô kôshûjo owned by Mori Arinori, the first Minister of Education, became a public school (present-day

Hitotsubashi University). In 1885, Tokyo Law School and Tokyo University merged, becoming the central school in which to educate future government officials. Examining Komachida's *gakusha* in light of the educational reforms, we find that he posited an 'apolitical' position within an overtly political realm. In other words, the conceptual figure of the *gakusha* that Komachida defined was realistically impossible. If Komachida had sought a position within the educational arena, the power dynamics that shape the political/education arena would have mobilized. It is thus not a coincidence that Komachida remains a student until the end of the story. However, what is important for us to note is that *Tôsei shosei katagi* conceptually posited a position outside of the already institutionalized sphere of success. At the time, the institutionalized path toward success was occupied by politicians, businessmen, and soldiers. *Tôsei shosei katagi* added a new subject position, namely that of a *gakusha*.

Part 3

Beyond Sovereignty and Subjection

THE FOLD, CINEMA AND NEO-BAROQUE MODERNITY

MICHAEL GODDARD

Introduction: Why The Fold?

It seems questionable to take Deleuze's concept of the fold, developed in relation to the philosophy of Leibniz and the art-historical period of the Baroque and apply it arbitrarily to the cinema.[1] After all, Deleuze has written extensively on the cinema, in works whose theoretical implications are far from being exhausted;[2] in fact they are only just beginning to have effects in Anglo-American film theory. Nevertheless, I would argue that the problems addressed in Deleuze's book *The Fold* are highly resonant with those in the cinema books and that the concept of the fold, first outlined in Deleuze's book on Foucault,[3] has a lot to contribute to an understanding of contemporary cinema. Furthermore, the association of the fold with the Baroque far from rules out its relevance to a contemporary practice such as the cinema since in *The Fold* Deleuze both refuses any art-historical delimitation of the Baroque, preferring instead to develop its concept more abstractly, and what is more, refers constantly to contemporary aesthetic practices and ways of perceiving the world including the cinema. After all, this concept was developed in relation to Foucault, and more specifically Foucault's attempt to re-think subjectivity in the *History of Sexuality* project,[4] and can in many ways be understood as Deleuze's own reconceptualisation of subjectivity outside of the realm of the subjection by means of which both he and Foucault had previously analysed it. It is therefore worth beginning with the concept of the fold as expressed in the *Foucault* book, before examining it in relation to baroque and contemporary aesthetic practices through a partial reading of *The Fold* itself, in order to arrive at whether a productive relationship between this concept and contemporary cinema can be developed.

Foucault, Subjectivation and 'the Foldings of Thought'

The concept of the fold is developed by Deleuze as a response to the impasse or deadlock comprised by the conflicts between and within the two dimensions that dominate the majority of Foucault's work: power and knowledge. This corresponds to Foucault's celebrated theoretical crisis in the problematic break between the first and second volumes of his *History of Sexuality.* In this gap Foucault abandoned his original project of a genealogical analysis of contemporary sexuality, in favour of an analysis of practices of the self in ancient Greece and Rome, conducted with an entirely different theoretical approach.

According to Deleuze (*F* 61-66), the dimensions of power and knowledge in Foucault's work are themselves characterized by irreconcilable divisions and conflicts. This is particularly the case with knowledge which is irreconcilably divided between the articulable and the visible, the statement and the diagram: Deleuze underlines the importance of the phrase that Foucault takes from Réné Magritte, that 'seeing is not speaking' and insists upon it as the key to Foucault's epistemology and ontology. This phrase was famously deployed by Maurice Blanchot in *The Infinite Conversation,*[5] and both Foucault and Deleuze rework Blanchot's formulation into a radical rethinking of subjectivation and exteriority. As Deleuze puts it: 'Perhaps this is the first area in which Foucault encounters Blanchot: "Speaking is not Seeing"' (*F* 61). Deleuze explicitly calls this an audiovisual problematic and goes as far as to refer to the cinema of Syberberg and Duras as models of its operations, thus underlining the links between his books on cinema and *Foucault.*[6] For Deleuze, neither the re-linking of words and things by means of the relations of forces, that is the dimension of power, nor the primacy of the statement over the visible, solves this problem, and Foucault therefore required a 'third agency' a 'non-place' (68), a new axis from which the two sides of the strata, of the audiovisual archive can be taken into account.

This dimension is first of all related to what Foucault had already identified as the force of the outside that 'continues to disrupt the diagrams and turn them upside down' (94). However this formulation is insufficient to constitute anything more than a supplement to regimes of power-knowledge, an insistence on their arbitrariness and limitation in relation to a wave of the outside capable of sweeping them away. Acts of resistance may participate in this force of the outside, but only to be restratified in new relations of power. The problem is one of 'crossing the line' (95), of no longer seeing things from the perspective of power but from the zone which escapes the operations of power and from which forces of resistance have the potential to emerge. This is of course a good description of Deleuze's own project, especially in his work with Guattari, but for Foucault, the theorist for whom the entirety of social life and discourse is permeated by power-knowledge, the idea of another dimension was a radical break that could only be pursued with the greatest caution and in an even more rigorous fashion than his previous analyses.

As Deleuze points out, this desire to cross the line is implicit from Foucault's earliest work, from his fascination with madness, through his engagement with literature especially that of Roussel to his identification with 'infamous men' (95, 82). Throughout his work Foucault supplemented his analyses of power and knowledge with the concept of a relation to the outside that was intimately related to the question of thought itself; as is evident from his engagement with Maurice Blanchot, his entire project was intimately related to this experience of the outside.[7] This, however, does not rule out any conception of an inside, despite Foucault's radical critique of interiority. Instead the interior must be reformulated as 'an inside that lies deeper than any internal world' (*F* 96) or in other words as the inside of the outside. According to Deleuze this concept is implicit in Foucault's analyses of the break between the classical and modern regimes of power in *The Order of Things*,[8] as different ways of folding the outside and constituting an inside, a depth, a density. Perhaps its strongest evocation is from *Madness and Civilisation* in which Foucault describes the Renaissance expulsion of the madman on the 'ship of fools' as follows: 'he is put on the interior of the exterior, and inversely [is] a prisoner in the midst of what of what is the freest, the openest of routes: bound fast at the infinite crossroads.'[9] This prisoner of the outside is, for Deleuze, both thought itself and also Foucault's particular conception of the double: the double is not for Foucault an exterior projection of the self, but the interior presence of the other, the 'self that lives in me as the double of the other'

(*F* 96). This interior of exteriority is clearly a conception of subjectivity, but in no way constitutes a recanting of Foucault's earlier critique of the subject; once we are speaking of a subject as an entity, we are already in the domain of power/ knowledge and therefore of subjection. Instead what is at stake in this folding of the outside is subjectivation, or the subject in a continual process of production that Foucault would analyse in the context of Ancient Greece and Rome in the second and third volumes of his *History of Sexuality.*

But why is this relation to the outside conceived of as a fold? To a certain extent this question will only be fully addressed in Deleuze's subsequent work, but for now there are two important consequences of conceiving of subjectivation in terms of the fold. The first is the idea of subjectivation as a relation to oneself derived from but autonomous from one's relations with others. If Foucault turns to ancient Greece it is not as an example of a society relatively free of the permeation of power-knowledge, and Foucault emphasizes the practices of the self he identifies are those of 'free men' defined by their place in a specific socially stratified and gendered hierarchy. Even less does Foucault see the Greeks as living in some greater proximity to being, in a world where the visible and the articulable were not yet divided allowing for a world-historical revelation of being or the unfolding of the Open, and Deleuze will go on to point out that the relation between Foucault and Heidegger is to be found elsewhere than in any ontological nostalgia (*F* 108 ff). The value of the model of ancient Greece is both less and more than this: it lies in the discovery of the bending of the outside to constitute an interiority through a doubling of force. This is the discovery of subjectivity not as an identity but as the result of daily practices of the self, which are practices of self-governing modeled on a relation to the outside: 'a relation which force has with itself, a power to affect itself, an affect of self on self ' (101). Why this is an important distinction is that it allows for a different domain to emerge that breaks free of both the moral codes of the domain of knowledge and exterior relations of power to constitute an autonomous realm of subjectivation that is no longer necessarily linked to domination. If this is a discovery of the subject, this is only as an after-effect of subjectivation which becomes an autonomous power in the sense of a capacity or a power to affect and be affected; underlying Deleuze's argument is the idea that this is as much a discovery of affect in the Spinozist sense, as it is of Greek or Roman practices.

Obviously it would be inconsistent for Foucault to maintain that these practices of the self, that are linked not only to the constitution of the self but to sexuality, could in any way be ahistorical or immune from reintegration into regimes of power-knowledge. As Deleuze puts it, Foucault is fully aware that over the long time period from the classical world to the present, 'the relation to oneself will be understood in terms of power-relations and relations of knowledge. [...] The individual is coded or recoded within a "moral" knowledge, and above all he becomes the stake in a power struggle and is diagrammatised' (103). This is the individual as the effect of power, as well as sexuality and subjectivity as the site of subjection familiar from Foucault's previous analyses. However, the recuperation of a particular mode of subjectivation belies the fact that it is continually re-invented in relation to new regimes of power-knowledge from which it detaches itself in a new way. This can already be seen in the differences Foucault identifies between the Greek emphasis on the body and its pleasures and the Roman/Christian focus on the flesh and desire, which is a completely different modality of subjectivation. The contemporary relevance of these shifting modalities can be seen in the tendency of Foucault to favour the paradigm of pleasure over desire, while Deleuze has tended to be a theorist of desire. This is not to say that either is advocating a return to an archaic conception of the subject, but rather that in different way they seek to re-invent contemporary modes of subjectivation by recourse to the memory of archaic practices. As Deleuze says, it is not so much that one identifies oneself as Greek or Roman, but that to some extent a Greek or Roman thinks in 'me' as a double or the folding of the outside of absolute memory.

This reference to memory is not arbitrary as folding is itself an operation of this absolute memory. Deleuze emphasizes a very important dimension of the shift in Foucault's thinking that occurs at this point. Whereas Foucault's previous analyses had focused on relatively short time periods corresponding to modernity and conceived of the outside as a kind of 'ultimate spatiality' (108), in the *History of Sexuality* books time takes precedence over space and the fold of subjectivation is conceived of in temporal terms as an absolute memory: 'Memory is the real name of the relation to oneself or the effect of self on self' (107). This Copernican revolution, which clearly echoes the one Deleuze diagnoses as taking place between the Movement-Image and the Time-Image in his Cinema books, is also what gives rise to a new confrontation between Foucault's thought and that of Heidegger; memory as the folding of the outside or subjectivation is co-extensive with forgetting and echoes Heidegger's phrase the 'forgetting of forgetting.'

Inasmuch as the present is forgotten in favour of the whole of the past, again an echo of the Bergsonism of the Cinema books, time becomes the ultimate exteriority whose folding is what constitutes processes of subjectivation in their autonomy from regimes of power-knowledge.

More than this, Deleuze claims that Heidegger's entire ontology is also based on a concept of the fold, that is, the fold of beings with Being. This conception of the fold is not restricted to Heidegger, and Deleuze claims that Foucault just as much took this idea from contemporary literature especially the avant-garde writer Raymond Roussel. As one of Deleuze's few other engagements with Heidegger is in terms of a comparison with the forerunner of the theatre of the absurd, Alfred Jarry, whose pataphysics he claims as a profound precursor to Heidegger's ontology,[10] it is clear that Deleuze's sympathies do not lie with the German philosopher. However there are more important reasons to distance Foucault's conception of the fold from that of Heidegger. For both Heidegger and Merleau-Ponty, according to Deleuze (*F* 110), the fold ultimately generates an opening in which seeing and speaking become inseparable and interlaced as part of the same fold of seeing-speaking whereas such a fusion remains inadmissible for Foucault whose insistence on their non-relation is maintained rather than abandoned by his conception of subjectivation. If there is any interlacing between the visible and the articulable it is only in the form of a stranglehold, a constant and reversible battle between the two forms of being, an apparatus of capture rather than a space of openness or liberation. Nor is the situation transformed in relation to the informal element of power, the relations of elemental forces before their codification in terms of knowledge. Unlike in phenomenology this is not the realm of savage experience but of strategy, the play of the unformed forces of the outside that are nevertheless subject to a strategic organization; this is the Nietzschean dimension of Foucault's thought that as Deleuze points out subtends his engagement with Heidegger. Still, this is not yet for Foucault the fold of being but merely another of its figures. It is only when force folds on itself to become self-action, thus constituting or hollowing out an inside from the outside that we arrive at the ontological fold itself. In this way Foucault arrives at an ontology that rather than being characterized by any nostalgia for a lost openness to being, instead is resolutely historical in that being is conceived of as inseparable from historically variable practices of self-constitution that express the shifting relations of force to itself. In addition to the Foucauldian questions of 'what can I know or see and articulate in such and such a condition?' and 'what can I do, what power can I claim and what resistances may I counter?' are added the equally historical questions of subjectivation: 'What can I be, with what folds can I surround myself or how can I produce myself as a subject? ' (114)

If this conception of the fold still remains opaque, and certainly far removed from the tradition of phenomenological ontology this is in part because it has a different history which Deleuze will relate in his next book to both the philosopher Leibniz and the aesthetic practices of the Baroque. Nevertheless the concept of the fold as the inside of the outside and in relation to practices of subjectivation is so central to Deleuze's subsequent conception of the fold that I would argue that the concept he develops can productively be understood as response to the Foucauldian questions outlined above.

The Fold, the Baroque and the Aesthetics of Subjectivation

Deleuze's interest in the Baroque, as Mireille Buyden has pointed out,[11] does not pre-exist his conception of the fold, and in both *A Thousand Plateaus*[12] and *Francis Bacon: The Logic of Sensation,*[13] it has no major function in his understanding of aesthetic practices; in the former it is merely lumped together with Classical art and it is Romanticism that introduces a profound break, while in the latter its play of light and shadow is merely considered a return to the Byzantine 'optical tradition' (Buydens 112). It is therefore not farfetched to claim that it was Deleuze's engagements with both the cinema and with Foucault that led him to a reconsideration of the Baroque, as a response to the problematics of subjectivation implicit throughout the former work and explicitly posed in the latter. In *The Fold* the aesthetics of the Baroque are privileged and seen as leading directly to both contemporary thought and aesthetic practices. This entails both an unconventional reading of the Baroque and of the philosopher Leibniz as the philosopher of the Baroque, both in terms of the concept of the fold; the modernity of this concept is however that it is the same one that characterized Foucault's 'inside of the outside' especially as expressed by both the Baroque house and Leibniz's concept of the monad.

For Deleuze, Baroque aesthetics departs from the Classical model of distinct forms and representation in favour of 'an operative function, [...] it endlessly produces folds' (*TF* 3). This can be on the most literal level in that Deleuze refers to the preponderance of folds of material, the textures of material objects and the distortions of curvilinear space as so many concrete examples of folding in both Baroque painting and architecture. However these folds that occur in matter, are only one level of the fold, which are supplemented by another level that Deleuze does not hesitate to call the 'folds of the soul,' and it is this second level that is related to subjectivation or the fold as we have been examining it in the work of Foucault. This co-existence of two levels is not arbitrary, but derives from both the tendency of having two levels in paintings related to heaven and earth respectively and especially the design of the Baroque house. Rather than reinforcing transcendence, this co-existence of two levels destabilises it by insisting on the interpenetration between the material and the spiritual. It is therefore worth examining the Baroque house, or at least Deleuze's version of it, to see how it could constitute an allegory for the labyrinthine operations of the fold.

The basic composition of this house is of a large lower level, open to the outside world, above which is built a closed private room, which in the place of any windows is decorated by folded draperies. This allegorical organization is the same as Leibniz's monad that will be examined next and which, while being materially located in the world, has a closed off soul or unity that Leibniz states also has 'no windows' (4, 27). We would seem to be a long way from Deleuze's philosophy as it is usually understood or materialist conceptions more generally, but before making rash judgements it is necessary to proceed further. If matter is conceived of as made up of folds rather than discrete units then as a whole it is porous and cavernous; an accumulation of labyrinthine folds within folds. This is what is being expressed in the Baroque tendencies towards not only folded and heterogeneous materials, but also a curvilinear conception of space. More than this, however, it implies a temporal dimension in which rather than a static outlook on reality, or an eternal structure, a painting or a building becomes an operation on external materials that folds them in a certain manner, implying at the same time their potential unfolding or refolding: in other words the aesthetic object becomes a duration, a relative stabilization of chaotic forces (5).

As Deleuze points out there is an affinity with this conception of the fold and organic life, which is similarly composed of folds and pleatings (7). From the Baroque perspective, while organic life is distinct from inorganic matter, both are subject to forces, which fold and bend their forms in a remarkable continuity; there is in addition to a spirit in beings a spirit in matter, a point of unity that paradoxically unifies a material undergoing continual change. The distinction is not between different types of matter but between different forces; while all matter is affected by external, active forces, it is only in organic matter that these external forces are supplemented by plastic forces, which hollow out an inside or generate endogenous rather than exogenous folds. Furthermore, organic life is not more natural, but rather more machine-like than inorganic matter in that it transforms the mechanisms of material forces into the constitution of a machine, that then has the capacity to transform its surrounding environment; in other words it operates by autopoiesis or self-constitution. This is the place of passage between the material and the spiritual: if the organism has the capacity not only to transform its own forces, but those of its surrounding matter, then it has become a kind of unifying machine for the interiorisation of the outside. This is the very process that generates a soul in the Baroque sense, a process that is entirely immanent, yet on another level to material processes.

This conception of the soul is therefore not as a dichotomy between soul and body but as an indissociable yet non-localisable relation between them that is the same folding of force by itself that was discussed in relation to Foucault. In a sense it is nothing more than the principle of movement on the one hand and duration on the other that enables a living being to traverse space and endure over time, hence the connection between Leibniz's philosophy with both Bergson's conception of the élan vital[14] and Deleuze's Bergsonist account of the cinema. The point is that this folding creates a space no longer dependent on the external forces from which it emerged, and therefore allows for an immanent conception of subjectivity, which will be examined next: Leibniz's celebrated figure of the monad.

Leibniz's conception of the monad is inseparable from his development of what Deleuze calls Baroque mathematics (*TF* 17) that as in architecture and painting is now based on curves rather than straight lines. The system of differential calculus that Leibniz developed is based on the variations of curves rather than the classical Euclidean geometry of straight lines, and its contemporary consequences go as far as the figures of Rene Thom's catastrophe theory and fractal geometry. The inflections or variations of curves or series necessarily refer to an event rather than a state of reality, and prioritise vectors of transformation or folds over rectilinear axes. This leads to a very contemporary reformulation of the object as an objectile, subject to continual variation and fluctuation that is more a process of modulation than a spatial mold. All of this was already implicit in Baroque architecture, but Leibniz's mathematics clearly underlines its contemporaneity.

Given this re-formulation, the subject is also reconceived as a 'concavity,' which is defined as a particular point of view. It is here that Leibniz's philosophy anticipates both contemporary perspectivalism and the cinema; if the subject as monad is defined as a point of view, it is clear that a film, sequence, shot or moment could be understand as a kind of monad, a point of view from a particular place. The crucial aspect of this conceptualization is that point of view precedes rather than expresses the subject, which is defined as 'what comes to [...] or rather what remains in the point of view' (19). According to Deleuze this subject is now a 'superject,' which is not so much the variation of a subject but a point of view on variation which gives rise to a subject. In other words the subject is what the exteriority of variation can be folded or enveloped in: a particular perspective. This enveloping in a point of view is what generates a soul through the inclusion of exterior folds. This is precisely Leibniz's Monad: it is self-enclosed in that it envelops and closes off a certain region of the outside, yet without the openness to this outside it would never be constituted. Perhaps it can best be understood as a process of complication: it complicates the divergent exterior variations by including them in a unity or point of singularity inseparable from these variations.

This raises the question of whether there is a single point of view that encompasses all the others, the monad of monads, which would be the point of view of the universal spirit or God. The problem is raised because each monad as a point of view on infinity potentially contains the world in its entirety as perceived from a particular place. The concept of a world-spirit or universal point-of-view is inadmissible however, since although each monad is in the same world, it sees this world from a particular perspective and therefore sees a particular region clearly and the rest increasingly vaguely. Therefore each monad is absolutely singular and could not be encompassed in any over-arching point of view. This is Leibniz's idea that points of view are incompossible, and therefore cannot be incorporated in a higher unity. Each monad implies a particular world that while the same world as that of the other monads, is at the same time an incompossible configuration of the world that is absolutely singular. In other words, the relations between monads considered as subjects and the world is one of actualization: 'subjects all relate to this world as if to the virtuality that they actualise' (26). The virtual world that each monad inhabits is the same, but each actualisation is entirely different, and only given in the foldings that a particular monad performs in relation to its virtual milieu. It is worth noting that Deleuze contrasts Leibniz's conception with that of Heidegger at this exact point, since instead of being-in-the-world, the relation of Leibniz's monads is one of being-for-the-world thus 'giving the world the possibility of beginning over and again in each monad' (26). The relation between the world and the subject is that of the fold, and it is this relation that is expressed in Baroque art and architecture, which can now be considered as the reduplication in matter of the monadic 'folds in the soul.'

Bringing together the conception of the monad with Baroque architecture, what does it mean to assert that the monad has no windows, by which anything could go in or out? In the case of the Baroque house this is achieved through the separation between the interior space of the upper room and the outside, a space which is entirely enclosed: no windows. According to Deleuze the architectural ideal would be a room of black marble, in which 'light enters through orifices so well bent that nothing of the outside can be seen through them, yet they illuminate or colour the décor of a pure inside' (28). These withdrawn interiors can be seen in the Baroque love of mirrors, *trompe l'oeil* effects and significantly the *camera obscura* which operates by bending and reversing light rays inside an otherwise closed internal space. Corresponding to this interior is the façade or false front that although riddled with holes, allows no direct access to the interior room. It is the separation of the façade from the interior that defines Baroque architecture and makes it an allegory of Leibniz's monadic subjectivity. In this situation the inside and outside are linked in a new way, particularly by the division into two floors. The ground floor is therefore just an extension of the outside, while the upper floor is the closed off monadic interior.

This organization is not only repeated in the baroque painting of El Greco or Tintoretto (30), but can be seen in contemporary aesthetic projects such as Mallarmé's conception of the total book (31). The book as monad that includes the whole world and yet is closed off from it, is a Baroque idea, and one that according to Deleuze can be applied to Leibniz's own writing: both Leibniz and Mallarmé dreamed of the total book, while nevertheless working in fragments. However, the monad is precisely this folding together of fragments, of the visible and the legible, the outside and the inside. As we saw in relation to Foucault, these two forms can never be entirely fused but nevertheless it is through monadic subjectivation that they may be re-linked whether through the unlocalisable connections between sound and image in contemporary cinema, or in this case the emblems and allegories of Baroque and Neo-Baroque writing.

These contemporary connections call into question the very concept of the Baroque, which has been a particularly problematic one in art history. There have been attempts to restrict the Baroque to architecture as well as to overly determined locations and time periods, that only function through the exclusion of much of what can be considered Baroque: there are after all Baroque tendencies in many cultural traditions, and they don't necessarily coincide with the conventional period of the Seventeenth Century. Other commentators have denied that the Baroque ever existed. More productive engagements with the Baroque have been in conceptual terms such as Knecht's 'Coincidence of Opposites,' or Christine Buci-Glucksman's concept of a 'dialectics of seeing and gazing' (33) but for Deleuze these definitions lack the necessary precision to fully define the Baroque. A more interesting attempt is Walter Benjamin's definition of the Baroque in terms of allegory understood as the autonomy of the fragment in relation to the whole (125). This conception is clearly influential on Deleuze, and is certainly exemplified by the Baroque taste for emblems and allegories which operate as just such fragments and which destabilise any concept of a single homogenous world. However, this is not sufficient to characterize the Baroque as it does not explain the relations between these fragments and both other fragments and the configurations in which they appear.

To sum up, the concept of the fold that Deleuze identifies first in relation to Foucault and subsequently in relation to Baroque thought and aesthetics, provides a complex conception of subjectivation, relevant to contemporary thought as well as practices. As such it is not so much a conception of the subject, but a way of conceiving the genesis of subjectivity, or how an interiority comes into being in a specific duration as the folding of a particular outside. In this way, Deleuze's book *The Fold* could be read as an unanticipated sequel to Foucault's *History of Sexuality* project, one that is even further removed from any conventional idea of sexuality or identity, but that has a strong relation to Foucault's concept of practices of the self; except that these practices are now taking place collectively in the sphere of aesthetic experience. It is still a case of an aesthetics of existence, but now conceived of as a way of inhabiting or actualising the world, rather than as a project of self-governing.

The question remains as to what this concept of the fold can contribute to an engagement with contemporary aesthetic practices, and with the cinema in particular. Rather than pursue all the multiple resonances between *The Fold* and modernity, I will focus on two inter-related points of connection between Deleuze's concept of the fold and cinema. These two points are the relations between the Baroque as Deleuze conceives it and contemporary aesthetic practices in general and the connections between the concept of the Fold and the operations of cinema as an apparatus that can be productively understood in relation to the concept of the fold.

The Baroque and Contemporary Aesthetics

Deleuze is, of course, not the first theorist to posit a direct link between the Baroque and contemporary aesthetics. Walter Benjamin, notably in his *Origin of German Tragic Drama*[15], and in his engagement with the poet Charles Baudelaire[16] saw the most radical potentials of modern aesthetic practices as being strongly linked with the Baroque. As Christine Buci-Glucksman has pointed out,[17] this is largely through a reversal of the romantic understanding of allegory. Instead of seeing Baroque allegory as an impoverished conventional sign in relation to the symbol by means of which a fragment can represent an absent whole, Benjamin saw allegory as a type of indirect language in which the fragment is wrested away from the economy of representation, and the allegorical figure is separated from meaning: 'through a veritable fragmentation of image, line, graphic art and even language it breaks up reality and represents time through hieroglyphs and enigmas' (Buci-Glucksman 70). In other words the allegory decentres the idea of the world as totality in favour of a fragmentary conception that is strikingly modern. As Buci-Glucksman points out, allegory 'anticipates the role of shock, montage and distancing in the 20th Century avant-garde' (70) through its privileging of the fragment over the whole and feeling over reason. This is precisely what Benjamin found developed in the work of Baudelaire whose poetry testifies to a world in fragments in which the shock of modernity announces itself by means of a modern re-invention of baroque aesthetics of allegory.

There is a very strong connection between Benjamin's account of the modernity of Baroque allegory and Deleuze's concept of the fold. However, whereas for Benjamin allegory was purely destructive of the concept and privileges feeling over reason, for Deleuze it is emblematic of a new manner of thinking as well as characterizing aesthetic practices. This is a crucial difference because it enables a richer account of what it is in the Baroque that is repeated in contemporary aesthetic practices, namely the fold as a modality of subjectivation and its relation to the world.

For Deleuze, the Baroque model of the monad is highly resonant with contemporary aesthetic practices since it is a way of thinking of subjectivity as process in relation to a world that is not given as a totality but as an infinite potential. Furthermore, the idea of works of art as the folding of divergent series in allegorical figures, characterizes not only contemporary tendencies in visual arts but also literature and music; Deleuze refers to the divergent series in the novels of Joyce, Borges and Gombrowicz (*TF* 81) as well as in serial music as examples of how this Baroque concept of the fold pervades some of the most radical examples of contemporary aesthetics. Nevertheless there is not an identity between this modern experimentation and the Baroque, since after all, Baroque systems, including Leibniz's philosophy, tend to rely on a concept of God, however immanently conceived.

For Deleuze the difference between Baroque aesthetics and the Neo-Baroque experience of the contemporary world can be seen in the difference between Leibniz's conception of incompossible worlds and Whitehead's contemporary conception of the event. The concept of incompossibility is one of Leibniz's most original contributions to philosophy, and as Daniel Smith points out, 'Leibniz here creates an entirely new logical relation of incompossibility, which is a relation that is irreducible to impossibility or contradiction. At the level of existing things, it is not enough to say that a thing is possible in order to exist; it is also necessary to know with what it is compossible.'[18] While there is an affinity between Whitehead's events or prehensions and Leibniz's monads, Leibniz's accounting for the divergences between monads as taking place in incompossible worlds is abandoned in favour of a motley world in which all the variations and divergences cannot be captured in expressive units. In Deleuze's words 'in the same chaotic world divergent series are endlessly tracing bifurcating paths. It is a chaosmos' (*TF* 81). This transformation from world to chaosmos necessarily has a profound effect on subjectivation, which ceases to be monadic and becomes dissonant or nomadic. This is because it is impossible either to contain or unify the entire chaosmos, or to select a defined position or stable point of view upon it: the death of the world leading to the destabilizing of the monadic subject. For Deleuze, this difference, which is expressed both in Art Brut and atonal or serial music, can be summed up as the transformation from Baroque monadism to contemporary nomadism:

> To the degree that the world is now made up of divergent series (the chaosmos) [...] the monad is now unable to contain the entire world as if in a closed circle that can be modified by projection. It now opens on a trajectory or a spiral in expansion that moves further and further away from a centre. [...] Stockhausen's musical habitat or Dubuffet's plastic habitat do not allow the differences of inside and outside, of public and private, to survive. They identify variation with trajectory and overtake monadology with nomadology. (137)

This is not however a rejection of the Baroque concept of the fold, but merely its reworking in relation to modernity and its breakdown of the unity of the relation between the subject and the world. It is this nomadic conception of subjectivity as the transitory folding of the chaotic outside that corresponds to the model of subjectivation that Deleuze identified in Foucault's project; nevertheless the monad and allegory still provide a crucial model for how this subjectivation operates, and both contemporary aesthetics and subjectivation can still be characterized in terms of the fold. It is in terms of both this connection and divergence from Baroque aesthetics that the relevance of the fold to the cinema should be understood.

The Fold, the Cinematic Apparatus and Spectatorship

At this point it is necessary to return to the question of the relevance of the fold to the cinema. There are several ways in which the concept of the fold seems particularly relevant to cinema as an apparatus, and its relations to subjectivity. The most obvious of these is that the concept of the monad as defined as a particular point of view. As Deleuze points out this is a very modern conception and is not the same concept as the point of view of classical perspective; in the classical conception, point of view belongs to a static subject and what they see is a representation, that is a window on the world that lies behind the image. In contrast, the monadic point of view is a particular actualization of a virtual world, a manner of seeing the world in a particular way that gives rise to a subject. In this way it is related to the conception of viewing positions in film studies,[19] although conceived in a more dynamic and metamorphic manner. Not only does the monadic conception of point of view reverse the relations between point of view and subjectivity, but it also constitutes a more precise and more abstract conception of subjectivity. In relation to cinema, the concept of the monad could apply to the viewer of a film, the film itself or any of its constitutive parts; even a single shot constitutes a particular point of view and thereby a subject, and through cinema's combination of successive shots, the capacity to include multiple variations enables a particular actualization of the world. Deleuze's description of the monad as seeing a particular part of the city clearly and other regions more vaguely, seems to suggest a cinematic experience of depth of field, just as the cinematic variations of light and framing resonate with the Baroque emphasis on charioscuro and curvilinear space. However, all of this is still to keep within the confines of the shot.

The combinations of shots through editing leads to another resonance with the fold, namely the conceptualisation of cutting as folding. What takes place when we view two different perspectives on the same event? It is only secondarily that we can say that what we see are representations of the points-of-view of cinematic characters. In the first instance, what we perceive is the folding of two or more views on variation into a more complex point-of-view. From this perspective it is not the individual shot that is monadic, but the overall sequence or film that constitutes a folding of views into a complex yet unified system. It would be arguable that this is more a collection of monads or a nomadic multiplicity rather than a unity, depending on the type of film that is being projected: perhaps it is only the type of cinema that Deleuze analysed in terms of the movement-image that gives rise to a monad, but the point is that the relations between successive shots can be productively understood as an operation of folding, rather than the more conventional concept of cutting.

Furthermore, this allows for a new conception of movement within a shot, since just as the sequence shot has been understood as cutting within the same shot, it can also be understood as a more continuous process of folding in which the shifting of point of view folds and unfolds the material of the outside. It is as much this transformation within a shot rather than the succession between shots that resonates with the concept of the fold, since it allows for the combination of subjectivation as a process of folding with the unity of a particular point of view, even if it has become mobile and dynamic.

Finally the temporality of the monad expressed in the idea of the fold as a temporary stabilization or actualisation of a continual flux is highly applicable to the cinema which as Deleuze has shown is above all a temporal art. While Deleuze does not use an explicitly Leibnizian framework in his cinema books on this point, the concept of cinema as a direct presentation of time has clear links to a Leibnizian or Baroque conception of the world. This is particularly the case since Deleuze explicitly associates the direct presentation of time in contemporary cinema with the opening of a spiritual dimension entirely immanent in the material world yet distinct from the transformations of matter. Like the Baroque house, the cinema for Deleuze is also constructed of two floors, the first of which consists of the transformations of matter in movement, and the second of which extracts from these movements a spiritual movement that Deleuze refers to as a pure optical and sound situation. The arrangement of these allegorical images that disrupt the distinctions between the real and the imaginary, the past and the present and the virtual and the actual results in an inorganic crystallisation of affect which Deleuze refers to as the crystalline regime of signs.[20] It should be clear that the Baroque aesthetics of folding, with its relation to the world of actualization rather than representation, and the indiscernability of the real and the imaginary through the cultivation of *trompe-l'oeil* effects and the *camera obscura* clearly anticipates this arrangement of cinematic signs. Furthermore the association of the temporal and the virtual with the spiritual, that is, as the crystallization of the outside into an interiority that is nothing other than duration, itself is a highly Baroque approach to both subjectivation and the spiritual.

In this regard it is worth noting that Deleuze refers to Leibniz twice in *The Time-Image,* the first time in relation to the still-lifes in the cinema of Ozu, which have clear spiritual resonances and the second time in relation to the concept of the 'powers of the false' of crystalline narration (125-155). This latter reference is interesting since it anticipates the fold by its association of contemporary cinema, the writing of Borges and non-Euclidean geometries. In this context Deleuze understands Leibniz's monadic conception of incompossible worlds as being the most ingenious and strangest solution to the crisis that time constitutes for the concept of truth. The concept of incompossibility is an attempt to save the concept of truth by positing different worlds in which a particular event does or does not take place; in one world the battle takes place whereas in another it doesn't so that the contingency of undecidable temporal alternatives is resolved. It is just a question of knowing which incompossible world you are in, depending on whether the event does or does not take place. However, in modern aesthetics these undecidable alternatives or divergent series are located in one and the same world, so that the event both does and doesn't take place in the same world. This is exemplified by the Borges story, 'The Garden of Forking Paths'[21] in which these undecidable alternatives become a labyrinth of incompossible but co-existing presents, giving rise to different pasts as undecidable alternatives any of which may or may not be true. In Deleuze's words this temporal undecidability 'substitutes the power of the false for the form of the true, and resolves the crisis of truth [...] but, in opposition to Leibniz, in favour of the false and its artistic, creative power' (Deleuze, *Cinema 2* 131). Perhaps Deleuze would not have needed to stress this opposition to the same extent had he already developed the concept of the fold, as it allows for the difference between the Leibnizian or Baroque incompossibility and its modern transformation to be understood as different yet related modalities of subjectivation, or different foldings that give rise to different subjectivities: the transformation from the Baroque monadic to the modern or rather modernist nomadic subject.

In the end the concept of the fold, from Foucault's reconceptualisation of subjectivation to Deleuze's analysis of Leibniz and the Baroque, is a tool not so much for understanding the past, but rather for a 'history of the present,' or in other words for grasping modernity as an event that folds and refolds its multiple pasts through particular practices. As such the fold is a productive concept not only for both a re-thinking of cinema and other modern aesthetic practices and subjectivation, but also provides the basis for a remapping of modernity itself outside of the now ossified discourse of postmodernity. Rather than continually asking ourselves the global question of what era we are in, it suggests a more specific interrogation of the practices we are involved with, how they actualize virtual forces, constitute particular modes of subjectivation and generate singular points of view. The concept of the fold therefore emphasises not only the modernity of the Baroque, but also the Baroque or Neo-Baroque tendencies of modernity. As Deleuze puts it, in the era of modernity: 'we are discovering new ways of folding [...] but we all remain Leibnizian because what matters is folding, unfolding, refolding' (*TF* 137).

Notes

1 Gilles Deleuze, *The Fold: Leibniz and the Baroque,* trans. Tom Conley (Minneapolis and London: Minnesota University Press, 1993). Subsequent page references to this text will appear parenthetically as *TF.*

2 See Gilles Deleuze *Cinema 1: the Movement-Image* and *Cinema 2: the Time-Image* (London: The Athlone Press, 1986, 1989).

3 Gilles Deleuze, *Foucault,* trans. Sean Hand (London: The Athlone Press, 1986). Subsequent references to this text will appear parenthetically as *F.*

4 See especially Michel Foucault, *The History of Sexuality Volume One: An Introduction,* trans. Robert Hurley (Harmondsworth: Penguin, 1981, 1984) and *Volume Two: The Use of Pleasure,* trans. Robert Hurley (London: Viking Books, 1986).

5 Maurice Blanchot, *The Infinite Conversation,* trans. Susan Hanson (Minneapolis: University of Minnesota Press, 1993).

6 See *F* 65.

7 See *Foucault, Blanchot,* trans. Brian Massumi and Jeffrey Mehlman (New York: Zone Books, 1987), esp. 'the Experience of the Outside,' Michel Foucault, 15-19.

8 Michel Foucault, *The Order of Things: An Archaeology of the Human Sciences* (London: Tavistock, 1970).

9 Michel Foucault, *Madness and Civilisation: a History of Insanity in the Age of Reason,* trans. Richard Howard (London: Tavistock, 1967), 11.

10 Gilles Deleuze, *Essays Critical and Clinical,* trans. Daniel W. Smith and Michael A. Greco (London: Verso, 1988), 91-98.

11 Mireille Buydens, *Sahara: L'Esthetique de Gilles Deleuze* (Paris: J. Vrin Librarie Philosophique, 1990).

12 Gilles Deleuze and Felix Guattari, *A Thousand Plateaus,* trans. Brian Massumi (Minneapolis: University of Minnesota Press, 1987).

13 Gilles Deleuze, *Francis Bacon: Logique de la Sensation* (Paris: Editions de la Difference, 1996).

14 On the Élan Vital see Gilles Deleuze, *Bergsonism* (New York: Zone Books, 1988), 91-113.

15 Walter Benjamin, *The Origin of German Tragic Drama,* trans. John Osborne (London: NLB, 1977).

16 See Walter Benjamin, *Charles Baudelaire: A Lyric Poet in the Era of High Capitalism* (London: NLB, 1973).

17 Christine Buci-Glucksman, *Baroque Reason: The Aesthetics of Modernity,* trans. Patrick Camiller (London: Sage Publications, 1994).

18 Daniel W. Smith, 'On the Nature of Concepts: Deleuze, Leibniz and the Calculus,' unpublished conference paper (Sydney: ASCP, 1999).

19 See for examples of this approach, Linda Williams ed., *Viewing Positions: Ways of Seeing Film* (New Brunswick, New Jersey: Rutgers University Press, 1995).

20 Deleuze, *Cinema 2,* 68-97.

21 In Jorge Luis Borges, *Labyrinths,* trans. Donald A. Yates (Harmondsworth: Penguin, 1970).

Taiwan Incorporated:
A Survey of Biopolitics in the Sovereign Police's Pacific Theater of Operations

Jon D. Solomon

From a normative perspective, Taiwan, the Republic of China, might be simply proceeding, with more or less difficulty, along a heroic path against the odds that repeats the processes culminating in the constitution of a modern nation-state, linking territory to language, people, and market in a struggle for popular sovereignty, or, as one recent work in English, part of a series dedicated to 'Taiwan in the modern world,' blithely proposes, 'national identity and democratization.'[1] Our goal in this essay is not to negate the meaning of this very real struggle, but to pose questions to the framework within which it acquires meaning.

In order to gain a cogent understanding of Taiwan's current situation that does not rely upon a narrative of historical repetition (establishing nation-State based on a 19th century ideal), it will be necessary not only to consider the filiation of power within Taiwan, but also to consider Taiwan's position within the nexus of sovereign power in the Pacific (if not around the globe). Given the complexities of today's world, we can no longer appeal to such problematic notions as, 'the current stage, at which the sovereign nation-state system still forms the mainstream of history,' nor to 'the [present] conditions under which the national polity forms the unique context of political institutions,'[2] without running the risk of masking new political and economic relations that cannot be construed through the normative model of State, and even popular, sovereignty. It is necessary, hence, for thought to make visible the exceptional status of sovereign power in Taiwan, to see it against the horizon of U.S. Imperial sovereignty, and to uncover the biopolitical aspects of the global crisis of sovereignty.

Largely determined by juridical, economic, and security considerations, Taiwan's relation to the United States requires certain caution on the part of those who would set a critique in motion, lest it be misconstrued for a kind of simple neo-colonialist argument. Of course, there are important, perhaps even determining facets of this relationship, such as the incorporation of important productive sectors in Taiwan, now one of the world's largest regions in the production of semi-conductors, in the formidable U.S. military-industrial complex, or again, the new kinds of diplomatic initiatives pairing the State with NGOs in development projects in Africa and Central America, which ought to be taken into account. Hence, it weighs heavily upon my mind to inform the reader that this paper simply cannot substitute for what I consider absolutely necessary but am unable to provide: a definitive, penetrating account of the relations between violence, the frontier, technology and production in the Pacific. However, Taiwan, the Republic of China, being such an exceptional place, ought to provide an excellent nodal point for understanding the complex relations between sovereign power, law, and technology in our world.

The work in this essay thus proceeds from this essential question: What would happen to perspectives on Taiwanese independence (or, if you prefer, Chinese sovereignty) if we no longer accept national subjectivity as the normative form of sovereignty at all but look instead at the real changes in sovereignty today? Our answer to this question is, in brief, that once we refuse this imperative, it becomes possible to see Taiwan's position in terms of a global process in which the exceptional situation of sovereign power, now typified by American martial rule, has become a permanent state of emergency and a global norm that affects the construction of sovereignty and national subjects everywhere.

The Logic of Sovereignty and Imperialist Expansion: The Status of Permanent Exception

Taiwan exists in an exceptional space. When we say 'exceptional,' we do not mean just different or superlative. We speak instead of the status of the exception, the inclusive exclusion, which is at the heart of sovereign power. Before we proceed to examine the specific position of Taiwan in relation to sovereignty, let us try to frame the concept of sovereignty in a way that will explain the working paradigm of this essay.

An understanding of sovereign power based on the notion of the exception most likely will invite association with the work of Carl Schmitt, a major German legal thinker of the 20th century who provided much of the theoretical basis for the Nazi regime. Although Schmitt ostensibly worked for the goal of buttressing the Weimar Republic, his ideas like his person lent active support to the Nazi cause. Our concern in this essay is neither with Schmitt nor with the debate around his work; instead, we follow the critique of Schmitt's understanding of sovereign power advanced by Giorgio Agamben in *Homo Sacer* (1995).

The novel force of Schmitt's work on sovereign power lies largely in identifying exception and decision as the essential elements of its internal structure. Of course, classical thought always construed the sovereign in terms of the power of decision, particularly the power to decide on the death of subjects, internally, and the power to declare war, externally. Schmitt, however, takes this further by recognizing that the position of the decision-maker itself is the key to regulating social relationships, and hence must be thematized. In Schmitt's eyes, the defining social relationship of the political is that between friend and enemy. In order for this potentially violent relationship to constitute itself as the essentially closed totality of a sovereign nation, it is necessary for there to be another position from which this relation can be apprehended in such a way as to distinguish it from a position that is simply foreign or external. The sovereign is thus that position which stands outside this relation. In contrast to Liberalism's theorization of the revolutionary situation at the end of Absolutism, however, Schmitt does not endow this position with an abstract rationality. For Schmitt, the position of the sovereign is fully implicated in the political configuration, yet also provides the only position from which it would be possible to adjudicate on it. Whereas Liberal thought posits a transcendental position of rationally formalized rules (the rule of law) that insures the basis of legitimacy for State power, Schmitt tries to ground it in the contingent fluidity of a deformalized, decisionist position.

For Giorgio Agamben, Schmitt's initial error occurs in the way in which he separates the position of the sovereign from the constitution of the political as such. Of course, the sovereign, by definition, should be a position above all others, hence, in a position of non-relationship. Yet Schmitt could only escape the possibility of relation by endowing the sovereign with a decisionist character of essentially ontological proportions.[3] Where Schmitt sees the distinction between friend and enemy as the essential moment in which political power is configured, Agamben finds that the non-relation of the excluded is the constitutive matrix for understanding sovereign power. In any specific, concrete political situation, this excluded position will be, by definition, theoretically representable, yet 'meaningless:' a meaning in effect without force. Hence, the position of the sovereign itself is but a clue — an effect — of the relationships that are themselves constituted upon the inclusion of something else by its simple, ostensibly unilateral, exclusion. This is the legitimating fiction of sovereignty in general, and it is repeated in the creation of subjects of knowledge — an idea to which we shall return in our conclusion. It is precisely this fiction that enables us — in spite of the knowledge that sovereignty never exists except as relationship (sovereign nations always come in multiple sets) — to conduct all manner of social actions with reference to a single sovereign totality and none other. Yet Agamben shows, in a series of wonderfully nuanced textual and historical readings, that the essence of sovereign power is the exception that includes something by excluding it. Hence, the sovereign position is the position that maintains a series of distinctions crucial to collective life: 'Sovereignty,' writes Agamben, 'is the guardian who prevents the undecidable threshold between violence and right, nature and language, from coming to light.'[4]

The second point on which Agamben fundamentally differs from Schmitt follows from the recognition of exclusion as the constitutive matrix of the political. Having framed the position of the sovereign in terms of 'guardian,' Agamben is able to relate the position of the sovereign to the violent operativity of the police. Indeed, the history of modern sovereignty, argues Agamben, shows a progressive entry of the sovereign into the figure of the police — to the point that in the 20th century, mass extermination occurs as a police operation administered without executive command.

This perspective entails, incidentally, the possibility of an understanding fundamentally different from that of deconstruction (not to mention dialectic). The deconstructionist would hold that, precisely because the logic of sovereignty rests on a determination of the political that is not based on the friend-enemy distinction but is rather based on the excluded, it becomes possible to describe a movement of ontological supplementarity at the heart of the history of sovereignty. Logically speaking, we would think of the subject of sovereignty not as the friendly side of the opposition between friend and enemy, but as the mixture of the two. Friend and enemy are simply two faces of sovereignty's attempt to self-ground itself without any other determination. This grounding can only be accomplished by a founding exception — a position 'given' to the sovereign and taken from the life that is condemned to exclusion. Being inherently unstable, this position requires a supplement. Deconstructive readings thus show that any 'thing' reveals itself to be insufficient in its own constitution and hence brings to light the organization of difference and the perpetual suspension of identity between two terms (identity *and* difference) through the supplement of a third, essentially unstable term. The relation between these terms is understood as a limit-possibility.

Faced with the deconstructive opening, Agamben leaves behind the notion of limit-possibility and heads towards a redefinition of ontology and politics in terms of non-relationship. The project that motivates his work is: '[to think] ontology and politics beyond every figure of relation, beyond even the limit relation that is the sovereign ban.'[5] Needless to say, the assumption of relation and representation is common to both contract theory and decisionist theory, and in this sense, Agamben's work point us towards a radically transformed field of political philosophy.

In order to pursue further the possibilities of non-relation for thinking beyond sovereignty, we would not only have to leave Agamben,[6] we would also have to thoroughly postpone our main concern here, which is the problem of sovereignty in Taiwan. It is wishful thinking indeed to pretend that complex problems of ontology and political philosophy can be summarily resolved. We have simply hoped to provide a *contextualization* for the meaning of 'permanent exception' rather than an explanation of all the issues involved. Let us turn the emphasis here toward the historical implications of this knowledge, which certainly bear upon our understanding of Taiwan.

Agamben holds that the history of the 20th century has been a process progressively revealing the essence of sovereignty. The 'breakdown' in sovereignty everywhere evident at the end of the 20th century has, in Agamben's eyes, brought to light what we were 'not supposed to see, namely what is apparent to everybody: that *the state of exception is the rule...*'[7] The state of the exception inaugurated by sovereign power is permanent in the sense that it is constitutive. Yet it is also in the nature of sovereign power to mask this essential feature of its constitution.

Let us reflect about why this permanent state of exception has been for so long — and continues to be — recognized as 'political sovereignty.' Michel Foucault, of course, advised us to think of sovereignty in terms of an 'ideology' that masks the deployment of power through 'technologies of the self.' Perhaps now we have finally arrived at an historical conjuncture when it is possible to follow the Foucauldian gesture in the opposite, yet complementary direction: now moving away from the self, towards the technologies of the collective subject, typified by national sovereignty. Here, it is necessary to depart from the Eurocentric imagination of the philosopher's discourse and return to the disavowed, founding supplement for the establishment of modern sovereignty: the creation of a territorial space called the non-West that did not possess 'sovereignty' and was considered to be open space, available for violent conquest outside the norms of European international law.

Here, we move from an ontological critique of sovereignty to an historical one — an historical critique that deserves considerably more elaboration than the schematic outline we are going to propose here. The schematic description may be useful, however, to the extent that it helps us imagine why the crisis of sovereignty, directly related to the history of European expansion, has entered a new phase in the age of the globe.

It is impossible to talk about modern sovereignty without relating it to the development of European expansion. The emergence of the inter-State system in Europe (normally traced to the Treaty of Westphalia) was concomitant with a new mode of appropriation/deterritorialization to which accrued the creation of a new subjectivity, the Western/non-Western binary opposition. Just as the subjectivity of the sovereign nation-State is constructed as the identity of a binary system characterized by the essentially non-democratic institutions of the national frontier, the national language, and the national currency, the subjective identity of the 'Unity of nations' that began in Europe itself is constituted precisely — and only — through the positing of a West/non-West opposition. Although this league of nations could be, and in fact has been, extended, quite unevenly, across the globe, what is in fact positively constituted is nothing other than the subjective identity of 'the West.' As others have observed, this identity is neither a geographical region nor a cultural unity, but a subject that gathers itself in discourse.[8] With the establishment of this totalizing and superior subjective position, the rest of the world was gradually formed into various different 'others' whose identity would be defined in relation to the West. Most of the 'non-West' only started to accede to political sovereignty after the Great War, while the entire process of decolonization itself only became fully irrevocable after World War Two. Hence, it is no exaggeration to say that the extension of sovereignty to an international league of nations spanning the globe is a very recent phenomenon. Recent enough for us to need to pose the question of the relation between sovereignty and the West/non-West binary: to what extent is the visibly apparent, global crisis of sovereignty today due to the fact that the 'outside' of the West is no longer discernible as it was during several centuries of Imperialist conquest?

With the supplement of exteriority no longer available, the essence of sovereignty as permanent exception becomes visible — even from a Eurocentric perspective. However, from an historical perspective that might be termed 'extra-European' (in the sense that it is not constituted as an 'Other' of Europe, but in a non-relation of equivalency), the essence of sovereignty could always be in the permanent state of emergency in which 'non-Western' countries (i.e., national subjects formed as 'Others' of 'the West') have existed for several centuries of colonial barbarism.

Taiwan: Ground Zero for the Enduring Crisis of Sovereignty in East Asia

The first step towards an alternative perspective on Taiwan amounts to refusing the decision foisted upon us by the nationalist appropriation of 'sovereignty.' It is only as the result of a long, European — and now irrevocably globalized — history (a history whose roots go back at least as far as the age of absolutism, when Jean Bodin advanced seminal ideas on the independence of the nation and the foundation of royal legitimacy in popular sovereignty) that we have become accustomed to the notion that 'sovereignty' refers to the independent, autonomous foundation of nation-States. Contemporary theorists, responding to the realities of a world whose complexity escapes the limits of national sovereignty, have posed questions to a whole constellation of problems surrounding the form of sovereignty itself, particularly the historical constitution of sovereignty as a world system and the philosophical constitution of sovereignty in terms of subjectivity.[9]

The framing of a problem in political philosophy is not independent of the way in which solutions are derived. Bartelson shows that the concept of sovereignty exemplifies the importance of framing, and suggests that it be treated as a concept contingent upon, rather than fundamental to, political science and its history.[10] However, it is becoming well known that outside a normative framework, sovereignty can only be understood in reference to what it excludes. In all contemporary accounts of Taiwanese sovereignty (except Chinese ones), this excluded yet intrusive other is unquestionably known to be the People's Republic of China.[11] Yet from the perspective of Chinese sovereignty, it makes sense to refer this position to that of the United States and Japan, both of which have played crucial roles, through treaties, declarations, and military deployments, in the international determination of Taiwan's status during the 20th century. How we view Taiwan depends in large part on what and whose sovereignty we emphasize.

There is another perspective from which the modern history of 'Taiwan'[12] reveals an enduring crisis of sovereignty—a crisis that is, in fact, common to East Asia, and ought to be related to the history of modern European (and Japanese) imperialism. This crisis is that of peoples subjected for a long duration to the barbarism of sovereignty's imperative normativity such that their political aspirations have been completely informed by the horizon of national sovereignty.

In the wake of the initial encroachment of Han settlers from the Ming Dynasty on aboriginal populations, there ensues 400 years of colonial baton-passes between Dutch, Portuguese, Spanish, and Japanese Colonial States, interrupted by Ming rebels-turned-pirate kings and Qing Imperial negligence, which culminates in a 'perfect' higher synthesis of domestic-foreign State negativity: mercenary remnants of a fascist State (the KMT Nationalist Party) are transported into puppet sovereignty by a United States government that is deeply preoccupied at the end of the Pacific War by its strategic agenda: to subsume Japanese sovereignty (ending Pan-Asianism) and to establish a juridical-police framework in the Pacific (indeed, the entire globe), which accords the United States exceptional status (Noam Chomsky will call it an 'outlaw superpower'[13]) while criminalizing China on account of its Communist aspiration (terminating the Communist alternative to Pan-Asianism).

Long before Communism, however, in the ruins of Chinese Empire and the shaky Republic that followed (1911), sovereignty had been developing, informed by European and Japanese colonial expansion. It had been developing into a state of exception for quite some time. Here, it is worth mentioning once again the need for an ongoing project to show that Chinese sovereignty was not inherited directly from the Imperium in a contiguous lineage, but was rather formulated in the exteriority of colonial power. Extraterritoriality, rather than the Imperium, ought to be placed at the center, not the encroaching margin, of our understanding of what sovereignty is for modern China. For this reason, the typical historical periodization of a 'semi-feudal, semi-colonial' status should be seen as a crisis of conceptual categories that calls for complete reformulation. We propose instead that Chinese sovereignty was maintained in the status of exception through the protocols of extraterritoriality, and that exception has almost always been managed by the State policing its territory and population (not 'defending the rights of citizens').

Taiwan, as a colony acquired by Japan from the Qing Empire, largely escaped the modern Chinese experience of sovereignty until 1945, when the KMT invests Taiwan with American transport. Significantly, the KMT governor's first act is to address the issue of sovereignty at the same time he grants validity to the previous colonial codes. Following this reintroduction of the permanent exception — a truly Chinese experience of modern sovereignty — there is a long period beginning with the Korean War in which the international status of Taiwan is declared — by Washington, acting as a police-judge — 'unresolved,' while Taiwan itself is ruled under the world's longest period of martial law. Once again, we are dealing with the exception made permanent — right back in the modern Chinese experience of sovereignty: a status of permanent exception.

The total mobilization of society maintained by the world's longest rule of martial law (1949 - 1987) in Taiwan was largely based upon five key elements: the identification of State interests with Party capital; the division of sexual labor that on the one hand required a total mobilization of the male population and on the other hand perpetuated a colonial distribution of women into social immobility through categories of either-prostitute-or-mother; the restriction of national space by controlling access to the mountainous outback, the open sea, and the air space above Taiwan; the discipline of 'national language' as a cover for instituting the privilege of a minority population; and finally the reduction of 'citizens' to mere populations and the system of ethnic identification cards that maintained a distinction between 'Taiwanese' and 'Mainlanders' (exiles from Mainland China who account for some 15% of the actual population) while maintaining aborigines (5% of the actual population) in remote spaces of restricted access.

Parallel to the domestic rule of martial law, the unilateral exercise of power by the U.S. since the end of World War Two[14] has kept sovereignty across the Pacific, and particularly in Taiwan (as well as China), in a virtually permanent state of exception. The proposition is worth repeating: Since the WWII defeat of Japan, America rehearses the entire Western Pacific region as a Theater of Operations in which it is the only sovereign nation — in truth, a sovereign lawmaker and law enforcer, the Judge-Police of the Pacific. This history is as well-documented as it is disavowed, although its justifications are simple: criminalize the enemy and reduce peoples in the region to populations subjected to forms of power and productive relations that actually cannot be understood through the model of sovereign politics, yet which maintain political aspirations immobilized in the desire-(of)-sovereignty.

I will cite one pertinent example of America's unilateral approach to sovereignty in the Pacific: according to wartime accords, the powers at war against Japan should have all been involved in drafting a peace treaty. However, the emergence by 1947 of the Cold War, the Chinese Revolution in 1949, and the Korean War in 1950, changed U.S. security considerations and the way in which the U.S. occupation of Japan was conducted into a virtually unilateral affair. Especially after the outbreak of war in Korea, Taiwan was now included in the defense perimeter of U.S. containment policy. Arrangements for the peace treaty with Japan, begun in 1947, followed a similar course. China and Russia, whose armies had diverted the bulk of Japanese land forces throughout the Pacific War, were excluded from drafting the treaty. The final treaty, concluded in San Francisco in 1951, was a United States production. China did not attend the treaty conference. Contrasted against this regime, the impunity, or again the status of exception, enjoyed by the East Asian nationalist State and its U.S. competitor/ally is particularly evident. Faced with what must strike any impartial observer ('impartial' means, minimally, that we do not criminalize our enemies, and furthermore, we recognize that our enemies do not constitute our politics as much as those whom we simply banish or exclude) as obvious, flagrant disregard for sovereignty and international protocol, let me voice what I believe to be common knowledge: given the military weapons systems in deployment since the end of World War Two, it is axiomatic that control of Taiwan would allow a third power effective ability to interdict the shipping lanes to and from Japan. Hence the description, 'Taiwan, the unsinkable aircraft carrier,' points us not only to China but to Japan, as well. If, we may suppose, Taiwan were to come under Chinese sovereignty, would not the whole strategic balance of U.S.-Japan production be seriously, perhaps fatally, threatened? With Taiwan under Chinese control, Japan would perhaps have to consider much more seriously the prospect of a Sino-Japanese alliance, rather than a U.S.-Japan security arrangement. Hence, the entire United States strategy in the Western Pacific must hinge upon maintaining a balance of power between China and Japan. One name for that 'hinge' is Taiwan — an area whose sovereignty, arranged by the United States in collusion with occupied Japan, was unilaterally declared 'unresolved' by the United States as the Cold War crept into its post-War Pacific protectorate. Other names are possible: obviously, Korea comes to mind; beyond any specific example, however, it is important to observe that although the four tigers (Korea, Hong Kong, Singapore, Taiwan) emerging out of economic expansion in the 1980s were called 'countries,' within a Cold War logic they might as well have been named 'front-line States,' that is, States without a nation whose entire population is subject (hostage) to the needs of Capital.

The Taiwan Relations Act: Incorporating Taiwan into America's Global Empire

With the end of martial law in 1987, and the first election by popular suffrage of Taiwan's head-of-state in 1996, thc discourse of sovereignty has apparently begun to erase the legacy of this painful history. The relation between the new, ostensibly democratic form of popular sovereignty, behind which often lurks the interests of local capital allied to global production, and the previous forms of sovereign power under martial law is invariably subsumed by a vague, progressive teleology which posits the neo-liberal state — a kind of fictive representation metonymically equivalent to the media presentation of the United States — as the ultimate direction of democratic development. This teleological faith prevents us from analyzing the ways in which democratic reform has actually served, not simply as a pretext for salacious private interest (which could be remedied by a return to public reason and a strengthening of the institutions that codify reason), but as an ideological interpellation of new subject positions that blend the biopolitics of sovereign power established during martial law to new forces of production and immaterial labor in the current conjuncture of unprecedented globalization.

Although democratization has reinstated the formal exercise of citizenship, the essential ingredients that formerly reduced citizenship to population remain in place: the sexual division of labor and juridical codes that favor patriarchal prerogative continue, language politics remain in a state of exception, and the system of citizenship laws and aboriginal population control remains fully in effect. Ethnicity, no longer marked on identification cards (except for aborigines), nevertheless remains on file in government archives.

In the meantime, democratization has not fundamentally improved the former identification of the Party-State with Capital. As Wang (1996) shows, democratic reform has changed the composition of the Party-State to reflect the movement of capital from State to private interests. In other words, the former Party-State has merely renegotiated a new alliance with Capital (or perhaps we should say that Capital has negotiated a new alliance redefining the Party-State), based not upon a minority exile population with a monopoly on State power, but upon an ethnically-mixed minority population of local private interests who appropriate the State apparatus for Private-Party ends.[15] This anti-democratic movement, which we can call the 'Private-Party State,' arose together with a parallel movement that increased Taiwan's incorporation into the global economy. Indeed, at several key junctures in the democratic reform, the United States exerted critical economic pressure upon Taiwan's monetary policy by calling for the 'internationalization of the New Taiwan Dollar,' creating pressure that seriously affected the development of domestic political reform.[16] Our thesis is that the powers of private interest and global hegemony that informed — even commanded — the democratic reforms since the end of martial law continue to maintain an effective link with the status of permanent exception previously instituted by martial law, maintaining sovereign power in a radically altered field of population, governmentality and biopolitics.

The difficulties encountered by President Chen Shui-bien, the first non-KMT head-of-state, elected almost by accident in 2000, could well serve as evidence of the profound resistance of the Private Party-State to democratization, and the continuing collapse of the political into economic categories. Equally important, and certainly even less well understood, however, remains the problem of Taiwan's incorporation within the U.S.-led global Empire.

It is well known that the Taiwan Relations Act (1979) that currently governs Taiwan-U.S. relations was the product of intense political lobbying and negotiation between the Executive and the Legislative branches of the U.S. government following President Jimmy Carter's decision to establish full diplomatic ties with the People's Republic of China. Even before it was passed into law, the TRA invited vociferous partisan debate within the United States, as well as in the P.R.C. and the R.O.C. Curiously, what interests participants in this debate are matters of principle and interest (if not simply 'principal' and interest — but the record of that investment is beyond this essay). It is impossible to find writers who seriously consider the significance of the TRA. For all writers, it seems, the TRA is simply an expedient means, a way for the United States of America to give *de facto* recognition to a front-line anti-Communist State from which it severed ties for considerations of *realpolitik*. In fact, the entire posture of *realpolitik* serves to produce a representation of Taiwanese people as victims, and unofficial diplomatic relations as humanitarian aid or service. This discursive structure (undeclared national emergency), of course, prepares in advance the ground for ultimate military intervention. Indeed, security is the main concern of the document, which 'authorizes' various relationships in order 'To help maintain peace, security, and stability in the Western Pacific.'

What is particularly remarkable about the TRA is that it excludes the government of Taiwan (the Republic of China) from diplomatic relations, yet extends full validity to all agreements with 'Taiwan' in effect before the end of diplomatic relations. Bypassing the State, the object of the TRA is either 'Taiwan' or the 'people *on* Taiwan.' Significantly, the preposition *on* stands in sharp contrast to the phrasing that precedes it: 'the people *of* the United States of America.' Internal State Department briefings about the island reportedly refer sometimes to the 'Taiwans' — a neologism that reflects with unprecedented clarity the confusion between population and territory that is at the heart of biopolitical power's new configuration of sovereignty within the discipline of crisis management and police power. Significantly, the TRA does not recognize a Taiwanese nation (which comprises 60% of the ethnic mix on the island), nor does it recognize identity based on the classic postulate of possession and property. But it does recognize 'life' *on* the island. This minimal recognition recalls once again Arendt's formula that links the decline of the nation-state to the end of the rights of man.

Before we consider the biopolitical implications of this formulation, let us observe that the TRA's management of State identity reminds us of the relation between the Federal Government and local States within the U.S. States whereby local states may not conduct independent diplomatic relations with other foreign governments but may carry on all manner of commercial, cultural, and representative links. Given Taiwan's current diplomatic isolation, its position vis-à-vis the U.S. Federal Government is very much analogous to that of a local State. This analogous inclusion of Taiwan within the Federal constitution of the United States is further confirmed by Section 4, Article 6, which states that for the purposes of the Immigration and Nationality Act, Taiwan will effectively be treated as an independent nation. In other words, documents ('passports') issued by the authorities in Taiwan can be officially recognized by United States government agencies as *de facto* national documents. Although we might be tempted to construe these documents as 'travel documents,' the recent experience of Mei-chin Hsiao exemplifies Taiwan's entry into a wholly different category.

Hsiao's case became public in Fall, 2000: working as an advisor for Chen Shui-bien's minority (non-KMT) government, Hsiao was threatened with legal action against illegal alien labor because she did not have R.O.C. citizenship. A U.S. citizen, born of a mixed Taiwanese (naturalized U.S.) and European American couple, Hsiao held an X-series (overseas) R.O.C. passport. In a public statement, Hsiao reported that when she consulted with the American Institute in Taiwan (AIT, the exceptional 'non-official' American Embassy established in Taiwan by the Taiwan Relations Act) about using her X-series passport to enter the United States (in case she would renounce U.S. citizenship), officials at AIT indicated that they could not issue a U.S. visa to holders of an X-series passport who did not bear documents showing permanent residency status and/or citizenship in another country. AIT could only treat the X-series passport as a 'travel document' rather than a truly national passport; holding such a passport, Hsiao would be treated by the U.S. government as a stateless person.[17]

This interpretation of Hsiao's passport raises questions about the status of R.O.C. passports in general: How can the U.S. view regular (non-X series) R.O.C. passports as anything *other* than 'travel documents'? (i.e, as national passports), since they are issued by a State which the United States does not recognize? The bearers of R.O.C. passports enjoy rights and obligations according to U.S. law and the protocols of U.S.-R.O.C. relations in place before the end of diplomatic relations. However, the documents themselves do not refer to any State recognized by the U.S. In this context, it is extremely difficult to understand why Hsiao's X-series passport would leave her to be considered as anymore 'stateless' than any of her compatriots by a government that does not recognize *any* R.O.C. state to begin with. Behind the apparent contradictions, we must seek a new conceptual category that fully accounts for the exception rather than attempt to paper over the exception by reasserting our faith in the normalcy of the rule. Hence, we propose that for the U.S. government, R.O.C. passports — which are admittedly *not* 'travel documents,' and yet refer to a State which the U.S. does not recognize — are primarily *identification papers* for an alien population with a government and no state — i.e., a fully biopolitical labor force — entering the discipline of naturalization. Here, the manifestation of racism is fundamentally altered — nicely captured by the concept of 'naturalization.' Indeed, that to which these 'identification papers' refer is not an ethnicity in the classic sense of the term — for that was the putative basis of nationality — but people apprehended simply as unqualified human life. In this sense, we detect an important discursive continuity between the ethnic identification codes of Martial Law and the TRA. Hence, the TRA should be seen as an exceptional measure that maintains Taiwan in the space of the exceptional state of undeclared emergency, prolonging Taiwan's sojourn at the very heart of the crisis of sovereignty.

From these two aspects of the TRA, we can see that the TRA effectively legislates treatment of individuals from Taiwan according to a domestic U.S. law process that essentially substitutes life for nationality, population for citizenship, and governmentality for sovereignty. In the event that the life of an individual bearing Taiwan travel documents residing in the United States was threatened by U.S. government agencies or other non-governmental vigilante forces (such as White Supremacist militia), that individual could not expect to receive the kind of support accorded to individuals of sovereign powers such as U.S. citizens abroad regularly receive. Under the TRA, Taiwan forms an undemocratic security border within which an ethnic population without citizenship is poised to acquire, given sufficient resources, U.S. residency. The real scandal, however, is that relations with Taiwan are handled under the protocols of U.S. domestic law. Our findings essentially confer with Micheal Hardt and Toni Negri, who write: 'the immanent concept of sovereignty [i.e., that of global Empire as opposed to territorial nation-States] is inclusive, not exclusive. In other words, when it expands, this new sovereignty does not annex or destroy the other powers it faces but on the contrary opens itself to them, including them in the network...*its space is always open.*'[18]

The recognition of a 'people on Taiwan' given by the TRA establishes a classic biopolitical category: live population, which, Arendt and then Agamben show by looking at stateless people, refugees, and camps, tends to reveal the emergence of a new political category, that of 'life' itself, life stripped of every determinate identity. This reduction to bare life helps us understand why Lee Teng-hui, first Taiwanese president elected by popular suffrage (1996), appealed to a concept of 'New Taiwanese' identity by recognizing community in the life on Taiwan. Hence, Lee's formula, that Taiwan is a 'community of life' (*shengming gongtongti*), is in fact a politically acute assessment of Taiwan's current position, although it is not something, as Lee thinks, that still awaits construction. The accuracy of Lee's assessment requires that an equally critical thought be applied to the contextual account of sovereignty.

One may ask why 'people on Taiwan,' whose lives, if not interests, are directly concerned, have not protested against this meaning of the TRA? Silence, especially in a non-coercive context, is often symptomatic of a certain desire that structures the formation of knowledge and action. Which is to say: one can maintain a dual, if conflictual, desire to acquire sovereignty at the same time one can desire to be incorporated into the constituent power of U.S.-centered Empire. This desire, it is no surprise, is born out of the insecurity of territory. It is important to note, additionally, that the TRA itself was passed at a time when the rule of law in Taiwan was still suspended by Martial Law. The meaning of 'domestic law' in this situation was understandably of secondary importance. Finally, I would observe in passing, that during the entire period of martial law in Taiwan, one finds a highly institutionalized, broadly accepted discourse throughout society about the criminal status of mainland China (labeled 'Communist bandits'). Nominally under R.O.C. jurisdiction, the Chinese mainland is regularly criminalized in legal documents of the period. Not just books and propaganda, but all products in general from the mainland are subject to control. Bizarrely, commercial relations with the mainland (officially non-existent, except through the mediation of Hong Kong and other third territories, but juridically codified, nonetheless) are referred to in terms of 'importation.'[19] No doubt, this usage itself was historically constructed through the long series of challenges to central authority that form modern Chinese history from the Taiping Rebellion up to the Communist Revolution. Once again, the language of sovereignty is completely insufficient to describe anything but — and this is no small feature — the desire of political movement in China. In any case, the meaning of law in the Republic of China is deeply implicated in an international politics of sovereignty and subversion in which the nationalist State itself is not the true sovereign power, but a police force maintaining productive discipline.

Peng Ming-min's seminal account of Taiwanese sovereignty, *The Legal Status of Taiwan* (1976), provides extensive historical discussion of the crisis of sovereignty in Taiwan. As a defense of Taiwanese sovereignty, the book marshals textual and documentary evidence to refute the claims of the other sovereign power: the People's Republic of China. The book does not consider the possibility of claims by other sovereign powers (such as Japan or the United States), nor does it consider the possibility that the historical praxis and concept of sovereignty has changed and is still changing.

It is certainly not incidental that this work was produced by an outstanding Taiwanese student seeking accreditation from the Faculty of Law at Tokyo University. Of course, since the beginning of the 1960s, Japan was a more or less congenial place for Taiwanese thinkers to prepare the theoretical groundwork of an independence movement. When we think of Japan at the start of the 1960s, we would have to think of the political and intellectual struggles around the strategic alliance with the United States. Certainly, by the 1970s, however, the U.S.-Japan alliance had stabilized, and opposition had been pushed into the discredited realm of radical terrorism. Within this milieu, we could be certain that the production within institutional sites as closely linked to government as the Faculty of Law at Tokyo University of elements for a discourse of Taiwanese independence cannot be easily dissociated from the general strategic interest of the U.S.-Japan security arrangement: to prevent the emergence of a Chinese sovereignty (if not a Japanese sovereignty, for that matter) capable of parity with the United States.

Our research shows that Taiwanese sovereignty needs to be seen as something that is included, virtually in domestic terms, within the *theater of operations* open to the sovereign police — U.S., Chinese, or otherwise. In the case of Taiwan, the terms 'theater' and 'act' must be rigorously taken at face value: this will help us remove the various productions of optical representation and dissemination (such as Hollywood films) out of the obfuscating category of so-called 'cultural imperialism' and begin to theorize them in terms of violence and logistics. This sort of genealogical perspective has the advantage of obviating culturalist assumptions that obfuscate the crucial articulation between sovereignty and subjective technologies during the transition from Colonialism to Cold War.

A 'theater of operations' comprises: logistics, communications, optical representation, and the capability to concentrate levels of disciplined force. As Paul Virilio persuasively argues,[20] twentieth century history shows that it is impossible at the limit to distinguish between advances in image reproduction technology and military weapons systems. The term 'theater of operations' was originally conceived during the global conflicts of the 20th century as a concept for strategic warfare. Perhaps we can use it today to depict, rather than delineate, the space and speed of power in an age when territorial sovereignty breeds only insecurity. In applying the term to depict the status of sovereign power in this age, we also wish to evoke important work by Jean-Luc Nancy that shows how 'operativity' has become an essential figure for understanding the predicament of modern sovereignty. In Nancy's work, 'operativity' describes the constitution of a subject (for instance, a national subject) through the production and maintenance of a common essence.[21] We use the term 'theater of operations' to describe the space opened by modern sovereign power and the space within which it operates.

Taiwanese Independence

The very designation 'Taiwan Relations Act' provides us an important clue, one that has been studiously ignored by thinkers of Taiwan's predicament. As the name of that truly performative 'act' so readily implies, in order to think Taiwan, it is necessary to think sovereignty not in terms of autonomy, but in terms of relation. In fact, one might characterize much of the new thinking in post-Marxism and post-colonialism as a turn from the thinking of a politics of the self-sufficient subject and sovereignty to a thinking of an ontology of relationship, of the proletariat as precisely that which is not a subject, and of the sovereign as that which is based on a permanent exception. As Hardt and Negri sum up, the concepts of modern national community, however, 'make the *relation* of sovereignty into a *thing* (often by naturalizing it) and thus weed out every residue of social antagonism.'[22]

The authors of *Taiwan's Legal Status* are indeed aware of the non-normative implications of sovereignty. Because Taiwan has never been constituted as a stable sovereign power, the authors must admit that an exclusively international framework, that is, a framework based exclusively on the normativity of an international community of sovereign States, is insufficient to explain Taiwanese history.[23] Yet there is no attempt to use this platform to seek a Taiwanese independence that would challenge the construction of precisely that normativity which has denied Taiwanese their own independence. As the Chinese title of the work 'Taiwan's position within international law' suggests, the book is primarily an attempt to fix the boundaries of the local constructions of sovereign power exclusively within a juridical discourse of supranational right. Such discourse represses historical difference. We never ask why *sovereignty* has become such an obsessive question around Chinese history and East Asia in general any more than we pose questions to the ponderous construction of international law's 'surplus of normativity and efficacy.'[24]

In place of these radically transformative questions, there is endless debate within the framework of cultural difference and cofiguration: did Chinese possess a conception of sovereignty? and/or what was the difference with a 'European' concept/practice? Whereas an earlier school of American sinologists, represented by John Fairbank, assert that sovereignty was an alien concept brought to China with the 'Western Impact,' a later generation of scholars, led by James Hevia's path-breaking work, asserts that, yes, China knew of sovereignty, but with a difference. To know whether China is the same or different is the obsession of a culturalism that never examines the desire motivating such massive institutional production of knowledge. Surely, it is because of a specific kind of power within history that we feel we must come up with an answer to the questions of identity and difference posed by the desire-(of)-sovereignty. Yet when we look at the history of sovereignty's desire as one of failure, we think it is precisely these answers to which questions must be addressed if we are to avoid reproducing the normative desire of sovereignty itself.

Considering just how explicit *Taiwan's Legal Status* is with a litany of rapacious, unethical maneuvers by various colonial powers around Taiwan, it is equally remarkable that the authors do not deploy historical knowledge to challenge the politics of knowledge and the political construction of sovereignty. What is it, then, that drives the authors, from the very outset, to subsume the political nature of the historical problem surrounding Taiwan to a court of international reason? If there is, as Taiwanese independence-oriented thinkers like Peng Ming-min believe, a lesson to be drawn from Taiwan's history, it is clear that no sovereignty takes

Taiwan itself as a central, core region of power. Rather, off-island-centered sovereignties lay claim to Taiwan, for various different reasons and histories, but always as part of a strategic gambit which itself forms the de facto framework of sovereignty during an age ('modernity') of intense international competition compressed by capital-imperialist global expansion. The standard position of Taiwanese independence would thus find the resolution to a painful history of external subjugation in the assertion of sovereignty whose core is located in territorial Taiwan. Although vociferous opponents of Taiwanese independence disagree, the appeal to territorial sovereignty as a final resolution of Taiwanese history is equally shared.

Change in the construction of sovereignty is one of the most common themes articulated by contemporary defenders of 'Taiwan,' who unimaginatively assert that the kind of ethno-territorial sovereignty claimed by the Chinese government is anachronistic. Needless to say, the enunciation of this position requires a certain disavowal of history. Anyone familiar with the 19th century history of the European-Japanese Imperialist penetration of the Qing Empire will immediately recognize a familiar motif in which impetuous Chinese sovereignty is always already anachronistic compared to the progressive, rationally-legislated sovereignty (in fact, the only real sovereignty) of the Powers (Europe and Japan). While subsequent generations of Chinese undertake enormous sacrifices to respond, sovereignty today is being restructured into a new kind of subjective technology, what Hardt and Negri call immaterial labor. And, as is true of material labor, outdated means of production incur greater moral opprobrium.

Our analysis of the hidden continuities between the TRA and Martial Law might suggest that settling the question of Taiwanese sovereignty would end the enduring violence that affects Taiwanese society due to the permanent state of exception into which Taiwan, from Martial Law to the TRA, has been thrown. Certainly this analysis cannot be refuted, and at this level, we must agree that maintenance of the *status quo* in China-Taiwan relations is the biggest obstacle to democratic development in Taiwan.

However, we must question whether even the regularization of Taiwan's sovereignty would remove Taiwan from its long sojourn in the state of permanent exception since Martial Law. Certainly posing this question means that the issue of Taiwanese sovereignty would have to be linked to the crisis of sovereignty around the world, including particularly the problematic status of sovereign power in China, and the emergence of biopolitics. Although resolution of Taiwanese sovereignty (for instance, as independent nation or as province of China) would grant some relative stability vis-à-vis the current situation, it would not resolve the predicament into which sovereignty has fallen since the 20th century.

After all the remnants of sovereignty's surplus of normativity have been washed away, the one unassailable narrative about modern Taiwanese history that remains would be the suffering that the enduring crisis of sovereignty has imposed for several centuries upon Taiwanese peoples (including, notably, decimated aboriginal populations completely denied the possibility for national aspiration). True Taiwanese independence would only come when Taiwanese peoples, in tandem with (other) Chinese peoples, have finally been liberated from this history and this imperative.

Taiwanese independence thus awaits the invention of an Asia that is not simply the 'other' of the West, nor the mirror image of the West's own worst fantasies of autonomous national subjectivity — typified by the nationalist appropriation of sovereignty. This invention, it may be worth clarifying, does not supercede, or substitute for, or follow in progressive fashion after, etc.... the construction of national sovereignty by non-Westerners, such as Taiwanese, who have been barbarized by the crisis of sovereignty for many centuries. However, the fact that Taiwanese are denied accession to the lethal normativity of sovereignty, yet remain subject to its imperatives and actively promote its consolidation, is a situation that must not be allowed to continue to be given (by Chinese, Taiwanese, Americans, Japanese, etc....) as a pretext for ignoring the equally real, global crisis of sovereignty around Taiwan — a crisis which no construction of normative, national sovereignty can resolve.

Beyond Sovereignty and Its Others

Without a doubt, the greatest change since the end of the Cold War in the status of sovereignty is the emergence of human rights and humanitarian intervention as a non-political arena. The best vision writers like Peng and Huang can provide is an appeal to international human rights, with which the authors end their argument for Taiwanese independence.

We know that at the back and at the core of Taiwan's status is a question about the relation between human rights and sovereignty. We can follow a persuasive line of argument developed by Arendt, Balibar, and Agamben[25] that shows how the concept of human rights is integrally part of the logic of sovereignty, and hence cannot be simply relied upon to counter or mitigate its effects. Agamben perceptively observes: 'It is almost as if, starting from a certain point, every decisive political event were double-sided: the spaces, the liberties, and the rights won by individuals in their conflicts with central powers always simultaneously prepared a tacit but increasing inscription of individuals' lives within the state order, thus offering a new and more dreadful foundation for the very sovereign power from which they wanted to liberate themselves.'[26] Once again, a glance at the Taiwan Relations Act is quite illuminating. As that document makes clear, human rights in Taiwan is ultimately indistinguishable from the rhetoric of military intervention.[27] After reading Agamben, we are neither surprised that the seminal work of Taiwanese independence seamlessly articulates human rights to a discourse of national sovereignty, nor can we uncritically accept the equation of the two. Our task is to go beyond these 19th century formulations (which 20th century history pushed towards unprecedented levels of biopolitical violence) and find new ways to theorize biopolitics and the community-to-come.

Undoubtedly, the difficulty of this future invention is compounded by the realization that going beyond sovereignty also necessarily means going beyond its others. Inevitably, this will bring a challenge to the construction of 'civil society' and its globalized variants. Liberal thought has always posited civil society as the legitimate bearer of resistance to the excesses of sovereign power. Our perspective exemplifies, however, the inadequacy of this formulation in the face of unprecedented change.

In the current conjuncture, the true bearer of sovereignty lies more and more with the category of 'life,' stripped down to bare, unqualified existence. This denuded life is now becoming almost exclusively construed through an ethico-techno-logical discourse of rights, which are constantly being expanded or upgraded; and total possession, which is constantly being honed down to new, intrusive definitions of the personal body.[28] Hence it behooves us to consider the body in relation to sovereign power, and to prepare the way for an understanding of a body that is consonant with non-sovereign politics.

In the course of this essay, we have concentrated on two main figures in the theater of operations opened by sovereign power: the sovereign police and the outsider (the excluded; but also, possibly, the non-sovereign community of the multitudes). By way of conclusion, we would like to introduce a third figure that instantly follows from these two, and indeed has been implicit throughout our narrative: the knowledgeable body.

It is well known that knowledge in the Human Sciences has been deeply intertwined with national sovereignty and language in the modern period. What we are beginning to see by looking at the crisis of sovereignty in Taiwan is the way in which sovereignty in general operates as a totalizing discourse *across* differences of nationality and language. The normativity of sovereignty is not only the default position for all accounts — regardless of language, ethnicity, and political position — of Taiwanese history, it is the *only* position. The utter uniformity with which all writers concerned with Taiwan — if not the entire Pacific Theater — simply accept the normative framework of international relations and the urgency to think the humanitarian, which is intrinsically connected to the discursive apparatus of military investment and intervention, is itself an indication of the need to rethink the position of the knowing subject and the social institutions that enable public knowledge.

At the very least, we need to begin to understand the eerie convergence between ostensibly ethnicized bodies and producers of knowledge about them. For an understanding of the knowledgeable bodies that operate in the theater of operations open to the sovereign police, nothing is more apposite than what Naoki Sakai terms the 'subjective technology of translation' — a term which refers to the creation of national language and national culture through a process of co-figuration. National language, hence national identity, is mutually produced in relation to the putative unity of an external 'other' in a process that includes the non-national only by exclusion. This *exclusion* is not evidence of a limit or impossibility so much as it is an indication of just how persuasive and widespread the juridico-ethic Empire of sovereign technology has become.

This perspective does not call for us simply to abandon sovereignty (ostensibly in favor of 'difference') in either our politics or in our conceptual understanding. Rather, it calls for us to engage the totalizing claims of sovereignty (and beyond that, of capital) with thought and praxis capable of producing new categories (e.g. an 'open totality,' ideas of non-relational equivalency that go beyond Same and Other, and/or proposals for a non-sovereign politics) that articulate the problems of biopolitics and globalization.

Notes

1 Alan M. Wachman, *Taiwan: National Identity and Democratization* (New York: M.E. Sharpe, 1994).

2 Jenn-Hwang Wang, *Shei tongzhi Taiwan?* [Who Rules Taiwan?] (Taipei: Juliu, 1996), 328.

3 An analogous problem appears in Martin Heidegger's attempt at 'fundamental ontology.' Cf. Jean-Luc Nancy, tr. Brian Holmes, 'The decision of existence,' in *Birth to presence* (Stanford: Stanford University, 1993), 82-109.

4 Giorgio Agamben, tr. Vincenzo Binetti and Cesare Casarino, *Means Without Ends: Notes on Politics* (Minneapolis: University of Minnesota, 2000), 112-113.

5 Giorgio Agamben, tr. Daniel Heller-Roazen, *Homo Sacer: Sovereign Power and Bare Life* (Stanford: Stanford University, 1998), 47.

6 We would want to turn our attention towards the work of François Laruelle. Cf. François Laruelle, *Théorie des étrangers*¸(Paris: Kimé, 1995) and François Laruelle, *Ethique de l'etranger: du crime contre l'humanite* (Paris: Kime, 2000).

7 Giorgio Agamben, tr. Vincenzo Binetti and Cesare Casarino, *Means Without Ends: Notes on Politics* (Minneapolis: University of Minnesota, 2000), 112-113.

8 Cf. Naoki Sakai, 'Modernity and Its Critique: The Problem of Universalism and Particularism,' in Naoki Sakai, *Translation and Subjectivity: On 'Japan' and Cultural Nationalism* (Minneapolis: Minnesota University, 1997), 153-176.

9 For an explanation of the historical constitution of sovereignty in terms of European colonial expansion, see Jean-François Kervégan, 'Carl Schmitt and "World Unity"' in Chantal Mouffe, ed. *The Challenge of Carl Schmitt* (New York: Verso, 1999), 54-74; also see Hideaki Tazaki, '*Konjitsu no Sei-Seiji no naka no Nîche* [Nietszche in Contemporary Bio-politics] in *Shisō* No. 919, Dec. 2000 (Tokyo: Iwanami), 164-174; for an explanation of the philosophical appropriation of sovereignty by subjectivity, see Jean-Luc Nancy, 'The Inopertaive Community' tr. Peter Connor, in Jean-Luc Nancy, ed. Peter Connor, *The Inoperative Community* (Minneapolis: University of Minnesota, 1991), 1-42; for a description of sovereignty and the importance of thinking 'non-sovereign politics' or 'sovereignty without subjectivity,' see Jean-Luc Nancy '*Ex nihilo summum (De la souveraineté)*' in Jean-Luc Nancy, *La création du monde* ou *la mondialisation* (Paris: Galilée, 2002), 145-172.

10 Jens Bartelson, *A Genealogy of Sovereignty* (Cambridge: Cambridge University, 1995).

11 For a collection of Chinese essays dealing with the problems of U.S. involvement in the determination of Taiwanese sovereignty, see: Xiaobo, Wang, ed., *Meiguo dui Tai zhengce jimi dang'an* [Secret files on America's Taiwan Policy] (Taipei: Haixia pinglun zazhishe, 1992).

12 We use the proper noun 'Taiwan' with reservations about the process of semantic recollection that would posit 'Taiwan' as an historical unity based upon the givenness of territory. We would want to know at what point in history does 'Taiwan' become an object of discourse, and further, at what point does 'Taiwan' become a site of subjective formation? Cf. Naoki Sakai's *Voices from the past* (Ithaca: Cornell University, 1994), which advances a revolutionary thesis about the subjective formation of Japan ('Japan'

did not emerge as a unitary subject of discourse until the 18th century). It is apparent that for much of its colonial history, 'Taiwan' was an extremely dispersed assemblage of disparate communities.

13 Cf., Noam Chomsky, *The New Military Humanism: Lessons from Kosovo* (Monroe: Common Courage, 1999).

14 In his most recent visit (2001) to Taiwan as part of a U.S. government delegation visiting both sides of the Taiwan Strait, Dr. Kenneth Lieberthal has suggested an end to 'unilateral' action by the U.S.

15 Cf., Jenn-hwan Wang, *Shei Tonzhi Taiwan? [Who Rules Taiwan?]* (Taipei: Juliu, 1996).

16 Wang, *op. cit.*, 119-133.

17 Cf. *Taiwan Ribao* (Taipei), 12/01/00, 5.

18 Micheal Hardt and Antonio Negri, *Empire* (Cambridge: Harvard University, 2000), 166-7.

19 Cf. *Guojia zongdongyuan faling zhuanji* [Compendium of Laws for National Total Mobilization] (Taipei: Ministry of Defense, 1978), 161-3.

20 Paul Virilio, tr. Patrick Camiller, *War and Cinema: The Logistics of Perception* (London: Verso, 1989).

21 Cf, Jean-Luc Nancy, *The Inoperative Community*, op. cit.

22 *op cit.*, 95

23 Peng Ming-min (Peng, Mingmin) and Ng, Yuzin Chiautong (Huang, Zhaotang), tr. Cai, Qiuxiong, *Taiwan zai guojifa shang de diwei* (Taipei: Yushan, 1995), 225.

24 *op cit.*, 180.

25 Cf. Hannah Arendt, 'The Decline of the Nation-State and the End of the Rights of Man,' in Arendt, *The Origins of Totalitarianism* (New York: Harcour Brace, 1979), 267 –304; Etienne Balibar, '"Rights of Man" and "Rights of the Citizen": The Modern Dialectic of Equality and Freedom,' in Balibar, *Masses, Classes, Ideas* (New York: Routledge, 1994), 39-59; Giorgio Agamben, tr. Daniel Heller-Roazen, *Homo Sacer: Sovereign Power and Bare Life* (Stanford: Stanford University, 1998); and Giorgio Agamben, tr. Vincenzo Binetti and Cesare Casarino, *Means Without Ends: Notes on Politics* (Minneapolis: University of Minnesota, 2000).

26 Agamben, *Homo Sacer*, 121.

27 Of course, the United States no longer maintains a mutual defense treaty with the Republic of China, yet the TRA is defined in terms of 'security interests.' In the absence of this agreement, the main document which covers Taiwan security within the theater of U.S. military operations would certainly be the U.S.-Japan Security Treaty. In its most recent modification, this treaty includes a clause which stipulates that the Japanese Self-Defense Forces will support the U.S. in defending against any military operation aimed against Japan 'and its environs,' including the Straits of Taiwan.

28 Etienne Balibar points out: 'Ever since old theological or theologico-political notions such as the "eminent domain" of God or of the sovereign over the entire earth have lost all significance, what has posed problems (and is today undergoing new developments) has above all been the possibility of extending the application of this principle of total possession to the human person itself, particularly when the human body, the use of its services and its capacities enters into commodity circulation. But

the question was never again posed whether the principle of total possession brings with it intrinsic limits, that is, whether there are not "onjects" that, by nature, cannot be appropriated, or more precisely that can be appropriated but *not totally possessed.*' Balibar, 'What is a politics of the rights of man?' in Balibar, tr. James Swenson, *Masses, Classes, Ideas* (New York: Routledge, 1994), 220.

Ritual Matters

Kenneth Dean and Thomas Lamarre[1]

Of the thousands of villages in Southeast China, virtually every one has a temple or shrine to the local tutelary divinity, the god of the earth. In addition to earth god temples, many villages also have temples to local, regional or empire-wide deities, as well as Buddhist monasteries or nunneries (in the village or on nearby mountains), and occasional Taoist belvederes. Lay Buddhist or 'sectarian' religious groups also have temples in many villages. Christian churches appear in a smaller percentage of villages. In most of the non-urban areas, a scattering of Taoist and other ritual specialists work out of their homes, as do a wide variety of local spirit mediums. Voluntary religious associations have developed in several regions, often developing additional ritual traditions.

At a wide range of important occasions in the life of individuals and families as well as on the birthdays of local gods, ritual specialists perform rites. Especially important are the Taoist priests or ritual masters. Most of the active temples — and a large number in Southeast China are very active — have temple committees that organize communal rituals, raise and dispense funds, and stage various entertainments in front of the temple (such as opera, marionette shows, puppet theatre and films) in conjunction with ritual activities. In brief, as all these different communities organize themselves around temples and their ritual activities, the contemporary field for popular religion in Southeast China is extraordinarily diverse and complex. [2]

If one attempts an overview or characterization of this field, it seems logical to conclude, as C. K. Yang does, that Chinese popular religion is 'diffuse' rather than 'institutional.'[3] Yet, if this field is not primarily or simply one of institutions, this does not mean that it is simply diffuse, that is, not in any way systematic or coherent. Nor can the field of popular religion and ritual activity be explained as glue in the cracks between institutions. Styling it as collective subjectivity, for instance, only evokes a kind of glue, an ultimately inexplicable kind of glue, and evades the question of how ritual works. Rather we need to think how this 'field' presents relations that are in some way systematic yet open to transformation. This is to think the 'diffuse' another way, and to look at how the complexity of relations entails a great deal of indeterminacy and unpredictability. Moreover, this is to think about how forms (say, the form of a ritual event) can be continuous over time yet transform. Which raises our basic question: what difference does the repetition of ritual activities make?

Figure 1: Taoist Masters performing at the Linshan Temple in Xianyou, Fujian, October 1999

This way of thinking is potentially very different from that associated with modernity and the modern. Thinking modernity puts the stress on rupture, on the break between the old and new, between the traditional and modern. We'd like to think other ways than modernity, to move beyond its ruptures and oppositions. But modernity demands (even slavishly begs for) critical attention precisely because it organizes so much of the practical knowledge about Chinese popular religion, in the West and in China. Especially problematic is the use of the logic of modernity to frame ritual activities as remnants or survivals of traditional, archaic or premodern modes, thus ignoring the contemporaneity of ritual activities in Southeast China (as well as the history of ritual practices). Of course, one can complicate the frame of modernity a great deal, by 'spectralizing' it, that is, looking at uncanny remnants of a past that haunt and trouble the present. Yet spectralizing modernity is only a first (and probably insufficient) step toward a more complex understanding of this field of popular religion. For, however much temporal leakiness or ghostly creakiness one attributes to the modern frame, this complex field remains at odds with the framework of modernity. This is largely because the ubiquity and productivity of contemporary ritual activities in Southeast China allows them to overspill the neat temporal frames that would have the modern present supercede, delineate and encompass ritual activities as remnants of the past.

Nonetheless, the question of how modernity continues to organize discourses on popular religion in Southeast China remains a crucial problem. This does not mean that analysis must always already be trapped in the logic of modernity. While we feel that it is important (and maybe inevitable) to discuss ritual in relation to modernity, we do not see modernity as an inescapable underlying totality that demands incessant efforts at deconstruction — efforts that are bound to fail, or rather, to succeed only by throwing modernity in an abyssal movement of infinite regression. Nor, conversely, is our goal to liberate ritual from modern discourses that attend it. Rather, as much as possible, we want to take seriously the logic of ritual practice and the implications of that logic for thinking other 'a-modern' temporalities. No doubt this is to implicate ourselves in something.

Epistemological Frames and Alternative Modernities

Of the many problems associated with the modern, the construction of a divide between nature and culture has had a profound impact on understanding the relation between ritual and modernity. Bruno Latour's work is relevant here for he shows how the modern brings about such a nature/culture divide by epistemological means.[4] To be modern, he says, is to live in a culture that has adopted forms of inquiry that separate its own operations from those of nature. To be modern is to live in a culture that defines itself by its acceptance and promotion of that separation. Scientific rationalism strips the natural world of cultural meaning. Nature comes to stand apart from culture as non-arbitrary, as a realm governed by unchanging laws that are deemed immune to human intervention. The non-arbitrary laws of nature are safeguarded by scientific method from the vicissitudes of linguistic difference, from the aimlessness of historical drift, from incommensurabilitites of belief. Any particular formulation of those laws, as well as any hypothesis concerning their factual consequences, remains contestable. Yet the immutability of nature remains. And it can be called upon to settle disputes. Once nature is set apart from culture as non-arbitrary, it becomes the arbiter of culture. For instance, when Western theories of sovereignty become confused about the foundations for popular rights and human agency, they establish a natural contract and equality between humans that precedes society — a non-arbitrary nature. Nature thus operates as a horizon of possible cultural agreement for the modern, of which sovereignty is just one. Latour's point is that the modern epistemological divide between nature and culture is inherently technocratic.

Enlightenment reason, in Latour's account, demands the production of epistemologically distinct domains within a culture — science, religion, politics — which are also modes of representation. The very notion of 'religion' then is a token of modern conversion. If a culture is capable of grouping certain of its operations under that category, it has already taken the turn. If the category is applied to a culture from the outside, that culture is already being prepared: primed for development (or disappearance). Latour's challenge to the modern can be seen as a twist on the critique of modernity as the production of space, as spatialization — but with an emphasis on epistemological divides and domains. From the standpoint of the modern, cultures thus separate out according to their willingness to accept the technocratic arbitration of nature. Some will persist in ways deemed epistemologically incorrect, insisting on other realms as a horizon of possibility — these are judged as supernatural, that is, neither natural by any scientific definition nor agreeably cultural. Culturally, these other realms are disagreeable because, by the modern definition, they are addressable only by belief, and faith is what is objectively non-negotiable. In other words, the modern demands that already operating horizons of possibility be consigned to religion. It is only by bracketing belief, by insulating mechanisms for the negotiation of differences from religion that a culture can begin to modernize. It is not required that a culture lose its religion. All that is required is for religion to be circumscribed as a separate domain, so that the arbitration can proceed on a technocratic basis, belief aside.

Latour's critique of the modern is a critique of modernization as the production of space, but in the dimension of epistemology: scientific knowledge and practices must sequester religion in order to establish the non-arbitrariness of nature, which in turn grounds a certain imagination of sovereignty and political representation. Modern technological networks reinforce, expand and refine these divides from the level of the quark to that of the globe and the cosmos. Yet Latour introduces a vengeful twist: for all its claims to have put an end to the intermixing of these domains, the modern (modernization) has simply recombined everything it claims to have separated — but on a vaster scale. If, in his account, we have never been modern (modernized), it is because modernization has simply enacted the same combinations as all those other non-modern cultures. The major difference is that the modern strives to make invisible its mixes.

While there are problems with Latour's model (to which we will return along the way), it does have the advantage of calling attention to the ways in which ritual is framed epistemologically in relation to the modern. For instance, in the fall of 1999, we attended, by invitation, ritual festivities at a temple in Linshan village, a small village on the Xianyou coast in Fujian province of Southeast China, in the company of some twenty odd ethnographers and sinologists, both from Western countries (England, America, Canada, Australia, France) and from Chinese regions (some local, some from farther afield — from Shanghai, Taiwan, etc). One of our number, Ken Dean, has been studying and participating in ritual activities in this village for many years, working closely with temple leaders and ritual masters. He was one of the hosts for the festivities. Within the group of invited 'observers,' there were a number of different ways of framing the ritual activities. The ethnographers from Western institutions (who might better be described as sinologists than ethnographers, for many received training within area studies rather than anthropology) showed the clearest sense of how to separate what was properly ritual from what was not. Their expertise led them to hone in on the activities of the ritual masters, almost to the exclusion of all else.

Linshan temple had hired two groups of ritual specialists, one composed of masters of Daoist scriptures, one of masters of Three-in-One scriptures.[5] They form two ensembles in front of the temple and, side by side, perform their choreography, now solemnly leaping and running in various patterns around a series of portable wooden tables (altars), stomping cosmological configurations into the sandy earth. These activities mark the first phase of a long series of ritual performances and trances designed to summon the deities who reside in the temple. The deities are called forth to partake of (and thus bless or somehow acknowledge) the bounty of the village and its neighbors. (In the course of the festivities, the villages in the temple alliance arrive with an incredible array of foodstuffs, often prepared and decorated, which are displayed in tents raised opposite the temple.) The sinologist-ethnographers directed their attention almost exclusively on the activities of the ritual masters, taking copious notes and photographs, comparing this particular pattern of ceremonies with others observed elsewhere in China.

Figure 2: Three in One Scripture Masters (left) and Taoist Masters (right) in front of Linshan Temple

Latour's account of the modern encourages us to ask whether such observation can figure as a neutral practice. Observation sets up and instantiates epistemological divides. Striking the stance of empirical neutrality sets the sinologists visibly apart from what they observe. Yet they are observed observing. The observation, though mutual, is not symmetrical. For the ethnographer to see himself observed does not change the nature of his activity, or who he feels himself to be. The weight he carries, in the form of cameras and recorders and notebooks, is the ballast of empirical validity. But what happens for various participants in the ritual activities? To be observed as from outside by such a weighty witness might be to see oneself circumscribed. As from outside — the ethnographer's 'neutral' presence dramatizes the cultural boundedness of the observed activities, and in dramatizing it, instantiates it. The nature of the activity immediately changes. Every act not shared by the ethnographic observer becomes a further confirmation of the separation. This separation also takes on a temporal dimension, for the sinological observer locates the ritual in relation to a traditional, sometimes archaic past that provides the authentic model. Ritual activities become measured for their authenticity. Thus the ethnographer becomes a personal emissary of the modernizing divide — from which he will also work to protect the culture he observes. The change in the nature of the observed activity is that it becomes a survival or a remnant — an attachment to a past separated from the wider present and promised future personified by the ethnographer.

This is a serviceable critique, as it goes. It draws attention to the ways in which neutrality is merely a modern epistemology that strives to introduce and sustain a divide between nature and culture, by cordoning off ritual activity in the manner of religion or religious culture — as something distinct from science and politics. Such neutrality (to repeat) is an inherently technocratic epistemology. In addition, in the instance of ritual practices in contemporary Fujian, sinologist-ethnographers seem especially insistent on establishing the pastness (and thus criteria for authenticity) of ritual practices. They are wholly interested in repetition as the same, as resemblance. Only on the basis of a modernizing temporal divide can they prevent ritual activities from bleeding into other epistemological domains.

This is especially difficult in contemporary Fujian, one of China's special economic zones, sometimes touted as the fastest growing area in the world. The transformations are amazing: ferro-concrete apartment buildings and hotels that soar into the sky in the port city of Xiamen sprawl into the countryside, following the new coastal highway, itself an impressive feat of engineering, six lanes cut across villages, towns, hills, inlets, and fields. And although construction gradually diminishes in size and scale from the city into the countryside, the scope of construction and reconstruction leaves almost nothing untouched, and blurs boundaries between urban and rural formations, if indeed such formations were ever entirely distinct. It offers undeniable evidence of social and historical transformations that cannot simply be enumerated and registered objectively.

Not surprisingly then, such transformations met with quite emotional responses from the assembled sinologists. While it should be noted that most of us were grateful, in the post-typhoon heat wave, for our air-conditioned hotel rooms, there was a constant refrain of objection that attended our travel from Xiamen to Fujian, and our tours around the region, a judgment passed on the disastrous ugliness of the rampant urban reconstruction so evident in an economically-prosperous area like Fujian or in contemporary Beijing. Objection to rampant development largely took the form of aesthetic anxiety — outrage over the blind destruction of local forms and customs, especially the loss of the beautiful older buildings in favor of ferro-concrete towers cloaked in bathroom tile. And such outrage over the cataclysmic transformation of Fujian province frequently extended to all of 'China' under its capitalist reconstruction. Anxieties crystallized around a sense of loss of tradition, of the past, which represented a sort of 'beautiful' continuity and connectedness to local customs, to history, and to the land.

Faced with transformation, the sinologists' impulse was to establish an epistemological divide between ritual activities and other domains, and to sustain the divide by recourse to a seemingly neutral divide between past and present. Ritual was marked as not modern. Thus sinologists avoid the problem of transformation on two fronts — ritual and historical — by recourse to an authentic and immutable past as manifested in ritual. In other words, they adopted the logic of modernization in order to frame ritual as a past in need of protection. The irony of such a stance is, of course, that it ultimately sides with modernization, for ritual activities only remain important insofar as they are seen as historically surpassed and therefore threatened.

Ritual activities in Southeast China, however, present a profound empirical challenge to this sinological romance of an authentic past in opposition to modernization. For it is simply impossible to submit that there exists a stable spatial and temporal divide between ritual activities and modernizing or globalizing forces. Basically, there is simply too much ritual activity. In the Puxian region of coastal Fujian, the area in which Ken Dean has done fieldwork over the past decade, ritual activities and temple organization are a part of everyday life. A survey of lineages, cults and ritual activities in over 600 villages conducted by Dean and Zheng Zhenman in this region over the past six years shows that, on average, the population of these villages is around 1,200 people — with the population of some villages as large as 6,000 or more. The survey found one hundred different surname groups in these 600 villages; while the average village had 3.4 surnames, some villages had as many as fourteen surnames, and others but one. The survey also located 1,639 temples in the 600 villages, an average of 2.7 per village (while some villages had as many as eighteen temples, 36% of them had only one temple). The 1,639 villages housed 6,960 god statues, representing over 1,200 different deities. Temples averaged 4.3 gods, yet some housed as many as thirty-one. Such figures do not support the image of traditional practices in flight before an encroaching, encompassing modernity.[6]

In the first lunar month of each year, each village holds its own procession of the gods, usually in conjunction with Taoist rituals in the temple and opera performances on stages erected in an open courtyard in front of, or adjacent to, the temple. Each village subsequently joins in a larger procession to the other villages in its ritual alliance. (123 ritual alliances, usually based in irrigation networks, link the 600 villages.) Combinations of several ritual alliances form still larger processions, which can involve over one hundred villages, and last up to a week. The network of local temple alliances is remarkably dense: with opera, for instance, a villager can attend performances 250 days a year. Moreover, the clusters of nested hierarchies between temples have allowed temple alliances to function as an unofficial second tier of local governance. The network with its hierarchies has gradually taken on many local administrative tasks. The success of temple alliances and ritual activities is astonishing in light of the destruction of these very temples and their alliances during the Cultural Revolution. Over the course of the past twenty years, a very large number of temples have been reconstructed, and village rituals renewed. In effect, even if one establishes the Cultural Revolution as the moment of temporal rupture between the traditional and the modern (which was one of its directives), ritual practices and temple alliances occupy an unstable position, neither entirely traditional nor entirely modern.

This returns us to Latour's problem with the epistemological divides of the modern. It is now probably clearer that, as a critique of ethnography or anthropology, Latour's account tends to set up and repeat the primordial encounter between the West and the rest — not entirely unlike the Western ethnographer or sinologist. In Latour's account, it is always the Western observer who introduces the divide; it is almost as if there existed some prior undivided wholeness before division. We do not wish to reject the possibility and even the necessity of concepts like the indivisible or the whole (*le tout*) that Latour's account opens, at least potentially. Yet we wish to signal that Latour's account tends toward a diffusion model in which Western divisions are first established then are disseminated. It may be, however, that those divisions within Europe are not indigenous to it. Divisions may arise at the site of encounter, neither inside nor outside. Because Latour retains a sense that modernity is indigenous to the West and external to the rest, he often seems to side with the old anthropology and sociology, however unwittingly. There is always a primordial encounter — the mainstay of a certain kind of anthropological thought. For instance, many of the sinologists who attended the Linshan rituals were observing these specific practices for the first time, which novelty they framed in the mode of discovery — as if this were a primordial encounter. Significantly, almost inevitably, the question then arose as to whether the rituals at Linshan temple were authentic, for they deviated from the elsewhere established patterns. In fact, some sinologists suggested that it was all rigged, just theatre! In other words, when the authentic past failed to emerge, discovery turned to disappointment, for the primordial encounter had failed — something had already altered and ruined the original practices. The question of whether 'inauthentic' ritual could nonetheless have effects remained unimportant and possibly unthinkable.

In the instance of ritual festivities at Linshan temple, in order to avoid reproducing the scenario of primordial encounter, one would have to have a better sense of how ritual activities have historically and discursively been framed in Fujian. This is crucial because part of the success of the modern (modernization) is its ability to locate, inhabit and intensify already existing divisions that are compatible with modernization. That is the very principle of modernization: selection of those traditional and historical patterns most in tune with the modern in order to effect a rupture with whatever is deemed unmodern. The modern is selective. Confucian notions of ritual may provide oppositions on which the modern may build, or Taoist oppositions for that matter. The sinologist might very well claim that it is not he, or the modern West, who has framed ritual as a distinct epistemological realm: already existing traditions such as Neo-Confucianism have done his work for him. He thus has license to naturalize the modern.

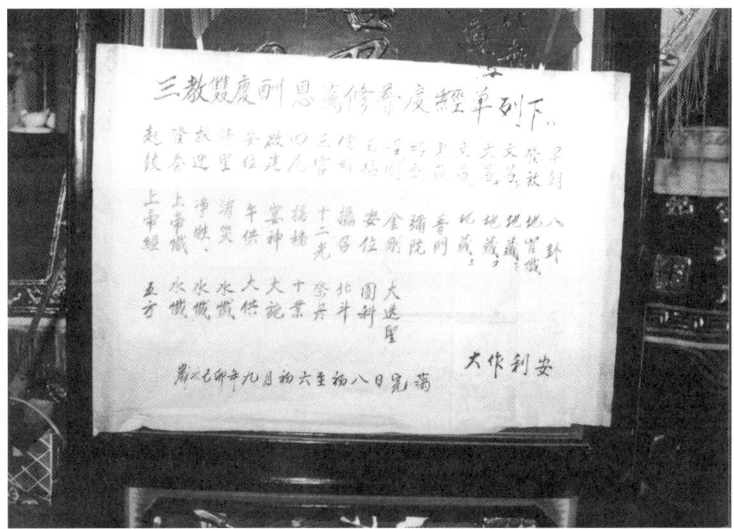

Figure 3: Program of Three in One (Confucian, Buddhist, and Taoist) Scriptures and Rites

This is where an archaeology of discourses on ritual becomes crucial for locating points of continuity and discontinuity between discursive regimes. Such an archaeological project is beyond the scope of this essay, but suffice it to say, in the history of Chinese thought, the relation of ritual or 'rites' to the State is of central concern. Moreover, there is a modern history of separation of religion from the State that takes many complicated turns and undergoes all manner of reversal (as with the Cultural Revolution). Nevertheless, even though the Western sinologist may found his observation of ritual practices on the basis of an epistemological divide between religion and science, one should not see this as primordial encounter or discovery. In fact, this is one of the older, well-documented and heavily-contested tricks of ethnography and anthropology: to act in the mode of discovery, and then to return to assure that nothing really has changed, in order to confirm that there was something real to begin with, which guarantees the possibility of continued (re)discovery and objectivity.

In the context of our participation in the ritual festivities at Linshan temple, temple leaders put a spin on our activities that challenged the ethnographer's neutrality. Temple leaders demonstrated a keen awareness of the problem of framing ritual as religion. They have to. Recent crackdowns on the Falunggong had made clear that to have one's activities framed as religion might prove disastrous. For one of the most important moments of modernization in China is that of the communist State, which has had its own versions of the modern separation of religion from science and politics. During the Cultural Revolution, temples in the Fujian region were largely destroyed. Subsequently, temples were reconstructed, and village rituals renewed. Gradually, money from Taiwanese and overseas descendants seeped back into the region, reestablishing temple registers and genealogies as well as more expansive and specific ritual practices related to these. Needless to say, the status of these revived ritual activities remains uncertain, productively and maybe necessarily uncertain. Should we think of the Cultural Revolution as a complete break with religious traditions? Are they now not really religion? Or, were they always not really religion, only mistakenly identified as such? To what extent are these new practices continuous and discontinuous with those previously slated for eradication?

Because such questions and interpretations have immediate political consequences, the temple leaders astutely frame ritual activities in a number of ways. Basically, they know how to observe the observer. Banners over the temple proclaimed a celebration in honour of the anniversary of the Communist Party and the reversion of Hong Kong — even though the dates for the temple's anniversary festivities were set with divination blocks, based on a completely different temporality than that of the State. Moreover, festivities included a series of speeches by various political figures as well as traditional theatre performances (puppet drama and opera). In many other ways as well, the boundaries between political and ritual, aesthetic and economic domains remained in flux. Under such circumstances, what would it mean to insist on framing ritual practices as religious and therefore distinct from other relations?

As for the Western and Chinese observers, they were duly observed, too — and recorded. Video records of the festivities include footage of the Western sinologists circling the ritual masters, snapping countless photos and making notes. Such videos are used largely for promotional purposes, to attract and impress Taiwanese and overseas benefactors and tourists. Western ethnographers are especially useful because they lend an air of authenticity and importance to the temple's activities. So much for the primordial encounter. In sum, it is impossible to deny that the modern gaze (both that of ethnographers and the modern State) frames ritual practices and introduces epistemological divides and domains that have an impact on the practices themselves. The temple leaders, however, seem adept at deflecting or refracting that gaze.

Figure 4: Three in One Masters read a memorial. Banners in the background proclaim the 50th Anniversary of the People's Republic of China and the return of Hong Kong to Chinese rule

On the one hand, this allows for an intersection of the communist State and global movements of capital — at ritual practices. It is an intersection in which ritual practices seem ever in danger of capture, of being caught between the State apparatus and global capital. The mutual capture of ritual by State and capital would frame ritual practices, once and for all, as something like heritage, local colour or traditions. This process is underway in many locations in contemporary China. The result would be an alternative modernity, a meeting of capitalism and communism that effects a rupture with, and reinscription of, two modernities. This rupture/reinscription proffers an effectively modern historical dimension to the meeting of two modernities, affording continuity and discontinuity with both. From this point of view, it should come as no surprise then that Southeast China is often thought as the model for a new China — that is, an alternative modernity that shifts and reinscribes the received patterns of totalization — as with those banners announcing the return of Hong Kong and the State's anniversary fluttering over the carefully reconstructed, incredibly prosperous and rapidly growing temple complex that attracts heritage tourists and scholar connaisseurs.

On the other hand, one might conclude that, by acknowledging and reinscribing various frames, the temple leaders have successfully broken the framing that strives to contain ritual forces. In other words, temple leaders are working with something like alternative modernity in order to allow ritual activities to produce their effects. In which case, alternative modernity is but an elaborate ruse. Temple leaders are not restoring or preserving ritual activities as traditions but giving ritual forces time and space to operate — in order to produce something else, something incommensurable with the modern. Temple leaders know that ritual practices strive to produce another world, an incompossible world, rather than an alternative modernity.

Alternative modernities entail displacement of an underlying totality (modernity); this displacement throws the origins of modernity into a dizzying spiral of infinite regression, because it is impossible to say that the original modernity was not always already an alternative modernity — otherwise how could it be displaced?

Incompossible worlds are rather like the parallel universes of science fiction. One might, for instance, conjure up a parallel universe in which the Cultural Revolution did not take place. Parallel universes, however, tend to preserve an notion of truth despite the reference to temporal diversity. It is simply a matter of knowing which universe you are in: the one with the Cultural Revolution or the one without it. Thus in Leibniz's case (as Goddard explains in his essay in this volume), there is a point of view that contains all the other points of view: God. But what is one to make of a world in which the Cultural Revolution both happened and did not happen? This is more like Deleuze's sense of incompossible worlds:

worlds in which a number of parallel universes co-exist and complicate a unitary point of view.

This opens another way of thinking about ritual activities in contemporary Fujian. They produce a world in which the Cultural Revolution both happened and did not happen, a world in which Marxism, communism, and capitalism all happen and do not happen. It is not that ritual practices are remnants or survivals that come from a time prior to all these. It is not simply that ritual practices are at once continuous and discontinuous with their past — despite the radical break with the Cultural Revolution, for instance, traditional practices appear renewed. Events like the Cultural Revolution are what allow for ritual practices to serve as a site for the construction of alternative modernities — for modernity's productive failure. While there is no doubt that ritual activities can be interpreted as archaic subterranean forces that subvert the imposition of modern totality, we think that there is another dimension to ritual, another temporal dimension — a looping or spiraling that allows for the folding of worlds with other worlds. This temporality is not merely cyclical, returning constantly to the same point of departure. Its looping or spiraling enables complication, fabulation or 'creative involution.' The play of historical continuity and discontinuity in Fujian ritual is not only that of rupture and reinscription (alternative modernity) but also that of folds, loops and spirals (fabulation and incompossible worlds).

In brief, instead the tired opposition between tradition and modernity that still confines Western sinological thought to modernization theory and Cold War politics, we propose thinking about the relation between (alternative) modernities and other (incompossible) worlds. To see in Fujian ritual activities the possibility for the formation of an alternative modernity is to see its suspension and alteration of the developmental logic of modernization or globalization. Clearly, as a special economic zone, Fujian province is poised between State capitalism and global capitalism, as if at a time of transition to some new stage of socio-economic development. One might even see this dialectically, as the emergence of a new stage that will produce a kind of synthesis of State and global capitalisms. The perspective of alternative modernities reminds us that whatever developments will take place, they will not proceed in a linear fashion on an established and predictable trajectory. They will defy teleological movement, whether developmental or dialectical. Local conditions — ritual activities and temple organizations — do not constitute an inert ground on which teleological development will take place. Local material conditions will incessantly shift any development sideways, so to speak. In fact, from the perspective of alternative modernities, straightforward development has always already been derailed — it is off track at its origins.

On the other hand, to see ritual activities in terms of the generation of incompossible worlds is to ask whether local conditions are fated to play the role of divergence-in-convergence. Are their powers of fabulation so weakened or compromised that we can only imagine them as derailing modernity and not making other worlds?

Looking at contemporary ritual activities in this way also recalls another thinker of ritual, Henri Lefebvre, who followed the transformation of village life in Pyrenees region of southwest France during France's rapid postwar economic reconstruction.[7] He looked at how modernization (managerial capitalism and consumer society) altered the rhythms and spaces of everyday life, with an emphasis on the transformation of village 'festival' (fête) into leisure. On the one hand, he rued the passing of the time and space of festival activities, and posited a rupture between the old and new that was impossible to overcome. On the other hand, in leisure activities, he saw the persistence of festival, albeit in diminished, compromised, and even negated form. And he held out some hope that festival, as otherness within the capitalist everyday of leisure might provide an immanent critique of capitalism, and even open new worlds. In other words, he saw festival at once dialectically and non-dialectically. Festival promised the advent of the 'total person' and the end of history — the dialectical end of dialectical movement — because something about festival and everyday life worked non-dialectically.

His notion of festival is not incompatible with Walter Benjamin's dialectical image, in which two temporal realities co-exist but whose difference cannot be dialectically sublated or overcome. Benjamin, too, stumbled onto the end of history (particularly as narration) in an apparently dialectical moment that no longer allowed dialectical movement. Thinking the everyday is important to this sense of the breakdown of the dialectical movement because the everyday implies a whole or all that is not compartmentalized yet is somehow systematic (though not in the usual sense of system). Even leisure, as Lefebvre shows, is not just a part or sphere or separate activity; it touches everything. Thus the political promise of everyday life is that it might enable the release of the creative potential of human beings on a daily basis — rather than a narrowly political revolution that does not transform everyday life (the Soviet revolution for Lefebvre). Nonetheless, Lefebvre remained very pessimistic about the possibilities for festival to end dialectical movement and to create a new world. He remained intent upon the possibility of the dialectical capture of ritual, as it were.

It is a shame that he never attended or followed festivals in Fujian province. For ritual activities in Fujian province suggest to us something like multilectical images — that is, the co-existence of not only present and past but of incommensurable presents and incommensurable pasts. Maybe here the dialectics of everyday life (the negative transformation of festival into leisure and heritage) not only meets its historical end but begins to generate new, incompossible worlds (fabulation and creative involution). Of course, the multiplicity of multilectal images is not a simple collection of fragments. Rather the multiple origins implicit in multilectal images generate a movement that is not attributable to any one origin; they imply a vector, a movement without origin (in the sense of without resemblance to any one origin). This is not to say that ritual activities absolutely cannot be captured by some kind of dialectical movement — maybe, under the pressure of capitalist development, temple festivals will transform into the managerial or post-Fordist capitalist everyday of leisure and heritage; or maybe State capitalism will force other transformations. We don't know. But we do know that the current sinological work on ritual, by framing ritual as tradition, does no more than provide raw material for someone else's dialectical movement, as if in all innocence (because a-critically).

Creative Involution

It is as if the village temple with its earth deity (or deities) stood at the centre of two different hierarchies and two different communities. On the one hand, there is the actual community with its temple organizations and leaders. On the other hand, there is the cosmological community with its liturgical organizations and ritual masters. In both instances, the temple gods are at the centre. Recent debates on the role of ritual in Chinese religion tend to stress the importance of one kind of organization over the other. Some argue that the Taoist liturgical framework plays the important structuring role, while others contend that the lay sponsors impose their meanings on the ritual. When the emphasis falls on liturgy, the argument is that ritual specialists go above the local gods to invoke higher cosmological forces. When the emphasis falls on lay organizations, it is individual contractual relations with the powers at hand (local gods) that come to the fore. What remains unexamined is the relation between actual (or local) and cosmological hierarchies or communities. Moreover, despite their different emphases, both sides of the debate presume a division between the secular and the liturgical or cosmological. The effect is to frame religious community and practice as distinct from secular or contractual community (composed of individuals) — a thoroughly modern divide.

The ritual view, however, submits that local powers are differentiated expressions of cosmological forces. There is no 'modern' divide. It is easy to understand why the ritual view creates some consternation. It becomes impossible to situate ritual practice comfortably on either side of the modern divide, as a premodern religious community or modern secular community — or even as an uncanny or untimely juncture of past and present. Moreover, another hallowed divide of the modern comes into question, namely, the teleological separation of nature and culture, in the specific form of man's instrumental triumph over nature. (Recall that this is why Latour sees the modern as inherently technocratic.) This instrumental view of nature is allegedly absent in traditional Chinese culture. But then, has this teleological divide really been so present in the modern West? Latour argues that, no, the West has all along been mixing nature and culture, crossing the divide — yet the West commits its energies to sustaining the illusion of a divide, simply to effect changes on a vaster scale. Less dramatically, Stephen Toulmin argues that nature has always been part of the modern equation.[8] He speaks of 'cosmopolis,' that is, different configurations of cosmos ('nature') and polis ('state'). His account introduces a way to think different cosmopolitical configurations — which potentially calls for a rethinking of values. Are certain configurations of cosmos and polis better? By whose terms? Under what conditions? Of course, a certain problem persists, for if one is to think in terms of configurations of cosmos and polis, then to some extent one already presupposes some kind of separation between the natural and the political.

Rather than assume a divide between political and cosmological organizations, we'd like to explore the ritual view, that there is not a divide. But there is differentiation: local powers are differentiated expressions of cosmological forces. Temple leaders and ritual masters are acting together (but differently) on a set of cosmopolitical relations — on a cosmopolitical configuration. Put another way, there is one centre but it is multiple. Not only can there be more than one deity, but also each resident deity is multivalent, embodying and emanating different qualities, which shift over time. It is the inherent multiplicity of deities that allows for temple and ritual alliances: among its many qualities, each deity has some that permit connection with the deities in other temples. This multiplicity also affords a point of intersection for the different organizations centring on the temple — for instance, temple leaders and ritual masters. Consequently, one organization cannot be given precedence or priority over another. From the perspective of the temple deities, the two organizations emerge together. Likewise, individual and community (if one wishes to use these terms) derive from one another, or more precisely, emerge together. Any individual or contractual relation with local deities or the powers at hand is equally a cosmological relation.

Nevertheless, this multiplicity is not an inert multiplicity, a neutral collection of differences. For deities are at heart unstable. Or, to be precise, we see deities as metastable. A physical system is said to be in metastable equilibrium (or false equilibrium) when the least modification serves to break the equilibrium. A prime example is crystallization. With super-saturated solutions and super-chilled liquids, for instance, introducing the smallest impurity with a structure isomorphic with the crystal serves as a seed for crystallization. Any system in a metastable state harbours potentials that are incompatible insofar as they belong to heterogeneous dimensions. This is why systems in a metastable state can only perpetuate themselves by dephasing, that is, by a change in the state of the system.[9] In the instance of deities, metastability is often evidenced in double personalities and multiple personalities. The deity of a village temple nearly Linshan derives from a woman drowned in a flood not so long ago. Such a deity clearly presents conflicting attitudes toward water. Is she a wrathful deity who must be propitiated to prevent her from calling forth another flood? Or is she a benevolent deity whom one should revere for her determination to prevent floods? Other deities similarly combine different, seemingly incommensurable traits and qualities. The point is that deities are not stable configurations of multiple traits. They are fundamentally ready to break; they are sites of difference, difference that is in some sense foundational. It is in this sense that they are metastable. One might think of this as a kind of cosmological differential. As a consequence, moving a deity from its perch in a temple is a powerful act, one that potentially alters an entire field of forces. Summoning a deity opens its fundamental asymmetry or instability. The question then is, what happens to this cosmological difference? How does it work in ritual? Is the goal of ritual ultimately to contain cosmological difference, to assure that, in the end, everything returns to what it was? Can one return to a metastable state?

Now there is no doubt that organizations centred on the temple frequently entail very coded hierarchical spaces. One has only to look at differential access to various zones on the basis of gender and rank to understand how heavily 'overcoded' temple organizations and ritual practices can become. Such rules and codes — from the organization of communal participation to the liturgical activities of ritual masters — are retroactive attempts to capture the cosmological differential. They frame and formalize the event retrospectively as a set of constant relations between standardized terms. These rules and codes then claim the role of foundation. They involve power formations that strive to constrain the processes of emergence and transformation. Apparently, the rules and codes that attend ritual events do little more than contain the forces of change, and to reproduce the same social structures. This is why ritual events are so often seen as fundamentally conservative, as mechanisms for reproduction of the status quo. Typically, the idea of ritual events as pure social reproduction is often evoked to establish a divide between the traditional (which rejects and stifles change) and the modern (which embraces change and innovation). However, to insist on seeing ritual events only in terms of repetition of the same ignores ritual's claims for transformation and change. And more generally, such a stance denies history altogether.

Again, this is why ritual proves so important to Western thinkers of the modern as different as Bakhtin and Lefebvre and even Benjamin. For Bakhtin and Lefevbre, there is a dramatic, seemingly uncontrollable eruption of difference in the carnival or festival, which disrupts existent hierarchies — the world turns upside down. Then the world returns, apparently right side up, as it always was. Has anything changed in the process? What is the relation between difference and repetition? Ritual presents a relation of repetition and difference that promises something that is not sheer reproduction of the same (pure retotalization). Nor does it entail the production of sheer difference (in the manner of capitalist detotalization). Difference is evoked and channeled in ways somehow at odds with modern capitalist regulation of difference, yet not entirely at odds with regulation. Ritual relates repetition and difference in a manner different from the restless detotalizing and retotalizing movement of capital. But does ritual's difference from capitalism afford some kind of resistance to it? Rather pessimistically, Lefevbre frequently signaled the impossibility of festival resistance (even though he never ceased his attempts to formulate its resistance): it invariably became leisure and thus complicit with managerial capital and consumer culture. Bakhtin, of course, is often accused of undue optimism, of generating heroically carnivalesque bodies.[10] Such are the broad questions that come with attempts to think ritual in relation to the modern, and in particular, modern capitalism. We feel compelled to add some others. Do global or macrohistorical teleologies leave no time and space for local entelechies? What manner of resistance do local entelechies enable? Is their potential for resistance best thought deconstructively, in relation to the West? What comes of thinking local entelechies constructively or productively — just more identities?

At this juncture, let's just say that Bakhtin and Lefevbre's accounts of carnival and festival help to underscore some the political stakes implicit in our basic problematic, namely, 'How do ritual events introduce and work cosmological, or rather, cosmopolitical difference?' At stake is difference from modern capitalism and within it.

On the occasion of the anniversary festivities at Linshan temple, the ritual event began with the Taoist and Three-in-One ritual specialists forming two ensembles before the temple, in the courtyard. Needless to say, preparations for the event had been underway for some months, but the ritual event started with ritual specialists setting up portable altars in the temple courtyard in order to generate a space heavily overcoded with symbolism — the altars are arranged in accordance with ritual patterns, and the ritual specialists dance and run between and around the altars in various cosmological configurations. This is the prelude to summoning forth the deities from within the temple — a shift in their situation that serves to transform their 'instability' into a force (or to dephase their metastability). The carefully prepared and overcoded space is designed to prevent a chaotic, undirected release of that force. The idea is to harness and guide it. This controlled relation to cosmological forces we will refer to as *sheng*, for it evokes self-cultivation, sageliness, and hierarchical codes. In terms of the practices of ritual masters, *sheng* implies controlled processes of self-transformation — techniques of visualization, the recitation of 'secret' mantra, performance of mudras (hand gestures enacted so fluidly and rapidly as to blur distinctions between signs), and choreography — all of which lead to identification with a divinity in a stepwise, encoded fashion. In effect, however, *sheng* simultaneously works within hierarchical overcoding and carefully decodes signs in order to move upward in the hierarchical ladder. As with the 'cursive' blurring of signs in mudra performance, the creation of zones of indistinction allows the movement to attain a higher level of coding — until the point that one reaches the divinity itself.

At the other extreme is what we call *ling*, which is best exemplified in spirit possession, that is, possession by a deity or demon — which involves trance, loss of self, spontaneous and uncontrolled bodily movements, and speaking in the voices of gods. In the course of the ritual event over many days, the ritual masters and spirit mediums will move between these two poles at various speeds and in different locations within and before the temple. In other words, by moving the metastable deities, the ritual event releases the force implicit in their fundamental asymmetry, and then establishes two different yet interrelated relations to that force — *sheng* and *ling* — what might be thought of as polar attractors in what is now a field of forces. *Sheng* and *ling* serve as polar attractors precisely because they themselves are paradoxical positions. In some respects, they replicate the paradoxes implicit in esoteric and exoteric approaches to religious experience. The esoteric approach claims that, in theory, anyone can undertake the intensive training needed to attain identification with the deity, but in practice, few are capable of such austerities, and very few reach the summit. The exoteric approach suggests that no particular training is needed since the deity already resides within, but as a consequence, there is no guarantee where or when (or even if) the deity will happen to you. These are two very different approaches to the force of cosmological difference, with different senses of how to gauge human interaction with deities. What is striking about the ritual events at Linshan temple is their evocation of both approaches in the form of polar attractors that organize the ritual field.

Between the poles of *sheng* and *ling* is a wide range of possibilities for viewing and participating in the ritual event. There are planned events and spontaneous events. As the deities begin to emerge, members of the community are drawn toward the site where the ritual masters dance and speak their invocations in the temple courtyard. Subsequent to the ritual harnessing their forces, the temple's gods will go out on a procession. Villagers carry the deities through the village and around its boundaries — drawing even greater numbers into the temple. This procession of the deities retraces boundaries and establishes the temple as a centre of sorts — an echo of *sheng* hierarchies. Yet this *sheng* fractures into multiple spheres of activity around the temple (in keeping with the primordial eccentricity of the deity centre, that has now been set in motion). By evening and over the next days, the courtyard space becomes dense with diverse, apparently unrelated or loosely related activities. In one corner, food is cooked. In another, financial offerings are recorded. In yet another opera or marionette plays are performed. Ritual music plays in another corner. Crowds fill the courtyard, bearing offerings, watching theatrical performances, or participating in that ritual actively performed intermittently before the temple. At various intervals, delegations from aligned villages arrive, frequently with brass bands and majorettes, sometimes with traditional music ensembles, and sometimes with palaquins bearing god statues or possessed mediums.

Figure 5: A possessed medium carried on a sedan chair in a procession in Xianyou

Although the procession of the deities' palaquin marks boundaries and a centre, the movement of the sedan chair of the gods also provides one of our favorite examples of participation that tends toward *ling*. A palaquin of the gods rushes into a crowd, born on the shoulders of eight elderly men. It begins to spin clockwise, rapidly, and then suddenly, impossibly it spins the other way. Several members of the crowd go into spontaneous trance, dancing around the gods' sedan chair. Some of them shoulder the poles, and the palaquin charges off into the crowd again. As the god statues move, the crowd moves with them, some of them moving into trance and entering into the palaquin's movement. The seat of the deities assumes a degree of autonomy and harnesses individuals to move it. At the level of movement at least, the gods assert their will.

As we've already discussed, there is a tendency in accounts of ritual to stress how the spontaneous is captured by the planned, or how the loss of the self is captured by overcoding and hierarchizing of self. The emphasis falls on recuperation of difference — the capture of *ling* in *sheng*, so to speak. Or, conversely, with respect to what we call *ling*, there is a tendency to construe it as ecstatic in a simple way — as a moment when the ritual event opens outside itself, to a simple outside. Either way, the ritual event becomes a machine for turning difference into the same. We'd like to challenge this way of positing an inside and outside to the ritual event, in which the inside always wins, recuperating and retotalizing what enters from outside. This is why we wish to stress the paradoxical quality of both *sheng* and *ling* (as different modes of relation to the deities' fundamental eccentricity or asymmetry).

There is a sense in which *sheng* elaborately lays out insides and outsides — hierarchical concentric circles — with the deity or deities at the pinnacle. The image is one of infinite ascent, a mountain whose peak vanishes into the sky, like that of deities within Linshan temple. Yet, because at the pinnacle one finds a fundamental asymmetry, instability or eccentricity, *sheng* also lends itself to an image of infinite crossing or lateral movement — each step upward toward the centre is, at the same time, a step sideways away from the centre — for this is a tricky, eccentric centre. No wonder there are so many esoteric codes and observations to keep the sagely one on track! What is important about *sheng* is that, however much it is territorializing or reterritorializing, *sheng* is not simply a matter of inside and outsides. It generates a finite territority with infinite surface. A useful image here is one common in contemporary popular culture: the hierarchical pantheon of the mandala dissolving into a digital fractal structure, and vice versa. *Sheng* might be thought of as cosmological fractality. It makes the relation between finite and infinite — in this case that between earthly community and celestial pantheon — seem manageable and controllable. Surely this is why esoteric approaches often have such an easy relation with the powers at hand, and with state formations.

Still, there is a paradox, partly because the relation between finite and infinite is not so manageable in practice or experience. Or, in another register, the problem is that, because *sheng* is all positions and thus surfaces, it is ultimately unable to contain anything; everything is at once inside and outside. *Ling,* on the other hand, is a kind of depth. Its depth comes not of a simple outside, nor is *ling* an inner depth (interiority) in relation to *sheng*. To some extent, it recalls the 'inside of the outside' evoked in Goddard's essay on the fold. The loss of self in trance, for instance, implicates an inside deeper than interiority, one that is also ecstatic (opening to outside) — limbs twitching and tongues speaking in response to the deities' passage. *Ling* might be thought of as the subjectivation of all the material and sensory paraphernalia of esoteric practices. In a manner of speaking, it entails connections between different sites or phases on the mountain. Basically, *ling* says, 'Every step up the mountain looks the same, so how do you know what step you are at? Any step might be *the* step.' It finds pure repetition across *sheng*'s hierarchical distinctions, in order to stage improbable, unlikely, magical connections between different times and spaces (phases) of sagely ascent. It decodes and deterritorializes coded objects and states, but most importantly, *ling* dephases. It treats *sheng* hierarchies as a metastable state in their excess of order and symmetry. In dephasing, symmetry is at once broken and retained.

Ling thus calls on the deity's eccentricity as a non-localizable force. Trance, for instance, makes the first step and the pinnacle indistinguishable — automatic identification with the gods, which comes with automatism, that is, tics and twitches and babble. Ritual instruments become playthings, and vice versa. We do not, however, see this as a matter of distinguishing and choosing between ritual implement and plaything (as some would have it).[11] A paper horse, for instance, hovers between toy and deity, on the basis of its potential for animation. Ritual masters, as they summon the deities from the temple, brandish a paper maché horse while they dance, and then paint eyes in the white sockets. The horse, having its eyes opened, opens its eyes and comes to life. Likewise, the deities' sedan chair is both ritual instrument and plaything, charging the crowds, forcing conversions, and leading crowds to the courtyard — animated and animating.

Figure 6: Paper horse

Thus the relation between *sheng* and *ling* is, in some way, non-relation. *Ling* is always undermining the coded relations of *sheng* yet has no purchase without them. *Sheng* continually brings *ling* into relation, but in fact, cannot relate anything without it. Their relation then is non-dialectical, and yet the co-existence of these two different modes of relation to the gods promises the emergence of something new — not just a combination or synthesis of two modes but another mode altogether. Clearly, this could be thought dialectically, and the new mode could be called modernity (or something like modernity, or an alternative modernity). This is to fix the outcome, to say that the ritual event has now ended, forever converged. Ritual, however, has not yet finished with the non-relation. And the co-existence of two modes of relation to deities — *ling* and *sheng* — continues to allow for two co-existent modes of relation — as two different takes on transformation. The paper horse, for instance, has two lives. In one life, it is a trivial sort of paper toy that is ritually blessed, encoded and elevated to ritual horse, albeit one without eyeballs. In another life, its eyes open, and it becomes an animated horse, but it is treated playfully, with all the inquisitive destructiveness that we children can bring to toys. These transformations involve two different ways of transforming or animating. The palaquin of the gods also has two lives, as do the ritual masters and spirit mediums who alternately perform rites by the book and fall into trance — as do watchers and participants. The difference can be thought of as that between spontaneous and controlled transformation, so long as it is acknowledged that the two modes of transformation are different but not distinguishable. It is a matter of differentiation not division or distinction.

The non-relation of *sheng* and *ling* explains the emergence of many different zones of activity in the courtyard and temple in the course of the ritual event: offerings, cooking, watching theatre, watching marionettes, playing music, and so forth. Topologically, the non-relation of *sheng* and *ling* assures that these events are somehow related to ritual activities but not in the manner of centre and periphery. Different degrees of *sheng* and *ling* coalesce at specific nodes of performance, usually around ritual objects (such as the palaquin, the horse, the incense burners, the temple doors, spirit writing or talismans, and so forth). Aesthetically, it is synesthetic or amodal experience that dominates. This is especially remarkable between nodes of performance: it becomes hard to see for the noise, and hard to hear for the colours; sounds hit you between the eyes, and the visible strikes between the ears (somewhere around the limbic system); this is about sensory excess generating sensory disintegration and re-integration (affect). So many co-presences make discrimination and contradiction impossible.

Yet this does not mean that there is nothing systematic at all. Even if the practices of ritual masters do not constitute a proper centre, there is no doubt that the ritual event would not unfold without their summoning of the deities. The movement of the deities inscribes a loop (in and out of the temple, around the village, around the courtyard, and so forth), generating nodes that spin minor resonant loops — some planned, others spontaneous — that become minor worlds in the sense that they are performative sites with coherent viewing positions. In this respect, the movement of the gods nicely fits the model of feedback and transformation. The deities are a kind of immanent cause — a non-localizable symmetry breaking that generates new phases by dephasing — the deities, like the metastable state, remain immanent in the phases. Yet the question recurs: what difference does it make, this looping? The concept of looping, with its autopoetic overtones, implies a certain kind of self-referentiality, and if one is not careful, closure, and potentially, a return of the same. The ritual event might be construed as pure recuperation or assimilation.

At this point, however, we can put this question about repetition and difference another way. The performative nodes that spring up around ritual objects such as the incense burner or the palaquin — or even around the opera performance — are like monadic points of view on the ritual event. For it is possible to see and experience the entire ritual event from one of these nodes. In fact, some villagers are clearly there for the opera, others to ogle the crowd or eat, while others arrive to entreat the deities. Of course, each node sees some parts of the event more distinctly and others more obscurely; each has its truth. They recall Leibniz's incompossible worlds: for participants at one node, it is as if certain other events do not take place. In the ritual event, for instance, there are participants for whom the horse's eyes do not open yet opera happens. As Deleuze remarks, temporality presents a great problem for the notion of truth, because, at every event, time bifurcates into different temporalities with incompossible truths[12]. Confronted with this problem, Leibniz resorted to an overall view, that of God, which lets you know whether you are in one world or another. Analogously, in the ritual event, one always has recourse to the deities in order to say, 'I didn't see the ritual masters summon the deities, but I know this took place, and so my experience is relative to that overall event.' In this way, the overall truth of the ritual event is preserved, and the formation of different nodes of performance and viewing positions does not undermine the position of the deities. So long as the deities provide some kind of overall view, the different nodes of the event do not become entirely self-referential; they remain open to the deities and to one another. Indeed the ritual event does imply something like a supreme or all-gathering witness — or heaven, or the pantheon of the gods. What to make of this gods' eye view?

Although we'd like to say that Leibniz's Baroque folds are a variation on Tang screens and Taoist ripples of non-contradiction, this is a rather long and complicated story that might only serve to sustain the Baroque as the point of reference. Consequently, we'll just point out a basic and crucial difference that arises between the ritual event and Leibniz's God and Truth. Above we suggested that there were two modes of relation and transformation implicit in Fujian temple deities. *Sheng* implied an excess of symmetry with its excessively hierarchized spatio-temporal formations — to the point that it comes close to a metastable state. One might think of the deities as the metastable state, while *sheng* is an initial dephasing that retains most of the metastable state. *Sheng* is like the symmetrical rings of ripples that result from a rock thrown into a pond, which retain so much of the molecular symmetry of water itself. Deities are an immanent cause, always immanent in *sheng*'s infinite hierarchies — a concept presented succinctly and directly in many mandala.

Ling is the resonance that arises between and across ripples. It is a resonance based on their semblance (not resemblance). It finds semblances across incommensurables. *Ling* thus presents a different mode of retention of the deities' metastability. One might think of a cork on a wave, which travels in a circle; it moves up, down and around yet returns to its initial point; it never moves forward or backward. The ripple is also a loop or temporal tic, a dimension of spatio-temporal symmetry from the expanding rings. *Ling* presents something like loops of semblance across something unfolding symmetrically in time and space.

From the angle of *sheng* and *ling*, we would have to say that the overall view that protects the integrity of the ritual event is never entirely transcendent. Commentators who wish to insist on transcendence in ritual or on transcendental causes usually call upon *sheng*. Yet even with *sheng*, the deities are immanent. And *ling* makes transcendent viewing possible everywhere, as if immanent. The ritual event calls on immanence to a far greater degree than Leibniz's God (which is not to deny this latter its share of immanence).

Ultimately, this immanence means that the ritual event is more open to temporal difference than Leibniz's monad. For each node has great potential for autonomy in relation to other nodes and the deities. This is precisely why ritual activities in Fujian province are able to serve as conduits for, and refractors of, state capital, global capital, and local economies. The danger, of course, is that local, state, or global formations will exploit the autonomies of the ritual event in order to frame the temporality of the ones against the others, simply and indifferently. At best one could hope for an alternative modernity. This is a real danger because the power of capital also lies in its immanence, in its ability to work within formations like those we have attributed to *sheng*, to transform its infinite finitude (rather like fractal surfaces) in an unfurling boundary of material expansion and incursion. This movement of capital tends to generate contradictions in the ritual space of non-contradictions, which then usually demand resolution in the form of local or national identity. Once non-contradiction is broken and contradictions appear, *ling* becomes a moment of dialectical contradiction (rather than multilectical non-contradiction), where the contradictions of dialectical movement are writ large in their terror and impossibility. The loss of self in trance becomes more like cinematic shock to the body.

The point of these observations is not to say that the immanence of ritual necessarily gives way to the immanence of capital. There is no march of history, and we do not wish to rue in advance an end that is not preordained. Nor do we wish to set the ritual event nostalgically or romantically against the logic of capitalism. Rather what seems important is to think an immanent causality that is not capital yet seems in many ways a semblance of capital. For the ritual event is not simply an obstacle to the movement of capital or a contradiction within it. It is a different kind of movement altogether, one that we've characterized as multilectical, as a kind of fabulation or creative involution. The ritual event thus asks us to think differently from capital but not oppositionally, which implies very different forms of resistance and of transformation.

Figure 7: Between economies — offerings at the Linshan Temple

A Wobbly Script

Thinking the ritual event in this way first demands a shift in emphasis from epistemology to ontology, and then to ontogenesis (prior to ontology). On the one hand, there is the problem of the epistemological framing of ritual activities as religion, that is, as distinct from science and politics. Sinological approaches to ritual practices resort to epistemological framing in order to guarantee the truth of their knowledge production. They divide the immanent whole of the pantheon of deities in order to reinforce an omniscient, transcendent perspective. Although they make ethnographic and historical claims, such approaches are far closer to a sociological understanding of ritual, which relies on a divide between tradition and modernity in the manner of modernization theory. On the other hand, there is the far more complex question of alternative modernities, and the challenge it presents to modernization theory. The idea of alternative modernity tends to posit resistance in the very inertness of traditions, as if their materiality slowed and thus spatialized the forces of the outside into a new, alternatively modern formation. This approach effectively challenges the simplistic relation to the past presented by modernization theory. Yet it often unwittingly unifies traditions under the sign of generalized negativity, often via the nation (Chinese modernity, Indian modernity, Japanese modernity, and so forth). If the formation of the nation can be seen as a somewhat contradictory response to the advance of capital (stabilizing what capital threatens to undermine yet ironically advancing the march of capital by providing it with workable units), then alternative modernity might be seen as a contradictory response to spatio-temporal homogenization.

In the instance of ritual activities in Fujian province, however, such a strategy tends to deny a dynamic role for ritual practices and their 'objects' (ritual implements, talimans, fetishes, and such). In fact, the alternative modernity strategy tends to deny a dynamic role for matter in general, for it sees materiality as the same as materialism (that is, materiality as quantity and quantification). Here we return to problem of the modern as an epistemological divide between religion, science and politics — and the problem of non-arbitrary nature.

Pietz's discussion of the fetish recalls Latour's tendency to think in terms of a primordial encounter between Western technocrats and natives.[13] Pietz makes clear what is at stake in the establishment of an epistemological divide. He writes of how Dutch traders, confronted with peoples who insisted on the power of specific objects (fetishes), concluded that they had a false understanding of cause and effect. These peoples had taken ordinary objects and invested them with subjective powers and values — fetichized them. In other words, in order to deny the fetish the power to construct worlds and histories, the Dutch traders had to insist that the fetishes were really just objects like any others. They had to ignore people's claims that these objects were somehow *materially* different from other objects. Nature, and matter itself, had to be qualitatively non-arbitrary, producing just more objects not differently endowed ones — what Ian Stewart dubs the mass-produced universe.[14] Objects lost their power to construct worlds, as Westerners made belief the central problematic in understanding the operations of fetishes, talismans, and ritual objects. This was crucial to the modern epistemological divide: true (scientific) knowledge dealt with cause and effect, which depended on the non-arbitrariness of nature as well as inertness of matter. From the perspective of Dutch traders, for instance, cultures with fetishes or talismans or ritual implements remained lost in a world of effects. They remained too close to nature, seeing it naively (qualitatively, in terms of effects) not analytically (quantitatively, in terms of cause and effect).

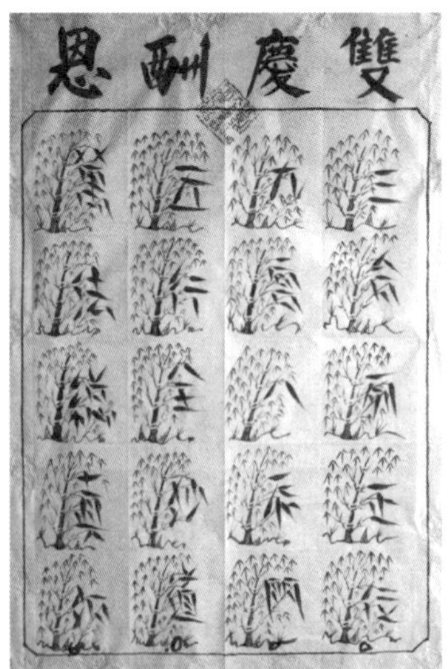

Figure 8: One of many sheets of writing posted on the outside walls of Linshan temple for the ritual festivities.

Ultimately, the idea of non-arbitrary nature functions to single out one world and one history, based on cause and effect. Other cultures come to be seen as survivals of prior historical stages (or simply non-historical), because history demanded a framing of nature scientifically, that is, as inert or passive (though rational). Fetishes and ritual objects are thus denied the power to construct stories, histories, or worlds. The introduction of modern epistemological divisions between science and religion works to undermine the notion of a material difference between ritual objects and any other object. Any claims for qualitative difference between, say, this ritual robe and that ordinary robe are attributed to subjective investment, or projection of value, or belief. For the moderns, Pietz and Latour seem to agree, objects lose all ontogenetic claims. For epistemological divides assured that only humans have the power to construct, invent, or create.

There is another take on the fetish that differs greatly from that of Pietz or Latour — that of Marx. While Marx might be said ultimately to ascribe a false ontology to the fetish, his approach is important because it does acknowledge the liveliness of fetishes — and, we'd add, the life of ritual objects. Naturally, it is possible to accuse Marx of making a questionable distinction between naïve perception and analytical or scientific perception.[15] Yet the luster of gold is not entirely beside the point for him. More importantly, although he would like us to demystify the fetish, this is clearly not so easy for him as it was for the Dutch traders. For Marx's fetish does have the power to construct worlds, however false they might ultimately prove. In the end, the falsity of certain worlds can be decided only on the basis of the ontological priority of the object over the fetish. That is to say, there is first the object (an ordinary object, associated with use value), then the fetish (an extraordinary object, linked to exchange value).[16] Thus Marx's account raises another kind of question, that of priority (and thus temporality): is the fetish first an ordinary thing and then an extraordinary thing? A great deal of historicizing and philosophizing depends on sorting out this priority, in order to jump-start linear historical movement. The movement from ordinary to extraordinary, because dialectical, quickly becomes complex. It becomes harder and harder to see the extraordinary object as merely derivative or secondary.

The interest of ritual objects —and there is a broad range: god statues, mudra, mandala, talismans, incense burners, paper horses, and so forth — is not that they reverse the priority of movement from ordinary to extraordinary, from object to subjective imputation of value (or from use value to exchange value). On the contrary, there is no such priority. A ritual object can be both ordinary and extraordinary, and be acknowledged as such. Once again we arrive at a kind of temporal loop or oscillation rather than a decisive break that inaugurates eras (divisible time) or dialectical movement. While this oscillating or looping might seem to imply stalemate or stasis, it is generative, precisely because it is a matter of an interaction between two forces. Naturally, in the course of ritual event, objects take on ritual functions in accordance to how they are situated and moved. A god statue in the temple does not behave in the same way as one in the palaquin. This is true of any number of other objects used in the ritual event. Previously, we talked about the retention of metastability in order to underscore the power implicit in ritual acts. At this juncture, we must add that this retention of metastability assures the co-emergence of ordinary and extraordinary qualities in ritual objects. When a ritual master says, 'This is no ordinary robe,' he truly means that the robe is not ordinary, yet his claim does not rule out the very ordinariness of the same robe. One might say that the object's extraordinary qualities derive from their positioning or situatedness. This is not a bad way to think about it, provided one does not forget that that situatedness is actually a material difference not a matter of belief or subjective projection of value.

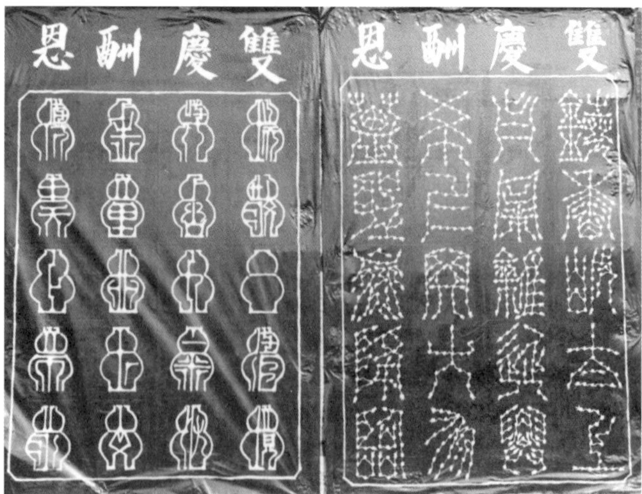

Figure 9: One of many sheets of writing posted on the outside walls of Linshan temple for the ritual festivities.

The different forms of talismanic writing, brushed on coloured paper and plastered on the exterior walls of the temple, provide a prime example. They are, in one sense, very ordinary. Glued on the temple walls, they are almost like posters or announcements, they are of the day and maybe of the hour— just so much decoration. There are, for instance, yellow sheets with a series of bamboo trees that have certain leaves accentuated to form characters — playful yet readable renditions of auspiciousness. Other sheets bear characters that are more like what is traditionally thought of as talismanic writing (*fu*) and diagrams (*tu*). There are blue sheets on which characters coalesce from what look like white tadpoles or snakes. Black sheets show characters that verge on star charts and diagrams. Still others present characters carefully re-worked into shapes that recall two jars: one atop another, with the bottom jar inverted. With different kinds of highly stylized characters, the line becomes faint between ordinary, readable characters and characters that are extraordinary, not intelligible to just any eyes. What is striking is that these are clearly scripts, meant to be somehow read — but how could you angle yourself to read them? What path could you trace with these patterns? There are many angles, many paths. This is one indication of the co-existence of multiple, oddly connected and disconnected worlds.

One might think of the power of such scripts in relation to the now-familiar production of alien languages in cinema. For instance, sound engineers take a known language or languages and tweak it, altering its tempo and intonations and pitch, often playing it backward. To hear it, it is speech to the ears. Yet it is incomprehensible. As such, the engineered alien tongue calls attention to the pre-semantic, a-signifying powers of language. Analogously, talismanic scripts evoke writing to be read yet cannot be read in any ordinary way. They, too, conjure up a pre-semantic or a-signifying force of language. One has the rhythms and intervals and patterns of writing without signification. Yet there is an important difference between cinema's alien tongues and talismanic writing. In film, the production of alien languages is intended to present an experience of the outlandish, exotic or creepy — it is largely a matter of sheer difference. The process is reversible technologically: you can reverse the tweeking and return to the initial language or languages. This is a simple schema of translatability and co-figuration. With talismanic scripts, however, the goal is to move beyond the mere difference of translatability, to go beyond a language that is just another language used by just another race or people. Crucial to talismanic writing is a sort of wobble that is not reversible.

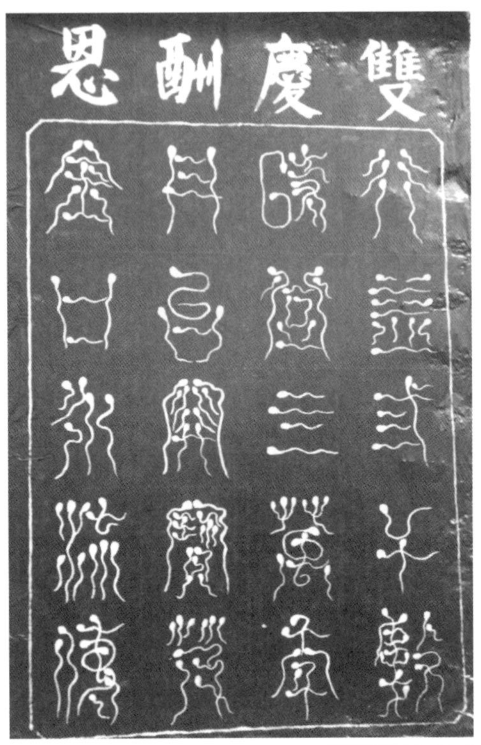

Figure 10: One of many sheets of writing posted on the outside walls of Linshan temple for the ritual festivities.

A range of procedures is used to produce talismans and diagrams — the repetition of elements, the mixing of familiar and unfamiliar elements, the alignment of characters or elements of characters with auspicious shapes or patterns — all of which underscore the sense of a relation of transformation rather than signification. And as is well documented, those who write these scripts undergo some sort of ritual preparation or purification — that is, they transform their body. What is striking is that, from the standpoint of calligraphic art (*shufa*), the brushwork of the resulting scripts appears weak. It is weak transformation, so to speak. Talismanic writing does not channel or harness cosmological forces in the manner of calligraphic art, with an eye to individuating each character while containing and balancing the individuation of each character — which is an apparatus of certain kind of imperial machine.[17] Calligraphic art insists on, or plays with, strength of line and the brushwork of character elements, even in the most cursive forms. Although the talisman writer also follows established models and patterns, the resulting lines and characters, however elaborate, appear weak. This weakness is that of a strange, extraordinary body, however. It is not the body of the master calligrapher, but of one overcome by the mutability of writing (the *ling* of trance) — it is the twitch of the relaxed arm. Only the established patterns (*sheng*, so to speak) prevent this writing from complete dispersal. There is a decided wobble to every element that threatens the overall harmony, which often calls on solid architectures to slow its drift — a swarm of bugs, a house of leaning cards, a bowl of wriggling noodles.

It is wobble that generates incompossible worlds between the ordinary and extraordinary. The alien languages of cinema are attempts at parallel universes (always already co-figured with the truth of the American globe). The stylistic differentiation of calligraphic art tends to produce concentric spheres of mobility — worlds within worlds, endless cloisters. Wobble allows for incompossible worlds within this world. It sketches out the field of modulation implicit in the materiality of writing. Like the ritual event, at the heart of ritual, scriptural wobble generates immanent points of otherness that allow the co-existence of autonomous experiences (and even economies) within its own, precisely because materiality matters for it. We can't say what will come of the encounter between global capital and the co-folding economies implicit in the ritual event. Maybe complication will be reduced to a simple containment or assimilation, or scuttled into complicity. Still, as the co-folding operations of talismanic writing shows, we will nonetheless need to think about the ways in which ritual 'matters.'

Notes

1. This essay is part of a larger collaborative project on the philosophy of ritual that includes Brian Massumi. We wish to acknowledge Brian's involvement with the project at various stages of its conception. In addition, we are grateful to SSHRC for its continued support.
2. Kenneth Dean, 'Local Communal Religion in Contemporary Southeast China', *China Quarterly*, No. 174 (June, 2003).
3. Ch'ing-k'un Yang, *Religion in Chinese Society* (Berkeley: University of California Press, 1961).
4. Bruno Latour, *We Have Never Been Modern*, trans. C. Porter (Harvard University Press, 1993).

[5] On Taoist ritual traditions in Fujian, see K.Dean, *Taoist Ritual and Popular Cults of Southeast China* (Princeton University Press, 1993). On the Three in One religious movement, see K. Dean, *Lord of the Three in One: The spread of a cult in Southeast China*, (Princeton: Princeton University Press, 1997).

[6] Kenneth Dean, 'Lineage and Territorial Cults: Transformations and interactions on the irrigated Putian plains', in *Belief, Ritual, and Society: Papers from the Third International Sinology Conference, Anthropology Division*, (Taipei, Academia Sinica, 2003).

[7] Of the many works by Henri Lefebvre germane to this discussion, *Everyday Life in the Modern World* (1968), *Critique of Everyday Life* and *The Production of Space* (1974) were the most important to our account, as well as 'The Everyday and Everydayness,' *Yale French Studies* 73 (1987): 7-11.

[8] Stephen Toulmin, *Cosmopolis:The Hidden Agenda of Modernity* (Chicago: University of Chicago Press, 1990).

[9] Our account of the metastable follows from that of Muriel Combes in *Simondon. Individu et collectivité* (Paris: Presses Universitaires de France, 2000), especially her explanation of the preindividual and the more-than-one (10-12). We subsequently extend the notion of dephasing (change of state) by reference to symmetry breaking as discussed by Ian Stewart in *Nature's Numbers: The Unreal Reality of Mathematics* (Basic Books, 1995).

[10] We're thinking here primarily of *Rabelais and his World*, trans. Helene Iswolsky (Bloomington: Indiana University Press, 1984).

[11] Giorgio Agamben, for instance, draws on this distinction in 'In Playland: Reflections on History and Play,' in *Infancy and History: Essays on the Destruction of Experience*, trans. Liz Heron (London and New York: Verso, 1993), 67-87.

[12] Gilles Deleuze, *The Fold: Leibniz and the Baroque*, trans. by Tom Conley (Minneapolis: University of Minnesota Press, 1993).

[13] William Pietz, 'The Problem of the Fetish,' in *Res* 9 (1985): 5-17; 13 (1987): 23-45; 16 (1988): 105-23.

[14] Ian Stewart, *Nature's Numbers: The Unreal Reality of Mathematics* (Basic Books, 1995).

[15] It is often remarked in cultural critiques of Marx that he rails, in a rather Victorian fashion, against the naïve attitude of the fetishist. Linda Williams even sees Marx's use of the term fetishism as one of old-fashioned moralizing abuse. 'He forthrightly accuses all under the commodity's spell of being like the savages who have given up their very humanity to a thing,' she writes in *Hard Core: Power, Pleasure and the 'Frenzy of the Visible,'* (Berkeley: University of California Press, 1989), 105. For a more materialist approach, see William Pietz, 'Fetishism and Materialism: The Limits of Theory in Marx,' in *Fetishism as Cultural Discourse*, ed. Emily Apter and William Pietz (Ithaca: Cornell University Press, 1991), 119-51.

[16] Jean Baudrillard questions the priority that Marx establishes between use value and exchange value in *For a Critique of the Political Economy of the Sign* (St Louis: Telos, 1981), and leans toward an inversion of that priority.

[17] See Thomas Lamarre, *Uncovering Heian Japan: An Archaeology of Sensation and Inscription* (Durham: Duke University Press, 2001).

Submission Guidelines

Traces is published in Chinese, English, German, Japanese, and Korean. Each article accepted for publication is translated into all the languages of the series. In addition to the languages of *Traces* publication, submissions in French, Italian and Spanish are particularly encouraged.

All manuscript contributors for publication consideration should be submitted in triplicate to: *Traces: A multilingual series of cultural theory & translation*, 388 Rockefeller Hall, Cornell University, Ithaca, New York, USA 14853–2502, A manuscript for submission should be prepared, in the first instance, with endnotes and not footnotes. The entire manuscript should be *double-spaced* throughout, including endnotes and block quotations. The author's name, address and email should appear only on a detachable cover page and not anywhere else on the manuscript. This applies to endnote matters where reference may identify the author. A disk version of the manuscript must be provided in the appropriate software format upon acceptance for publication.

English language submissions should conform to the reference system set out in the *14th edition of The Chicago Manual of Style*, following the guidelines for endnotes and not footnotes. Examples of the preferred style may be consulted throughout this issue of the journal.

Submissions in languages other than English, please provide the following references in the order listed:

Books: Author's full name/Complete title of the book/Editor, compiler, or translator, if any/Series, if any, and volume or number in the series/Edition, if not the original/Number of volumes/Facts of publication — city where published, publisher, date of publication/Volume number, if any/Page number(s) of the particular citation.

Chapter in a Book: Author's full name/title of the article/Title of the book/Full name of the editor(s)/Inclusive page numbers of the chapter in the book [follow the above guideline for Books, for the rest].

Article in a Periodical: Author's full name/Title of the article/Name of the periodical/Volume (and number) of the periodical/Date of the volume or of the issue/Page number(s) of the particular citation.

Unpublished Material: Title of the document, if any, and date/Folio number or other identifying number/Name of collection/Depository, and city where it is located.

Public Documents: Country, state, city, county, or other government division issuing the document/Legislative body, executive department, court, bureau, board, commission, or committee; Subsidiary divisions, regional offices, etc./ Title, if any, of the document or collection/Individual author (editor, compiler) if given/Report number or any other identification necessary or useful in finding the specific document/Publisher, if different from the issuing body/Date.

For all subsequent references to already cited reference: Author's last name/ short-title form/Page number.

Submission of an article implies that it has not been simultaneously submitted or previously published elsewhere. Authors are responsible for obtaining permission to publish any material under copyright. Contributors will be asked to assign their own copyright, on certain conditions, to *Traces*. For further guidelines, please contact the *Traces* office: <Traces@cornell.edu>.

Acknowledgment: Traces is receiving support from Hitotsubashi University, Japan Foundation, New York University, and the Dean of the College of Arts and Sciences, Asian Studies Department, and the East Asia Program at Cornell University.

Traces Publishers

Traces Editorial Office
350 Rockefeller Hall
Cornell Univeristy
Ithaca, NY 14853-2502
USA
traces@cornell.edu
fax: +1.607.255.1345

Jiangsu Education Publishing House
31, Ma Jia Jie
Nanjing 210009
P.R.China
traces@1088.com.cn
tel: +86.25.3303497
fax: +86.25.3303457
(Chinese Edition)

Hong Kong University Press
14/F Hing Wai Centre
7 Tin Wan Praya Road
Aberdeen, Tin Wan
Hong Kong
China
hkupress@hkucc.hku.hk
http://www.hkup.org
tel: +852.25502703
fax: +852.28750734
(English Edition)

Iwanami Shoten
2-5-5 Hitotsubashi
Chiyoda-ku, Tokyo
Japan
tel: +81.3.5210.4000
fax: +82.3.5210.4039
(Japanese Edition)

Moonhwa Kwahaksa
5–15 Chungjung-ro 2-ga,
Seodaemun-ku, Seoul
Korea
transics@chollian.net
tel: +82.2.335.0461
fax: +82.2.335.1239
(Korean Edition)